AF544778

A Material Legacy

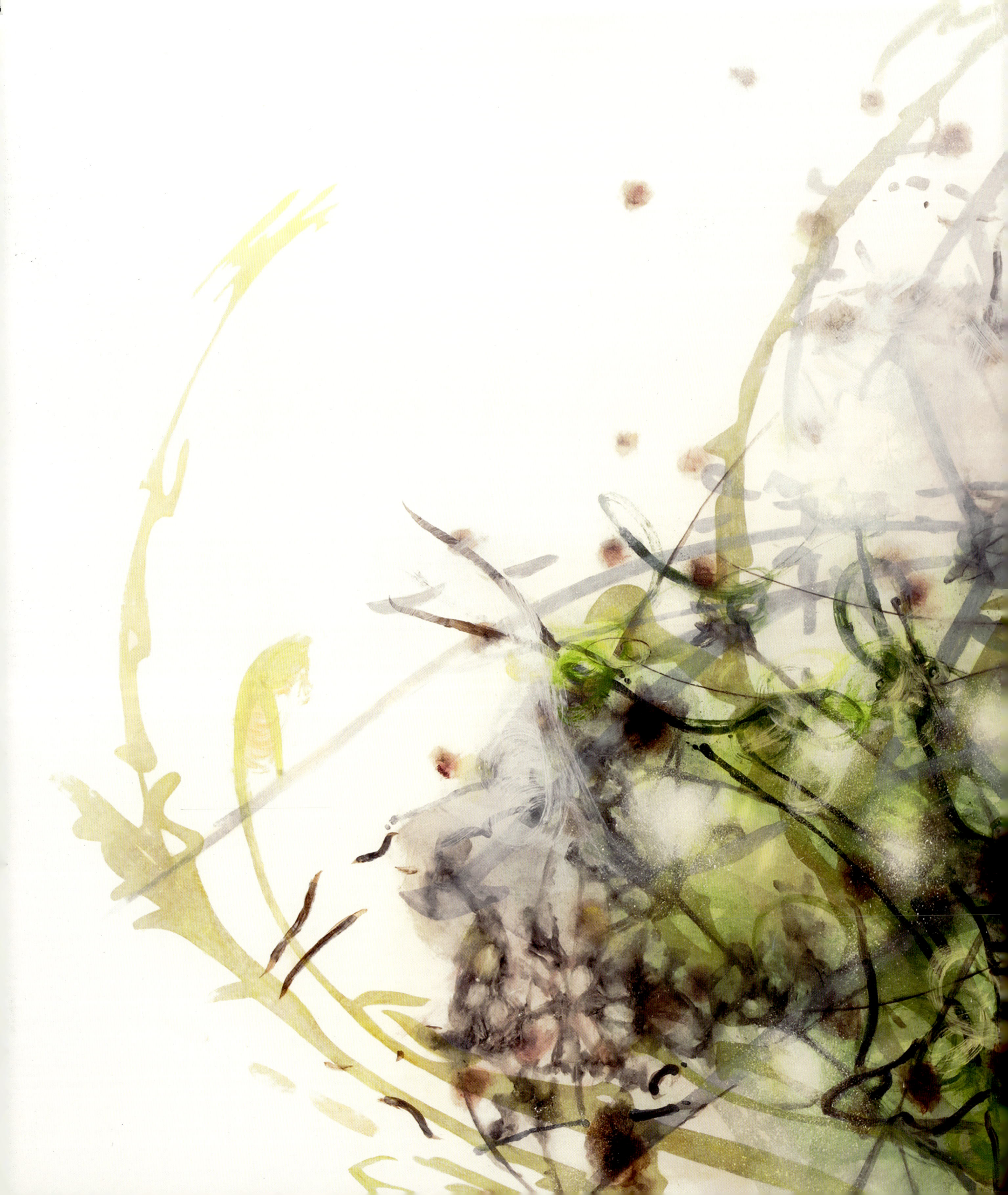

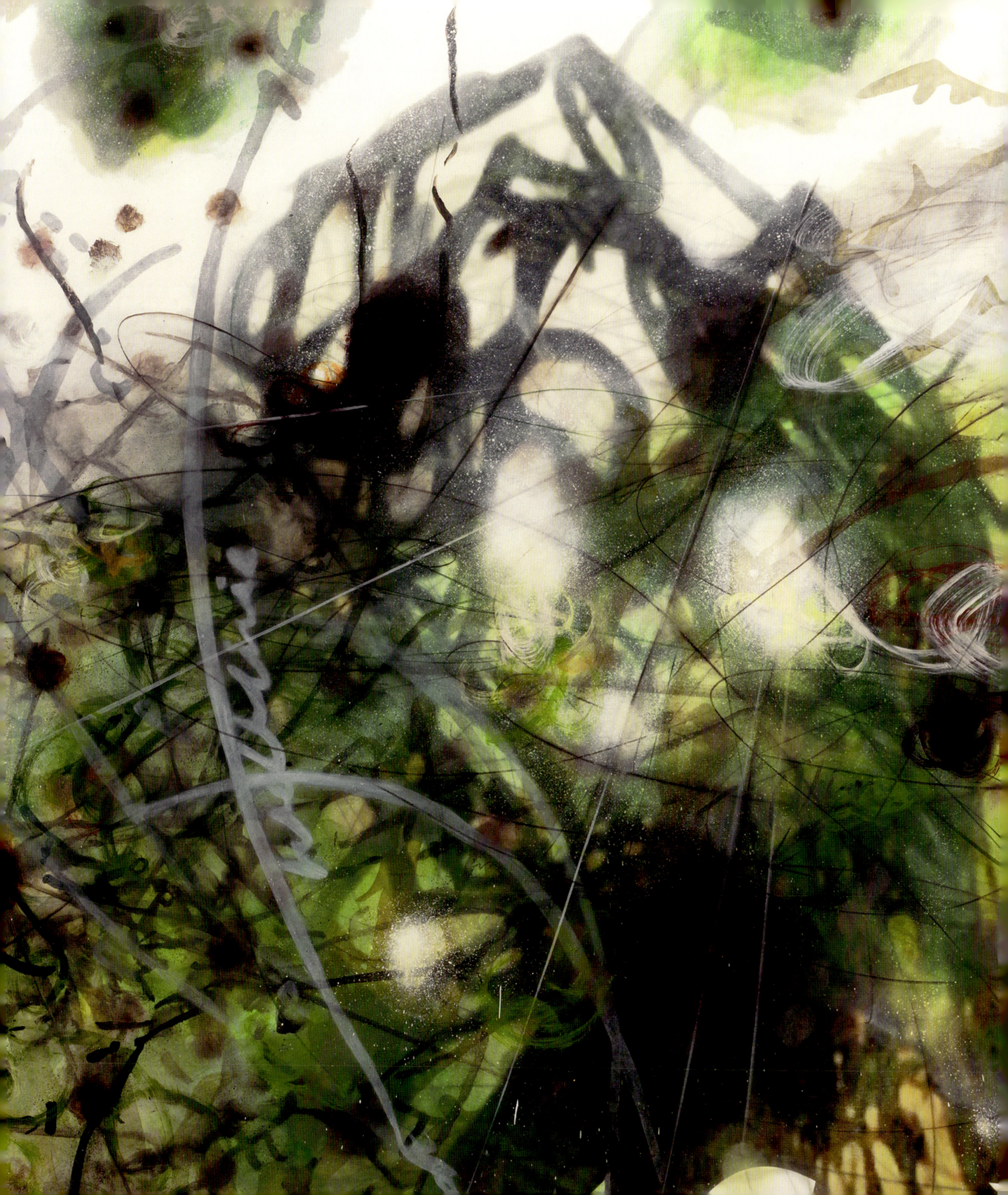

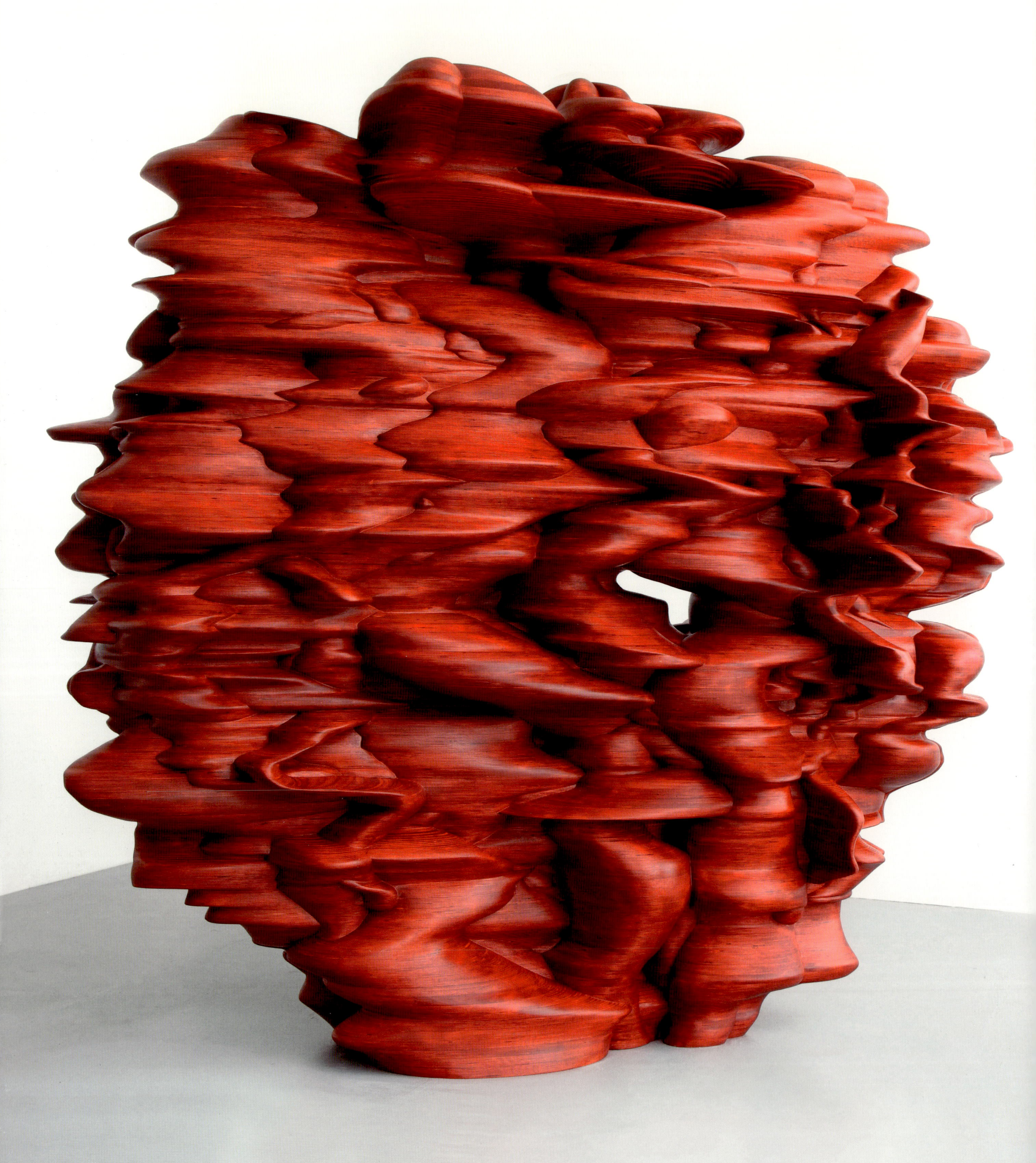

A Material Legacy

THE NANCY A. NASHER AND DAVID J. HAEMISEGGER COLLECTION OF CONTEMPORARY ART

EDITED BY MARSHALL N. PRICE

Nasher Museum of Art at Duke University | 2016

Published on the occasion of the exhibition *A Material Legacy: The Nancy A. Nasher and David J. Haemisegger Collection of Contemporary Art*, organized by the Nasher Museum of Art at Duke University and curated by Marshall N. Price, Nancy Hanks Curator of Modern and Contemporary Art.

NASHER MUSEUM OF ART AT DUKE UNIVERSITY
February 18–June 26, 2016

PRINCETON UNIVERSITY ART MUSEUM
July 30–October 30, 2016

Nasher Museum of Art at Duke University
2001 Campus Drive, Durham, North Carolina 27705
(919) 684-5135
www.nasher.duke.edu

Cataloging information for this title is available from the Library of Congress.
Library of Congress Control Number: 2015955588
ISBN 978-0-938989-40-0

Distributed by Duke University Press

A Material Legacy: The Nancy A. Nasher and David J. Haemisegger Collection of Contemporary Art is made possible by the Nancy Hanks Endowment, Katie Thorpe Kerr and Terrance I.R. Kerr, and Kelly Braddy Van Winkle and Lance Van Winkle.

This exhibition would not be possible without generous loans from the Nancy A. Nasher and David J. Haemisegger Collection.

Nasher Museum exhibitions and programs are generously supported by the Mary Duke Biddle Foundation, the late Mary D.B.T. Semans and James H. Semans, the late Frank E. Hanscom III, The Duke Endowment, the Nancy Hanks Endowment, the Courtney Shives Art Museum Fund, the James Hustead Semans Memorial Fund, the Janine and J. Tomilson Hill Family Fund, the Trent A. Carmichael Fund for Community Education, the Neely Family Fund, the E. T. Rollins Jr. and Frances P. Rollins Fund for the Nasher Museum of Art at Duke University, the Marilyn M. Arthur Fund, the Sarah Schroth Fund, the George W. and Viola Mitchell Fearnside Endowment Fund, the Gibby and Michael B. Waitzkin Fund, the K. Brantley and Maxine E. Watson Endowment Fund, the Victor and Lenore Behar Endowment Fund, the Margaret Elizabeth Collett Fund, the Nasher Museum of Art General Endowment, the Friends of the Nasher Museum of Art, and the Office of the President and the Office of the Provost, Duke University.

Production and coordination by Reneé Cagnina Haynes

Copyediting by Katie Adkins Brennan

Design and typesetting by Julie Klugman Braude

Set in Monotype Modern, News Gothic, and Stempel Garamond

Color separations, printing, and binding by Puritan Capital, Hollis, New Hampshire

PL. 26 Matthew Ritchie, *Link of Nature*, 2014 (detail). Oil and ink on canvas. 78 x 116 x 2 1/2 inches (198.1 x 294.6 x 6.4 cm).

PL. 4 Tony Cragg, *Versus*, 2011. Wood. 110 1/4 x 116 x 39 1/2 inches (280 x 295 x 1003 cm).

Contents

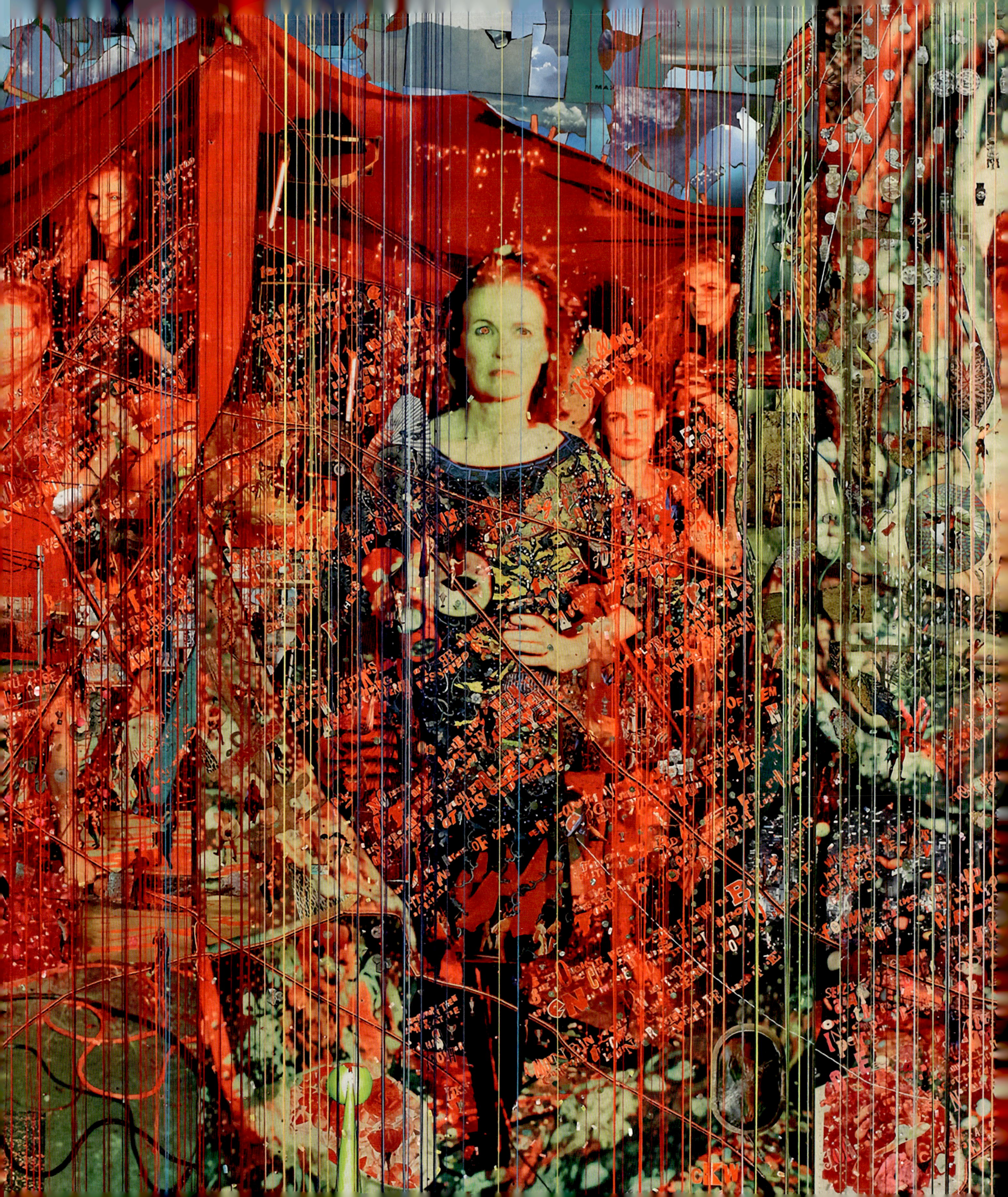

Directors' Foreword

It is fitting that the art museums of Nancy Nasher and David Haemisegger's alma maters should collaborate on an exhibition showcasing, for the first time, artworks from the private collection they have been quietly building over the past two decades. Nancy and David met on their first day as undergraduates at Princeton University, from which they graduated together in 1976. Nancy received her law degree from Duke University, from which her father, Raymond D. Nasher, had graduated in 1943, and as her father before her, served on Duke's Board of Trustees from 1999 to 2011.

Raymond and Patsy Nasher made innumerable trips from Dallas to Duke University during the extended period it took to realize their vision and insistence that Duke build a significant art museum, and one designed by an internationally renowned architect, if it wished to compete with other top research universities in the nation. Nancy and David always accompanied Ray on these trips, standing beside him in wholehearted support and participating in every aspect of the planning, from the selection of the site to the choice of the architect, Rafael Viñoly. All three generously offered wise advice and support to Michael Mezzatesta, director of the then Duke University Museum of Art, who knew the family from his years as curator at the Kimbell Art Museum in Fort Worth. Both Nancy and David served on the original Nasher Museum of Art Development Committee for the new facility, and Nancy served on both search committees for the directorship of the Nasher, backing the Nasher's first director, Kimerly Rorschach, who successfully launched and professionalized the new museum while at the same time articulating a clear direction foreword. Since 2013 Nancy and David have been extremely supportive of the second director of this institution and have been the best sounding board a director could possibly have.

Since Ray passed away in 2007, Nancy and David have stepped in as major benefactors to the Nasher Museum of Art at Duke University, naming a curatorship and a lecture hall and creating one endowment for a visiting curator and another for acquisitions. Since its inception, they have been a steady presence on the Nasher Museum Board of Advisors, which Nancy now chairs, generously sharing their time before, during, and in-between board meetings. Nancy and David have become the face of the Nasher Museum, attending the museum's major events on and off campus. Now, they extend their support and generosity by helping realize *A Material Legacy: The Nancy A. Nasher and David J. Haemisegger Collection of Contemporary Art.*

At Princeton, Nancy has been a longstanding and passionate participant in the Art Museum's Advisory Council, a twenty-member board charged with guiding the museum's director, advocating for the museum to the university leadership and to university alumni, and generally helping to assure the museum's vibrancy as one of the nation's oldest collecting institutions. Nancy and David's shared passion for art and architecture continues to make a compelling contribution to the work of the council; indeed, Nancy's particular passion for and understanding of how critical space is to the experience of art makes her an incomparable advocate on behalf of the museum's need for expanded space. The intimacy of their relationship with art—learned, perhaps, from Nancy's parents—leads them to a shared conviction that such a relationship should be afforded to every Princeton student. Their encouragement has made a remarkable impact during a period of significant institutional growth and change, when a number of new initiatives have been launched to make art a powerful part of the experience of the entire university community. Nancy and David made an impressive statement upholding this belief when, toward the close of Princeton's recent university-wide campaign known as Aspire, they made an exceptional financial commitment that endowed the Nancy A. Nasher and David J. Haemisegger, Class of 1976, Directorship of the Art Museum.

Over the years many exhibitions have celebrated the collecting eye that guided Ray and Patsy Nasher. It is our great pleasure to join in presenting the first exhibition to celebrate the bold and inspired collecting carried out over many years now by Nancy Nasher and David Haemisegger. We are proud to share in their support, and to recognize the impact of their leadership at both our universities.

Sarah Schroth
Mary D.B.T. and James H. Semans Director
Nasher Museum of Art at Duke University

James Christen Steward
Nancy A. Nasher—David J. Haemisegger,
Class of 1976, Director
Princeton University Art Museum

PL. 16 (OPPOSITE) Elliott Hundley, *eyes that run like leaping fire*, 2011 (detail). Wood, soundboard, ink-jet print on Kitakata, string, pins, paper, photographs, plastic, wire, and found embroidery; 98 1/2 x 240 5/8 x 11 3/8 inches (250.2 x 611.2 x 28.9 cm).

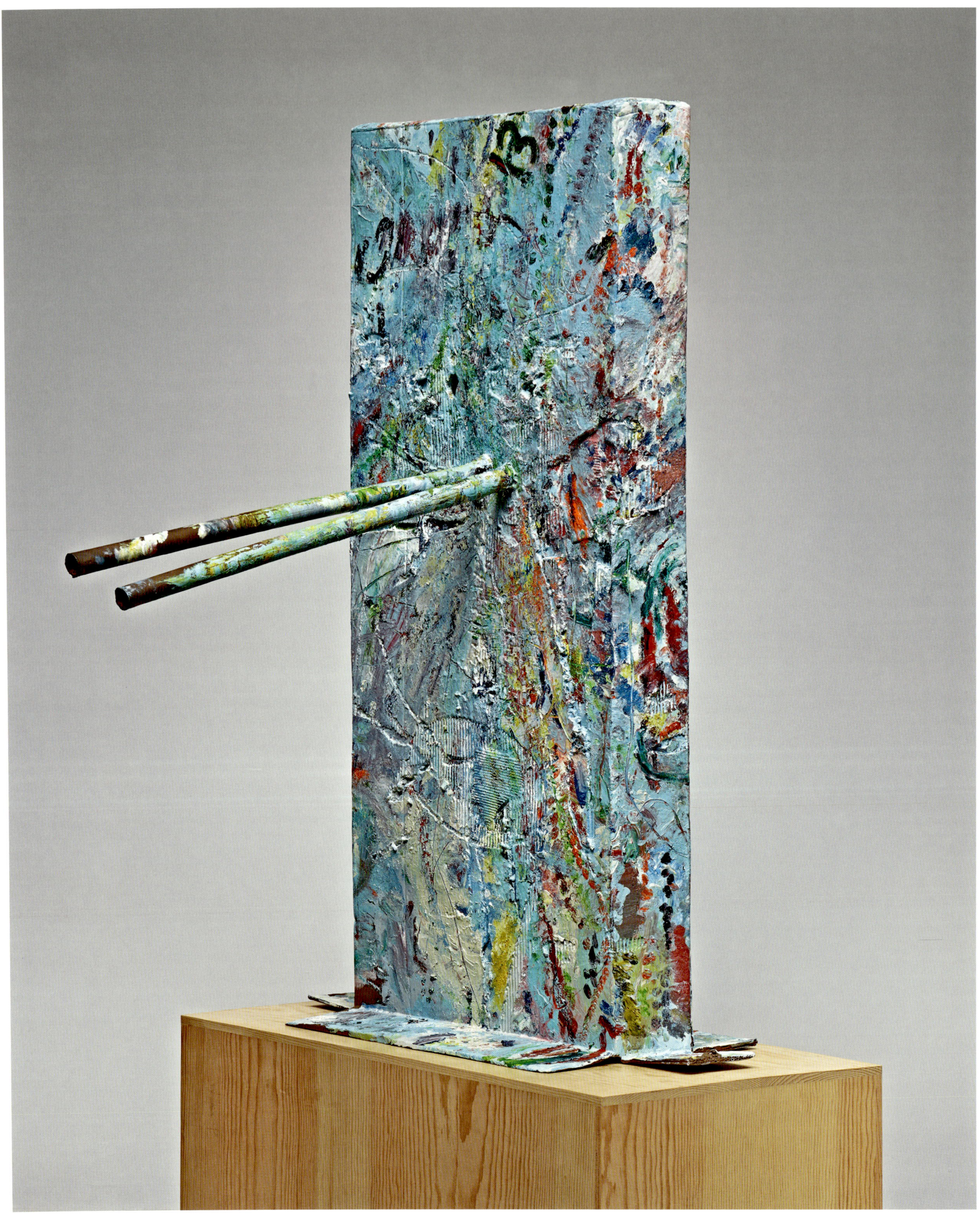

PL. 12 Mark Grotjahn, *Untitled (Pretty Lost Blue for My Girls, Italian Mask M30.b)*, 2013. Painted bronze, 52 3/4 x 33 1/2 x 38 inches (134 x 85.1 x 96.5 cm).

Acknowledgements

The Nasher Museum of Art at Duke University is proud to present *A Material Legacy: The Nancy A. Nasher and David J. Haemisegger Collection of Contemporary Art*. Many people justly deserve to be acknowledged for their roles in the development and execution of this exciting exhibition.

Above all, of course, we are grateful to Nancy Nasher and David Haemisegger for graciously agreeing to show their works of art as a collection for the first time. These works have held pride of place in their home in Dallas and at their landmark property, NorthPark Center, where Dallas residents have grown accustomed to viewing them every day.

Thankfully, Nancy and David have been as generous with their time and energy as with their collection. They have worked closely with Dr. Marshall Price, the curator of *A Material Legacy*, hosting him numerous times in Dallas, offering wise advice on his selections for the show, and contributing to plans for the exhibition design, without ever imposing their will or interfering with Marshall's vision. They are very special patrons indeed.

At a time when he was still relatively new to his post at the Nasher Museum, Dr. Price enthusiastically embraced the project, skillfully overseeing the coordination of every detail, from the creation of a cogent curatorial concept to the planning of the superb installation. His illuminating essay for the catalogue is thoroughly researched, well thought out, and beautifully written.

The entire Nasher Museum staff labored tirelessly to make this wonderful exhibition a reality. Chief curator Trevor Schoonmaker guided Marshall and the collections team with characteristic grace and intelligence. The inexhaustible devotion of Reneé Cagnina Haynes, exhibitions and publications manager, brought this catalogue, as well as other aspects of the exhibition, through to completion. Molly Boarati, assistant curator, and Chanelle Croxton, curatorial assistant, contributed invaluable research assistance and were instrumental in the preparation of this project. Kelly Woolbright, registrar, skillfully coordinated the packing, unpacking, and transportation of the exhibition, while exhibition designer Brad Johnson and team have prepared and mounted yet another stunning show.

We also warmly acknowledge the dedication of both designer Julie Klugman Braude and copyeditor Katie Adkins Brennan, who brought this catalogue to life through their thoughtful and untiringly meticulous work.

This exhibition would not have been possible without the assistance of many of the NorthPark staff. General manager Billy Hines's specific knowledge of the works of art was invaluable to our installation. Taylor Zakarin, manager of arts programming, and Andi York and Andrea Atkins of the Nasher Haemisegger support staff all provided crucial help throughout the organizing process.

The camaraderie of James Steward, director of the Princeton University Art Museum, provided essential guidance and support necessary to bring this project to its full potential. We are excited that the exhibition will travel to his institution so that a broader audience will have the opportunity to experience the collection that Nancy and David have so presciently assembled. For this, we owe James and his team a special debt of thanks.

Additionally, our sincere thanks go to those who have provided the Nasher Museum and its exhibitions program with ongoing financial support. Without their commitment, the museum's programming would not be what it is today. This exhibition in particular is made possible by the generosity of the Nancy Hanks Endowment, Trent Carmichael, Katie Thorpe Kerr and Terrance I.R. Kerr, Kelly Braddy Van Winkle and Lance Van Winkle, and Lisa Lowenthal Pruzan and Jonathan Pruzan.

At Princeton, the entire museum staff has, as usual, contributed to making the project a success, but particular thanks go to T. Barton Thurber, associate director for collections and exhibitions, for providing overall curatorial guidance; Mike Jacobs, manager of exhibition services, for devising a beautiful installation plan in the museum's all-too-constrained spaces for temporary exhibitions; Alexia Hughes, chief registrar and manager of collections services, for overseeing all registrarial aspects of bringing the collection from Durham and then assuring its safe return to Dallas; and Caroline Harris, associate director for education, and her team, for considering how to present and interpret such rich and diverse contemporary objects for both expert and novice audiences as well as how to assure its impact on the university's mission of teaching and research.

Sarah Schroth
Mary D.B.T. and James H. Semans Director
Nasher Museum of Art at Duke University

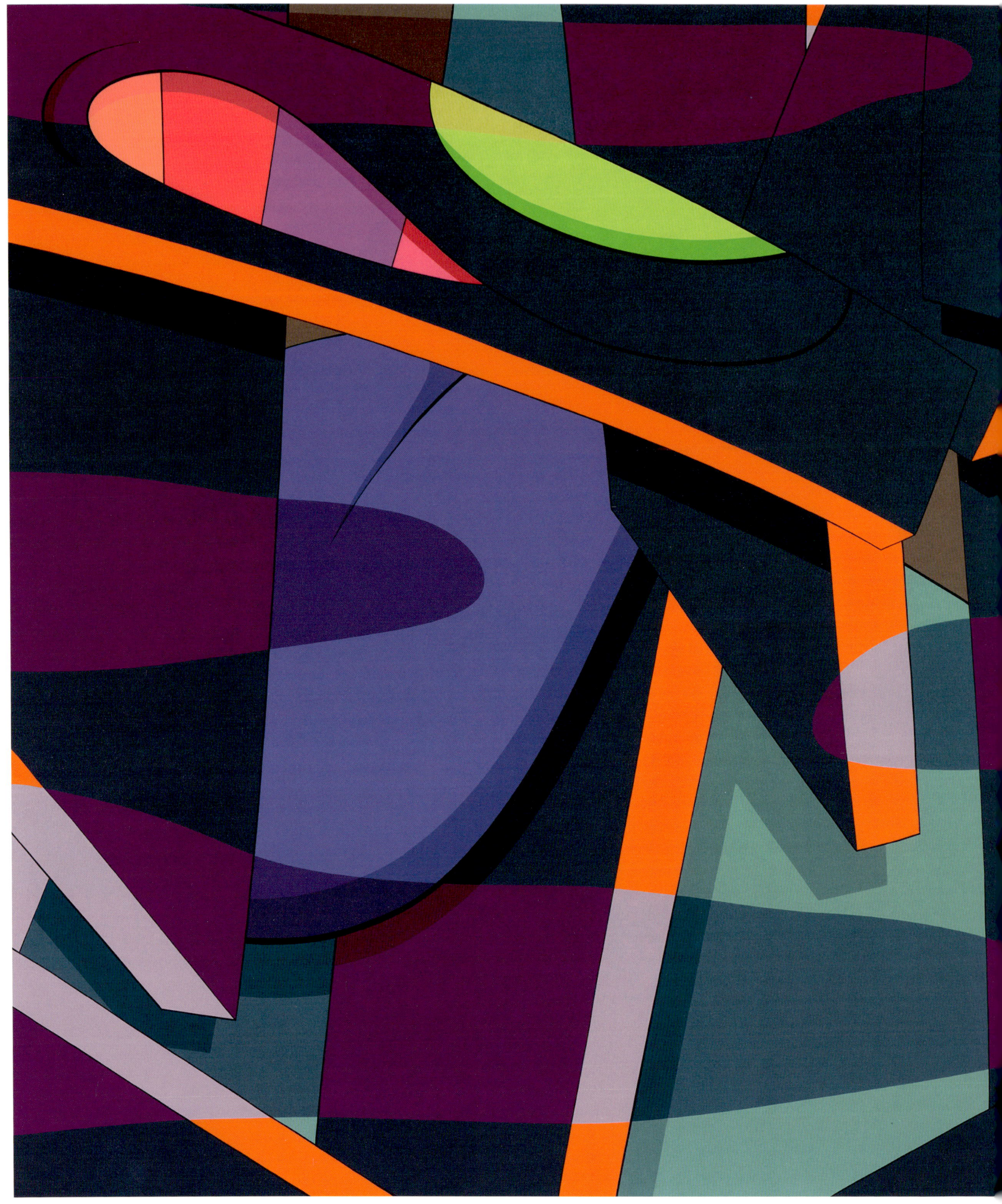

PL. 19 KAWS, *Untitled*, 2015. Acrylic on canvas, 72 x 120 inches (182.9 x 304.8 cm).

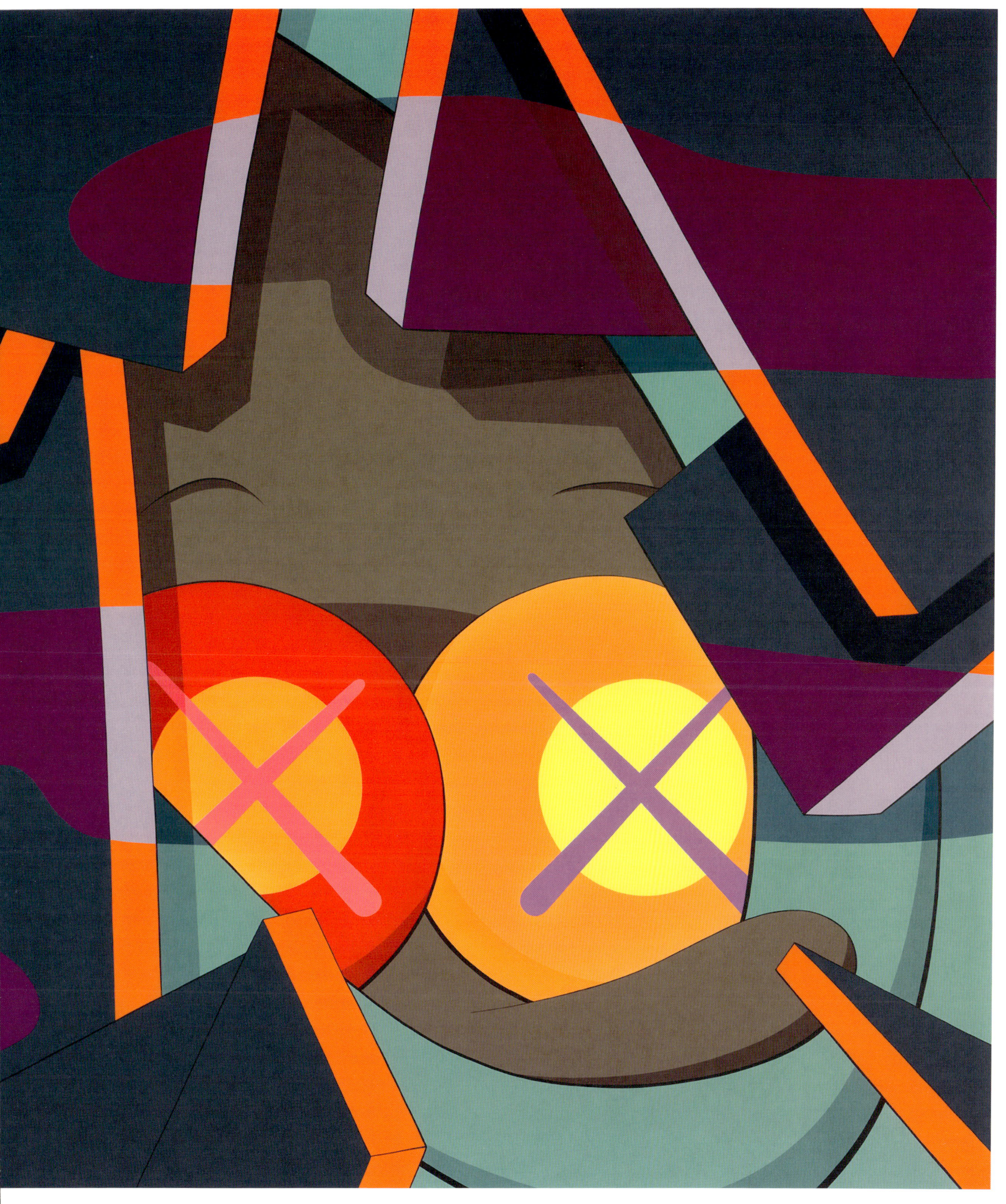

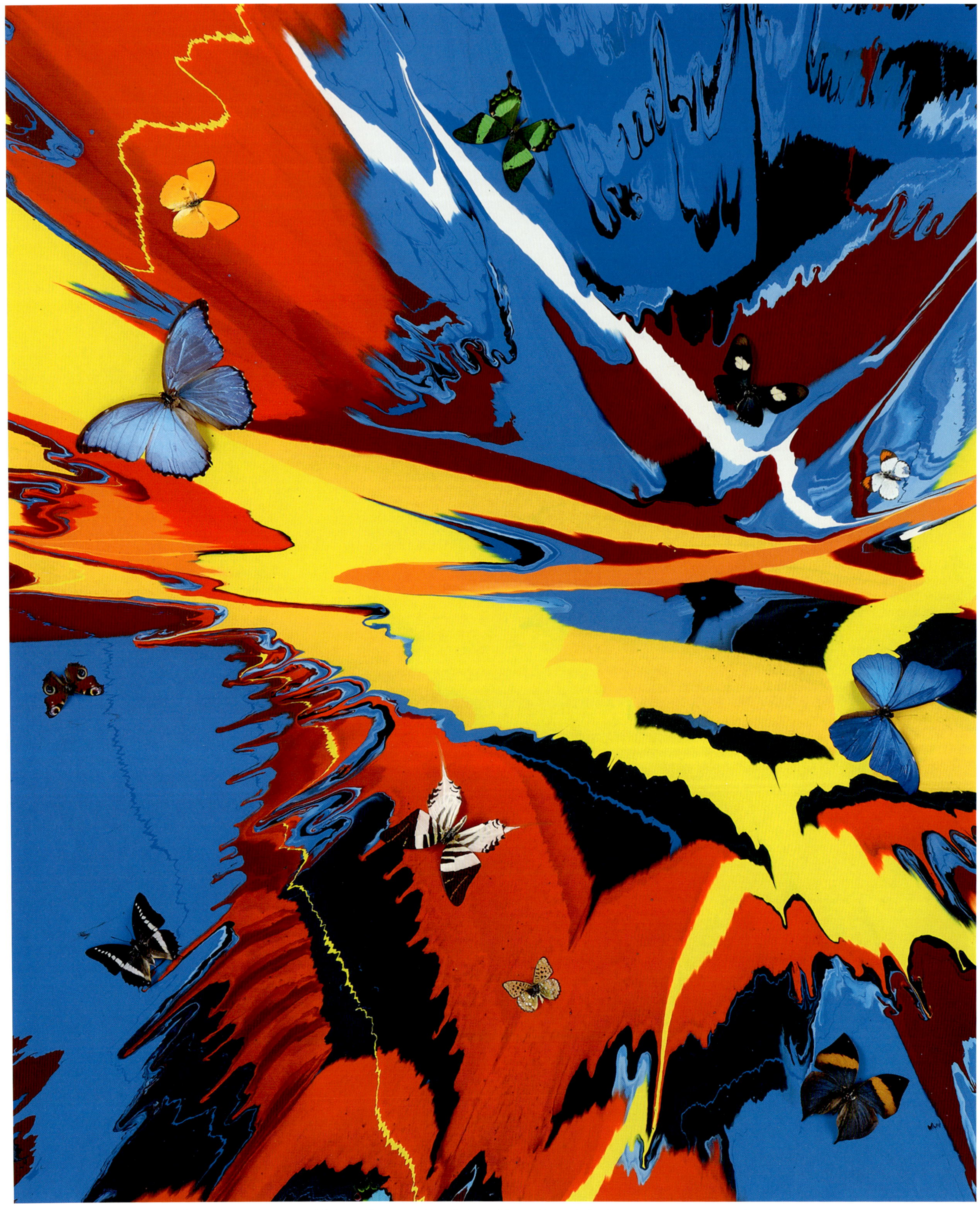

PL. 13 Damien Hirst, *Beautiful Superheroes Painting (with Butterflies)*, 2007 (detail). Butterflies and household gloss on canvas, 48 x 48 inches (122 x 122 cm).

Introduction: Notes on Collecting Patterns in the Nasher Haemisegger Collection

Sarah Schroth

The act of collecting, according to one definition, begins with the feeling of affection or inclination for an object, to fancy possessing it, give one's mind to it. From there, the acquisition of one object leads to another until a mass is formed. Every collection exhibits patterns based on the qualities of the persons who assemble it. Their personalities, backgrounds, values, intellectual and emotional lives, and financial means all play a part.

The first collections in the Western world were formed by the Greeks, who compiled sacred objects in temple treasure rooms, offerings to the gods protected by a special caretaker. The idea of a treasure room was carried over to the medieval period, when high-ranking ecclesiastics in charge of the cathedrals of Europe collected luxurious liturgical vestments, ritual objects made of gold and precious stones, and jewel-encrusted reliquaries made to preserve and display pieces of the holy cross, for instance, or parts of a martyred saint's body. These cathedral treasuries still exist today, filled with glittering symbols of wealth and power meant to impress the masses.

It was not until the sixteenth century that collecting in the modern sense began at princely courts. Rulers and courtiers competed with each other to accumulate rare and precious objects brought from around the world, which they placed together into a *Wunderkammer*, a room of wonders. The Wunderkammer contained assemblages of objects ranging from natural specimens to elaborate examples of silver- or goldsmithing. These rare marvels were primarily collected for the purpose of scientific interest or education. During the Renaissance, Italian city-state rulers and popes commissioned paintings, sculpture, and architecture from the likes of Raphael and Michelangelo. Although great patrons of public and semipublic spaces, the Italians were not the first to gather together art objects for the sake of owning a collection as a manifestation of status. The Hapsburgs were the first megacollectors in Europe, importing large numbers of artworks from Italy and Flanders to decorate their residential palaces. King Philip II of Spain owned over 1,500 paintings alone, and he passed his passion for collecting onto his heirs. He invented the tradition of buying multiple works from a favored artist—he had the largest collection of Titians. The courts of England, France, and Germany soon followed in a race to possess the greatest number of fine paintings and sculptures, while in the Netherlands, merchants filled their homes with portraits and cabinet paintings by Vermeer, Rembrandt, and others. Thus, the art market as we know it dates to the seventeenth century.

Nancy Nasher and her husband David Haemisegger belong to these traditions. As art patrons, they commission works for public spaces. As collectors, they have amassed great numbers of artworks (close to 580 works thus far and growing), and they often express their admiration by acquiring multiple works by the same

FIG. 1.1
Andy Warhol, *Portrait of Nancy Nasher* (second version), 1980. Silkscreen on canvas, 40 3/8 x 40 3/8 inches (102.6 x 102.6 cm). Image and artwork ©2015 The Andy Warhol Foundation for the Visual Arts, Inc. / Licensed by Artist Rights Society (ARS), New York, New York.

artist. They inherited a passion for collecting from Nancy's parents, Raymond D. and Patsy R. Nasher, who were architects of a truly great private collection of sculpture. And yet, when curator Marshall Price and I proposed the idea of an exhibition of works from their collection, Nancy and David had an immediate visceral reaction. "We don't have a *collection*," they protested. "We are just buying what we like. We don't think of ourselves as *collectors* exactly."

Their reaction rang a very specific bell for me. In *The Evolution of the Nasher Collection* catalogue in 2005, I had written about the first time Raymond and Patsy were asked to display their collection in Dallas:

> In 1978, William B. Jordan, director of the Meadows Museum and dean of the School of the Arts at Southern Methodist University, approached the Nashers to propose an exhibition of their collection for SMU's temporary exhibition gallery . . . Patsy was so unsure that an exhibition could be made from their works that she feared Jordan might lose his job. There was not a conscious motivation in 1978 to win attention and praise. Instead they were buying what they liked and wanted to live with—considering their acquisitions a gift to themselves and part of their daughters' education.

The hesitation expressed by both generations of Nashers is common among collectors who are exhibiting their works in public for the first time, especially if they feel they are still in the act of building a collection or do not yet identify themselves as collectors. It can be uncomfortable for them to expose their inner lives as reflected in their choices, to show objects for which they have felt affection and have grouped together without a conscious unifying purpose or particular focus in mind. But Nancy and David carry a heavier-than-usual burden. As a girl, Nancy witnessed her parents, especially her mother, become part of the vibrant contemporary art scene, commissioning Andy Warhol to paint family portraits (fig. 1.1) and buying Jean-Michel Basquiat's work before he was a star. She was there as they built a remarkable collection and formed close relationships with top dealers and sculptors of their day. Nancy's boyfriend from Princeton, an impressionable twenty-two-year-old David Haemisegger, became a part of the family around the time Raymond and Patsy began to identify themselves as serious collectors and focus their efforts on modern and contemporary sculpture.

As the exhibition *A Material Legacy: The Nancy A. Nasher and David J. Haemisegger Collection of Contemporary Art* illustrates, Nancy and David have made good use of their background. They have closely observed and gained considerable knowledge by paying attention to what, when, and how Raymond and Patsy collected. As Patsy indicated above, their collecting was always meant to be an education, a family affair, and Nancy and David have proven to be excellent students. Now they are becoming master collectors themselves.

There is plenty of evidence to show that Nancy and David learned valuable lessons from the Nashers' example, as they have embraced many of the same ideals and best practices: the importance of sharing the collection with the public, the benefits derived from constant study of the art market, the value of wide exposure to all kinds of art, the acceptance of some guidance from professional curators and dealers while also maintaining an independent stance, and the personal pleasure and insight gained from knowing the artists whose work they collect. As collectors in their own right, however, Nancy and David are expanding upon these ideals and adding new goals.

Always respectful, Nancy and David waited their turn, devoting real time and copious energy in forming their own private collection only after Raymond passed away in 2007. Both Nancy and David worked hard until they had the financial security to create a serious collection. That security comes from the considerable success of their investment in NorthPark Center, the shopping center Raymond built fifty years ago with stores set among world-class sculptures. Nancy and David purchased NorthPark Center from Raymond in 1995 and proceeded to transform it dramatically. In 2006, they opened a $250 million renovation and expansion, doubling the size of the original shopping center. Their vision for the new NorthPark added another dimension to Raymond's original mission of

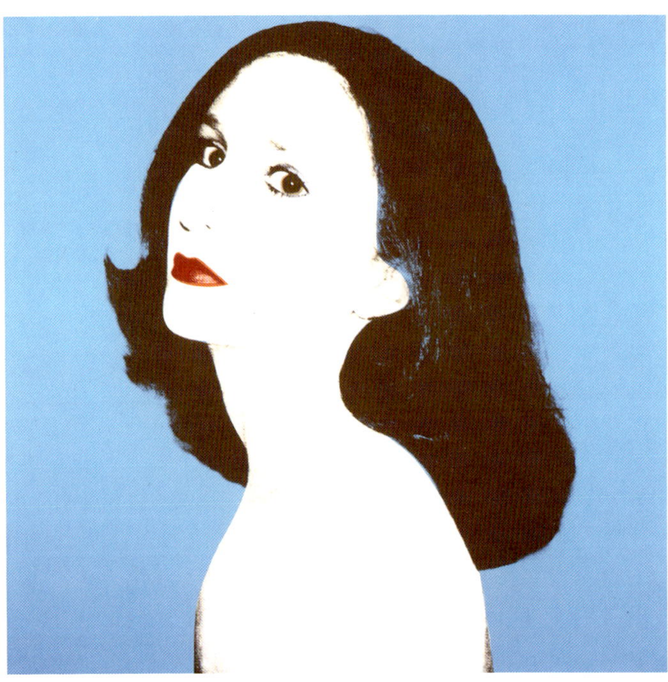

1.1

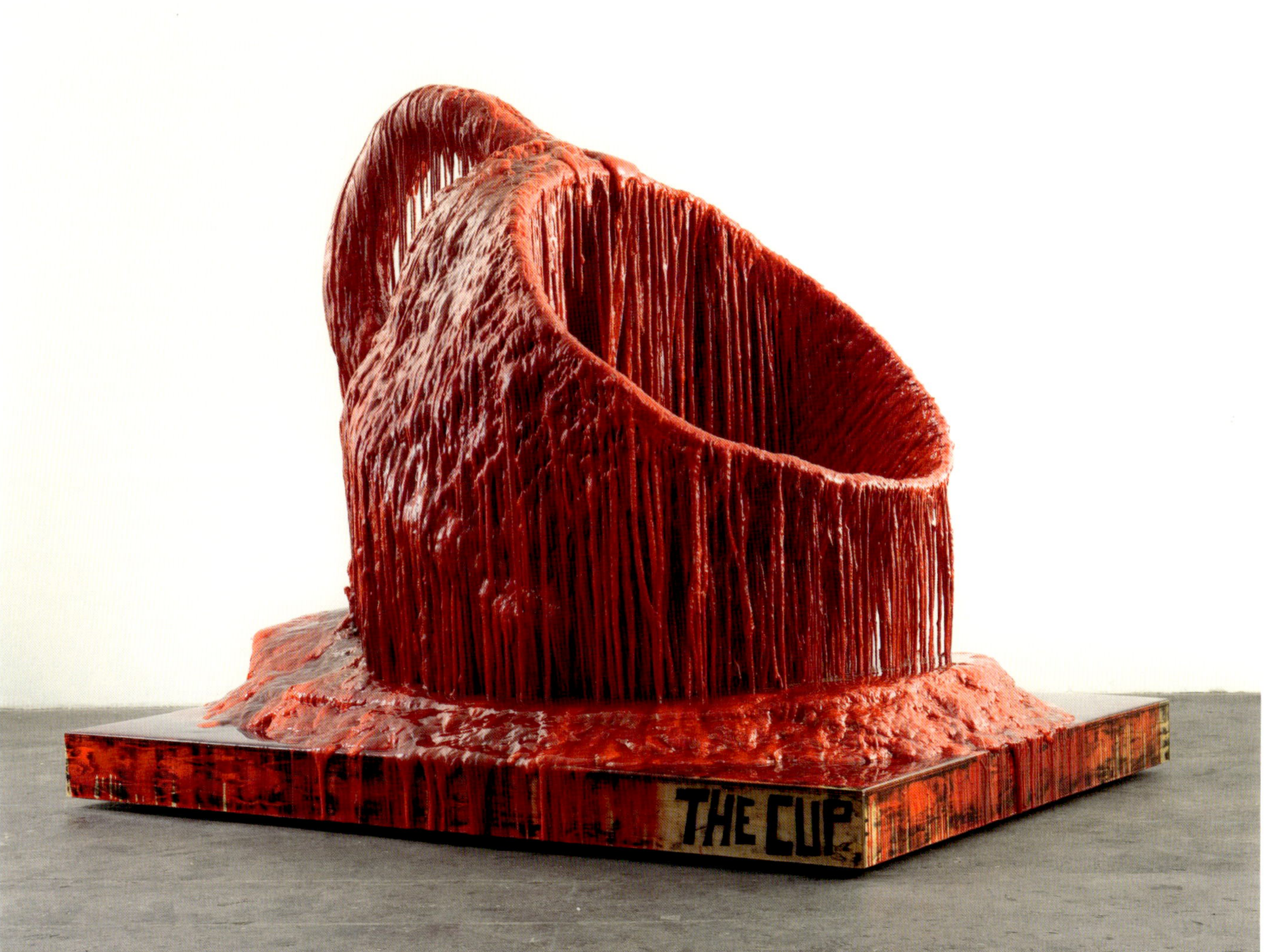

FIG. 1.2
Sterling Ruby, *The Cup*, 2013. Foam, urethane, wood, and spray paint; 92 x 115 1/2 x 88 inches (233.7 x 293.4 x 223.5 cm). ©Sterling Ruby.

1.2

combining low- and high-end stores to reach all segments of the population. In the new spaces, Nancy and David have brought in designer stores and luxury retailers, a gamble that has turned a handsome profit.

After Raymond's death in 2007, ownership of the majority of the sculpture from the Raymond and Patsy Nasher Collection was transferred to the Nasher Foundation. Nonsculptural works were dispersed, with many sold at auction to raise funds for the Nasher Sculpture Center, the museum built in Dallas to house the Nasher Collection. Nancy and David acquired from the Nasher Foundation the pieces they could afford at the time. Their choices reveal a wish to preserve some of the important historical milestones in the life of the Nasher Collection, such as the first major purchase by Raymond and Patsy—Ben Shahn's *Tennis Players*, bought in New York in 1954—and the New Guinea basket mask Patsy found, along with its corresponding print by Henry Moore. Morris Louis's painting *Aleph Series VI*, 1960, which always graced the parents' dining room, is another work they did not want to leave the family.

They also purchased from the Nasher Foundation the lovely *Torso in Space* by Alexander Archipenko, Georges Braque's *Hyman*, and a small work by Alberto Giacometti. They have added to their own holdings sculptures that have become synonymous with NorthPark: Jim Dine's *The Field of the Cloth of Gold*; Jonathan Borofsky's *Five Hammering Men*; Barry Flanagan's *Large Leaping Hare*; Frank Stella's enormous aluminum relief *Washington Island Gladwall*; Alain Kirili's *Rediscovered King*; and the site-specific earthwork commissioned for NorthPark from Beverly Pepper, *Dallas Land Canal*.

In the 1970s, Patsy had astutely acquired complete sets of prints produced by pop artists. Now Nancy and David own the serial prints Patsy purchased by Jasper Johns, Robert Motherwell, Dine, Stella, and Warhol. At this stage in the history of the Nasher Haemisegger Collection, prints are the second largest group, behind sculpture. Relatively affordable, prints are a good place to start a collection. In the 1990s, Nancy and David decorated their home, as well as office suites and hallways, with bright, colorful prints by David Hockney and Howard Hodgkin.

On their honeymoon in London in 1990, they made their first purchase together: Roy Lichtenstein's

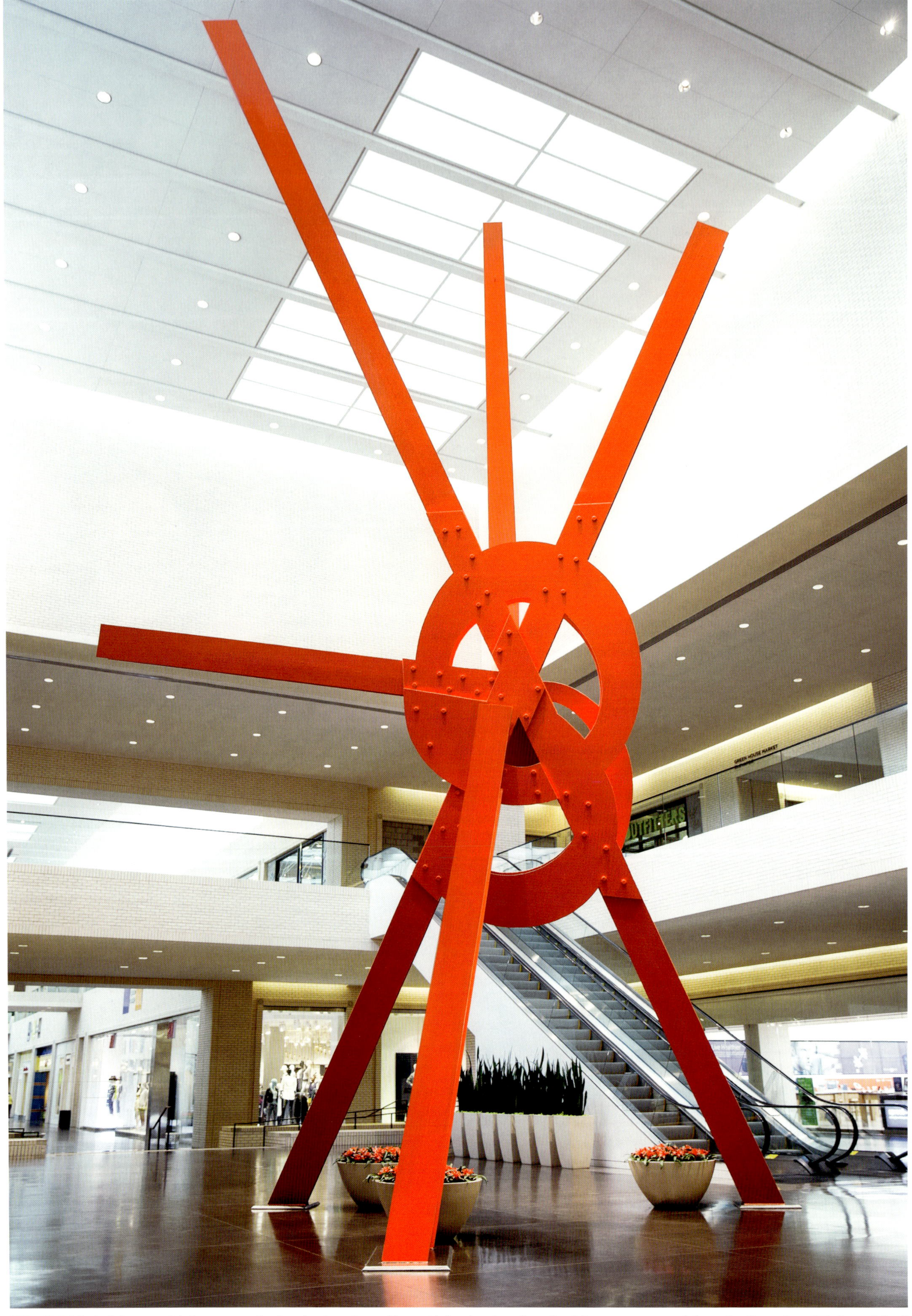

FIG. 1.3 Mark di Suvero, *Ad Astra*, 2005. Steel and paint, 48 x 25 1/2 x 25 1/2 feet (14.6 x 7.8 x 7.8 m). Image courtesy of the artist; Spacetime CC, Long Island City, New York; and Paula Cooper Gallery, New York, New York. © Mark di Suvero.

Bull Profile Series from 1973, six lithographs in which a realistic rendering of a bull in the first print progressively morphs into total abstraction by the sixth print. It was a cerebral purchase. Nancy and David had firsthand knowledge of Lichtenstein's work, including the painting *Reclining Bather* from 1977, purchased by Raymond and Patsy in 1978. Nancy and David had chosen to acquire an important, earlier work by the pop artist. After the *Bull Profile Series*, Nancy and David bought other prints by Lichtenstein, which are experiments with new media and date from two succeeding decades.

The purchase of the Lichtenstein series predicts certain patterns of collecting seen today in Nancy and David's collection: keen interests in material, artistic processes, and the continuity of the legacy of the Nasher Collection.

But while both Nancy and David obviously admire Raymond and Patsy's accomplishments and strive to preserve their legacy as patrons, they are clearly developing their own identity as collectors. The world has changed since the Nashers were able to focus, locate, and purchase classical modernist sculpture. In their collecting activity, Nancy and David are proving their ability to keep pace with those changes. Without a doubt, they are creating a twenty-first-century collection. In the

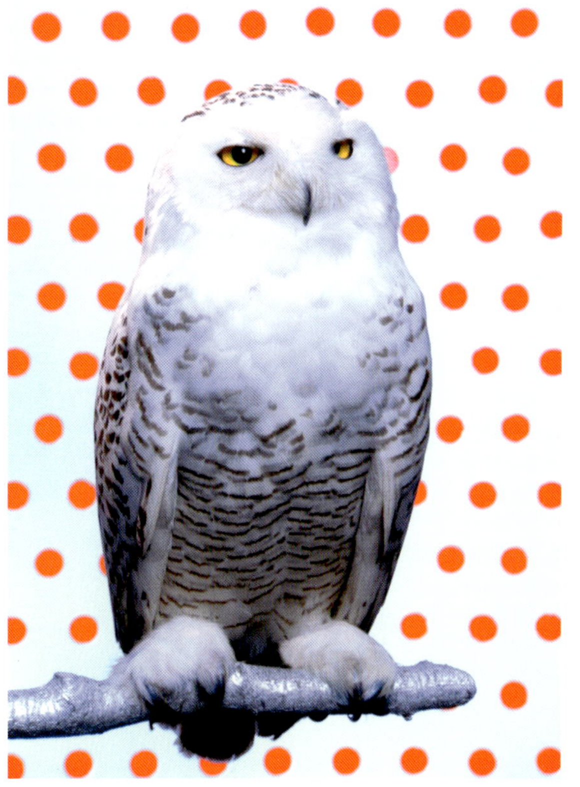
1.5

FIG. 1.5
Robert Wilson, *KOOL (Red)*, 2006 (still). High definition video, edition 2/2; 44 3/4 x 24 x 9 inches (113.7 x 61 x 22.9 cm). Music by Robert Wilson and Peter Cerone. Commissioned and produced by VOOM HD Networks. © Robert Wilson.

FIG. 1.4
Iván Navarro, *BED (Water Tower)*, *Ladder (Water Tower)*, and *ME/WE (Water Tower)* from the project *This Land is Your Land*, 2014. Neon, wood, painted steel, galvanized steel, aluminum, mirror, one-way mirror, and electric energy; edition 1/3; 189 x 105 1/8 x 105 1/8 inches (480.1 x 267 x 267 cm) each. Installation view, NorthPark Center, Dallas, Texas.

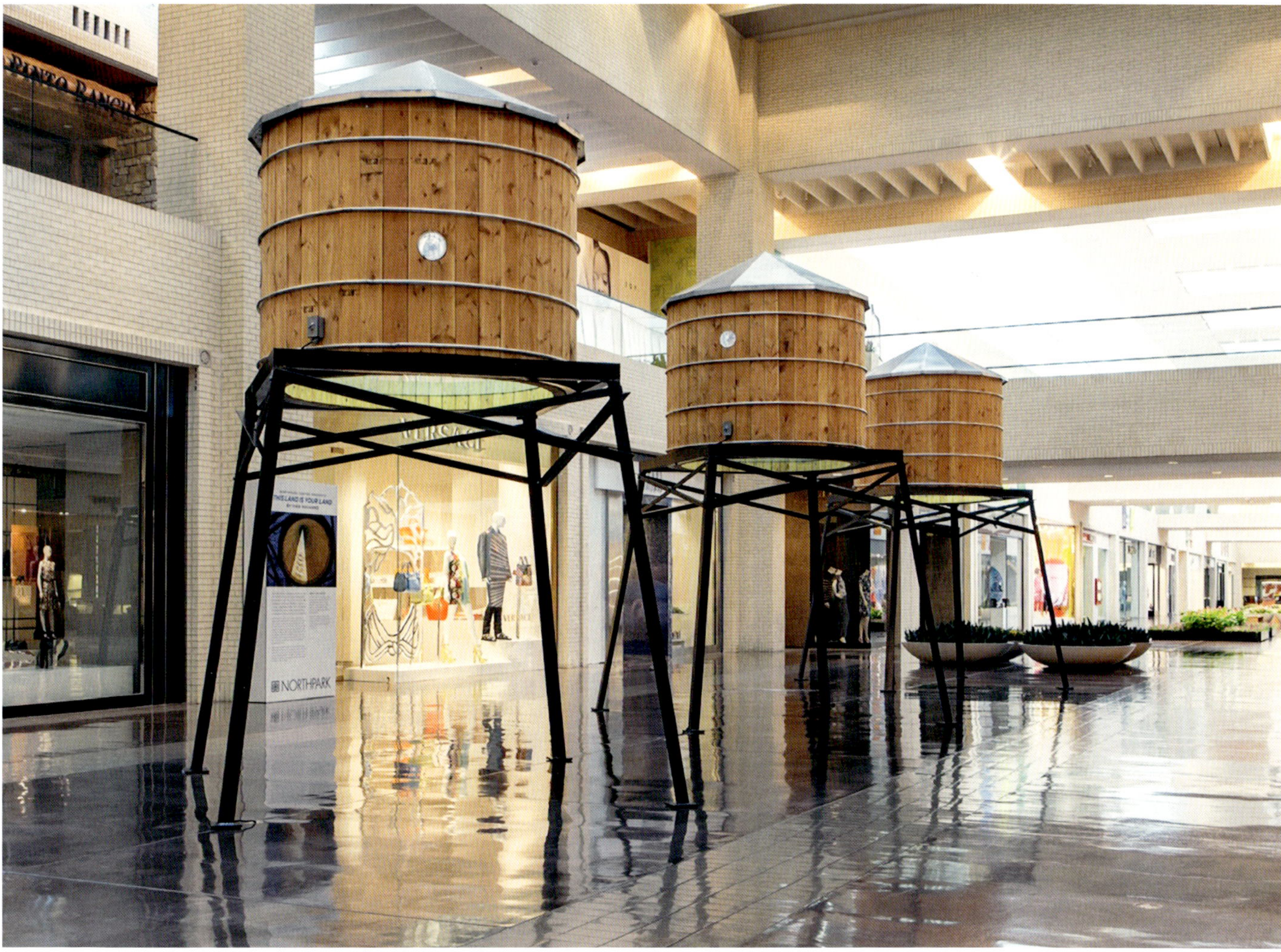

1.4

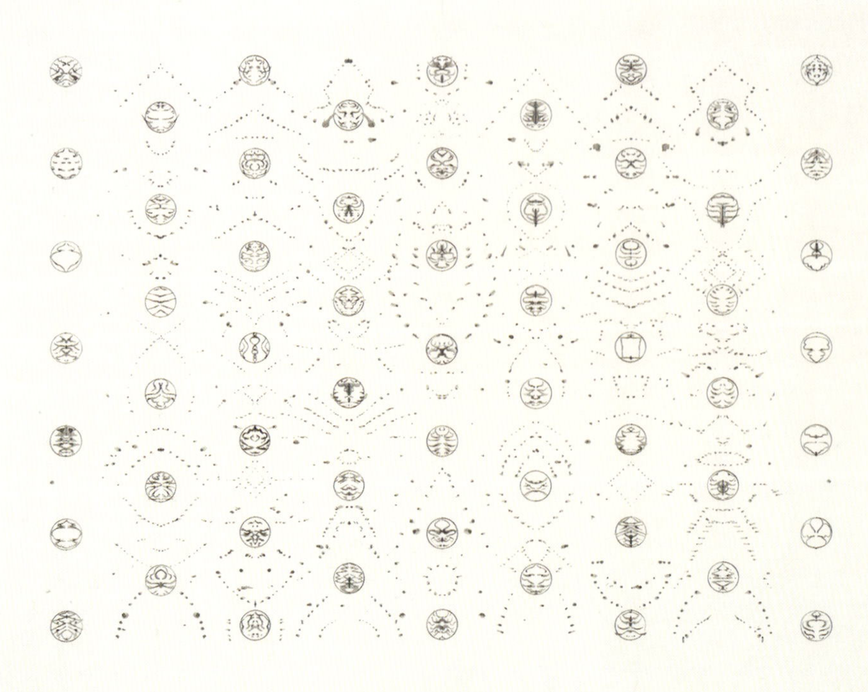

1.6

FIG. 1.6
ANONYMOUSE (Bruce Conner), *INK-BLOT DRAWING, JULY 25, 1999*, 1999. Pencil, pen, and ink on Strathmore Bristol paper; 23 1/8 x 29 inches (58.7 x 73.7 cm). ©Conner Family Trust, San Francisco, California / Artists Rights Society (ARS), New York, New York.

last five years, a period of considerable momentum, the majority of the works added to the collection date from 2011 to 2015. There is an exciting diversity, from an elegant marble-and-thorn piece (pl. 24) and a bronze by Giuseppe Penone to a painting and four lithographs by Takashi Murakami, and a 2015 ink-jet print with spray paint on polyester by Julian Schnabel (pl. 27), a new direction for this artist better known for his paintings.

Unlike the Nasher Collection's focus on sculptures of bronze, steel, and stone, the Nasher Haemisegger Collection contains a balance of media. Thirty-three percent of the collection is sculpture; prints make up twenty-nine percent; painting represents twenty percent of the collection; video, photography, and conceptual art represent ten percent; and eight percent are drawings. And, as Marshall Price points out in his catalogue essay, the collection betrays a true interest in the materials artists use for self-expression, from fabric to plaster or cardboard. Nancy and David have included work by the best sculptors of today, often in depth: Thomas Houseago (pl. 15), Ugo Rondinone, Sterling Ruby (fig. 1.2), Edmund de Waal (pl. 5), Rachel Harrison, Liam Gillick (pl. 8), Rachel Whiteread (pl. 33), Teresita Fernández (pl. 7), and others. When they do have the opportunity to acquire works by older sculptors represented in the Nasher Collection, they always buy recent work, such as the three works by Anthony Caro made in 2012, just before the artist died (including pl. 3), and Anish Kapoor's *Full Moon* (pl. 18) from 2014.

Nancy once described her experience as a teenager watching Beverly Pepper weld the plates of Cor-Ten steel for *Dallas Land Canal*. It impressed her that a woman was engaged in a sculpture technique normally practiced by men. Female artists are almost nonexistent in the Nashers' collection. Nancy and David clearly seek them out. To date, there are a total of twenty-one works by women artists in their collection.

Nancy and David are also putting their individual stamp on the art at NorthPark by making it a venue for contemporary art. They commissioned an interactive mobile app for touring the art on site and have employed a full-time manager of art programming. Nancy and David are acquiring monumental works specifically intended for NorthPark, public art that could not easily fit a domestic setting. For the soaring, two-story atrium entrance in the NorthPark expansion, they acquired the forty-eight-foot Mark di Suvero work *Ad Astra* (fig. 1.3), made in 2005. It has become the landmark symbol for their expansion and a meeting place for shoppers, visitors, and theatergoers. It pays homage to Raymond's forty-seven-foot di Suevero *Eviva Amore* (2001), which features a similar design and was chosen as the anchor piece for the garden of the Nasher Sculpture Center. But, whereas Raymond's di Suvero is bare Cor-Ten steel, unpainted, Nancy and David's di Suvero is completely painted in a strong, happy color. They also added a colorful multiform by Joel Shapiro made of wood—*20 Elements*, 2004–2005—which contrasts with the starker bronzes that Raymond purchased. Love of color plays a central role in many of the purchases Nancy and David have made. A recent example is the purchase of paintings and a large multimedia work by Elliott Hundley (pl. 16).

When Nancy and David saw Chilean artist Iván Navarro's *This Land Is Your Land*, his monumental commentary on the immigrant experience created for Madison Square Park in 2014, they arranged to have it moved and installed at NorthPark (fig. 1.4). For the first time in NorthPark history, they are commissioning a special work from Leo Villareal, an LED sculpture based on his *Buckyball* series. These acquisitions recall the energy, passion, and pure daring Patsy showed at this stage in the development of the Nasher Collection. The Navarro and Villareal works are as adventurous and forward-looking as Patsy's purchase of Jeff Koons's *Louis XIV* from his first show at the Sonnabend Gallery in 1986. Risk-taking, appreciating originality of subject matter or technique, and trusting their instincts are collecting habits manifested in the Nasher Haemisegger Collection.

Another trait is the development of genuine friendships with art dealers. The Nashers had a noticeable chemistry with the dealer Edith Halpert. A good number of the blue-chip international artists in the Nasher Haemisegger Collection—Christian Marclay (pl. 21),

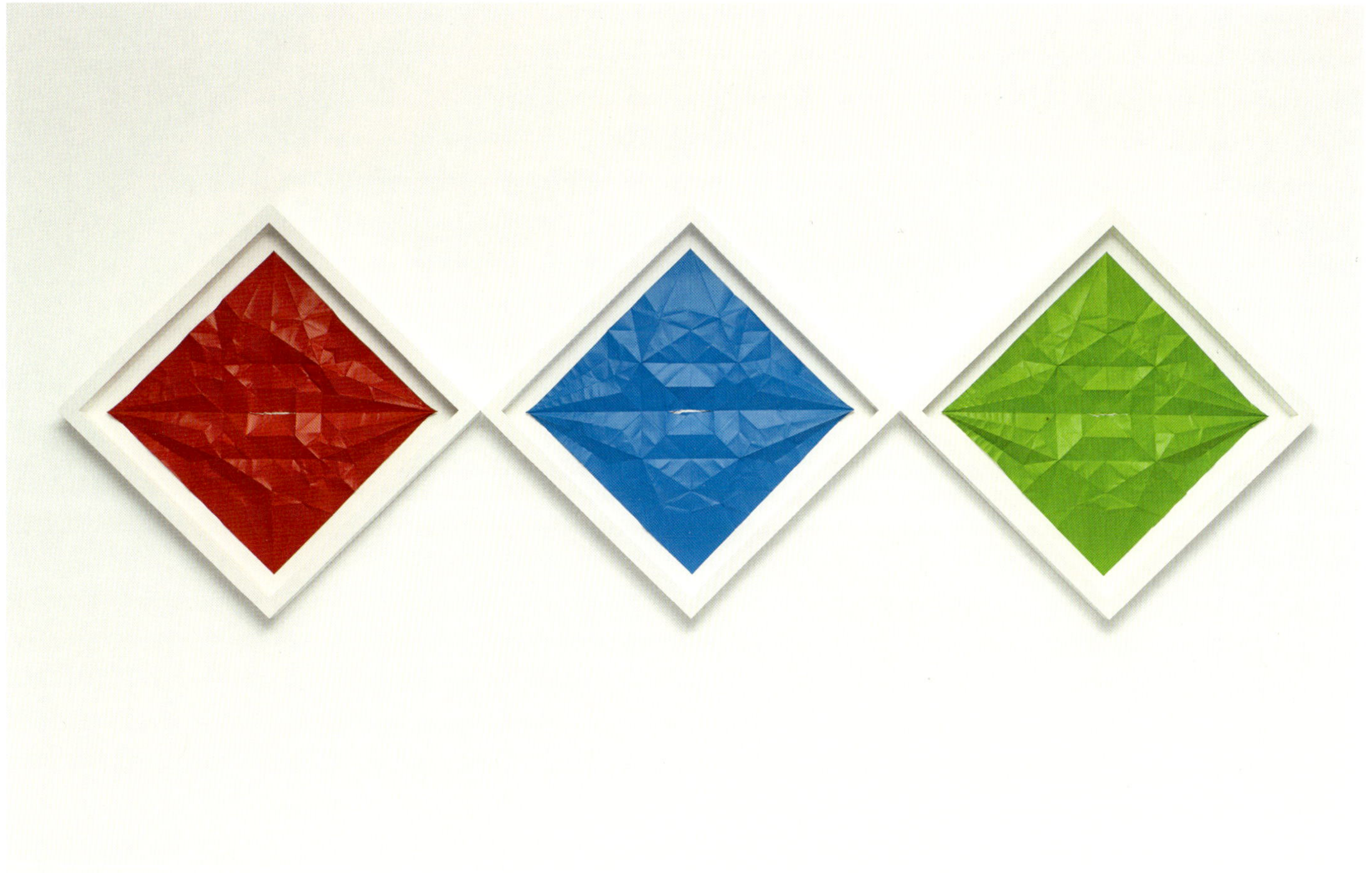

1.7

FIG. 1.7
Tom Friedman, *Dragons*, 2014. Paint on paper, 33 1/4 x 33 1/4 inches (84.5 x 84.5 cm) each. Image courtesy of the artist and Stephen Friedman Gallery, London, England. ©Tom Friedman. Photo by Stephen White.

FIG. 1.8
David Bates, *The Deluge II*, 2006. Oil on canvas, 66 x 48 inches (167.6 x 121.9 cm). Image courtesy of the artist and Arthur Roger Gallery, New Orleans, Louisiana. ©David Bates. Photo by Tom Jenkins.

Sherrie Levine, Charles Gaines, Robert Wilson (fig. 1.5), Christopher Wool (pl. 35), and Bruce Conner (fig. 1.6)—came from the Paula Cooper Gallery. Paula Cooper is not only a source; they highly value her input. Although the relationship with Paula Cooper is the strongest, they have acquired from all of the top dealers and galleries: Galerie Lelong (Jaume Plensa and Alfredo Jaar, pl. 17), Gagosian (Damien Hirst, de Waal, Ruby), Hauser and Wirth (Houseago), Barbara Gladstone (Rondinone), Goodman (Penone), among numerous others.

Loyalty to certain artists they believe in is another discerning attribute. They have amassed five paintings and four sculptures from Tom Friedman (fig. 1.7), four sculptures and two paintings by Houseago, including the plaster cast for his bronze in their collection, and a total of twelve works by David Bates (fig. 1.8). They are currently in the process of adding important earlier works to their pieces by Ken Price. They invest in living artists and enjoy supporting them, often purchasing works in more than one media from an artist.

Another collecting pattern Nancy and David have adopted is a kinship with artists. Some collectors fear they might be persuaded to buy a work because of the artist's personality and therefore avoid direct interaction with the artist. Nancy and David, however, know most of the artists they have recently collected. Many

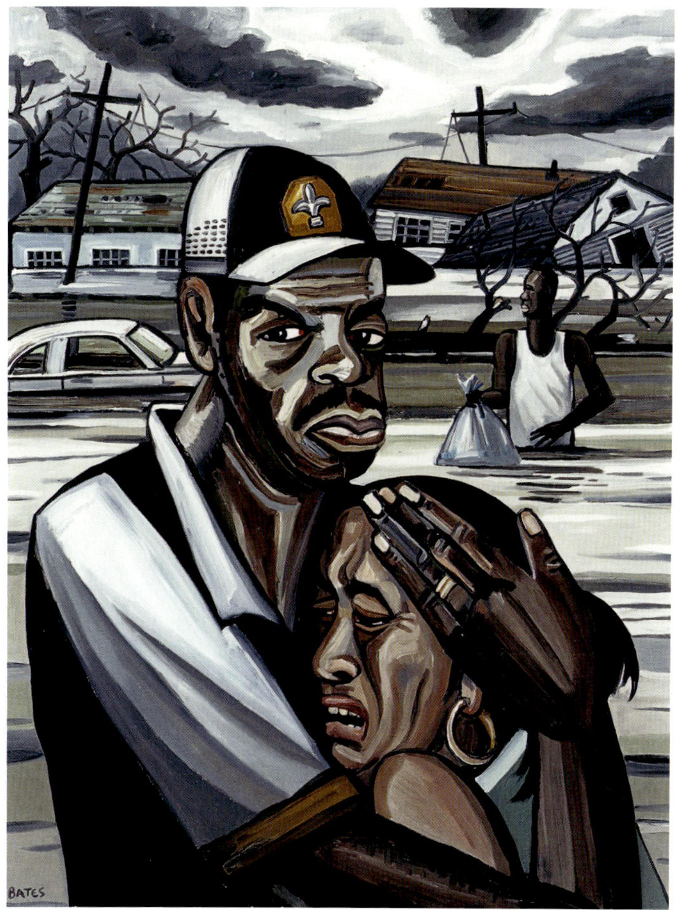

1.8

FIG. 1.9
Melvin Edwards, *Gulley Hammer*, 1980. Welded steel, 9 7/8 x 7 x 8 inches (25.1 x 17.8 x 20.3 cm). Image courtesy of the artist; Stephen Friedman Gallery, London, England; and Alexander Gray Associates, New York, New York. ©Melvin Edwards / Artists Rights Society (ARS), New York, New York.

FIG. 1.10
Melvin Edwards, *Level*, 1973. Welded steel and barbed wire, 6 1/4 x 13 3/4 x 12 7/8 inches (15.9 x 34.9 x 32.7 cm). Image courtesy of the artist; Stephen Friedman Gallery, London, England; and Alexander Gray Associates, New York, New York. ©Melvin Edwards / Artists Rights Society (ARS), New York, New York.

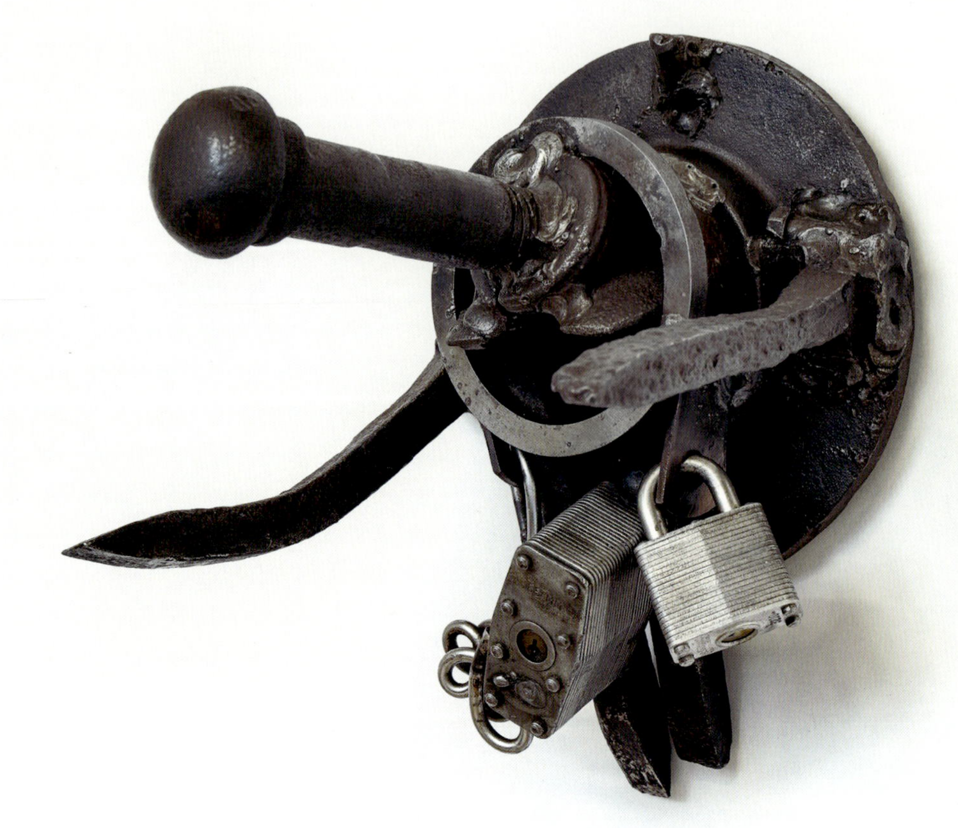

1.9

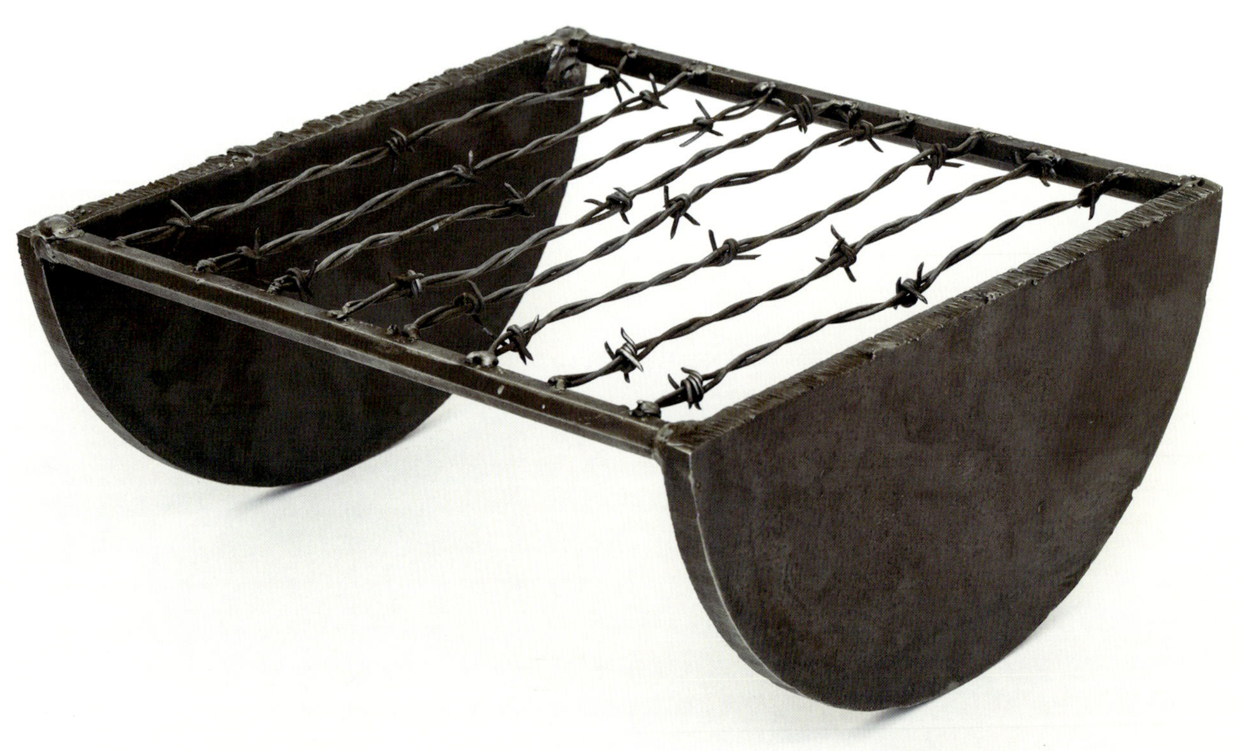

1.10

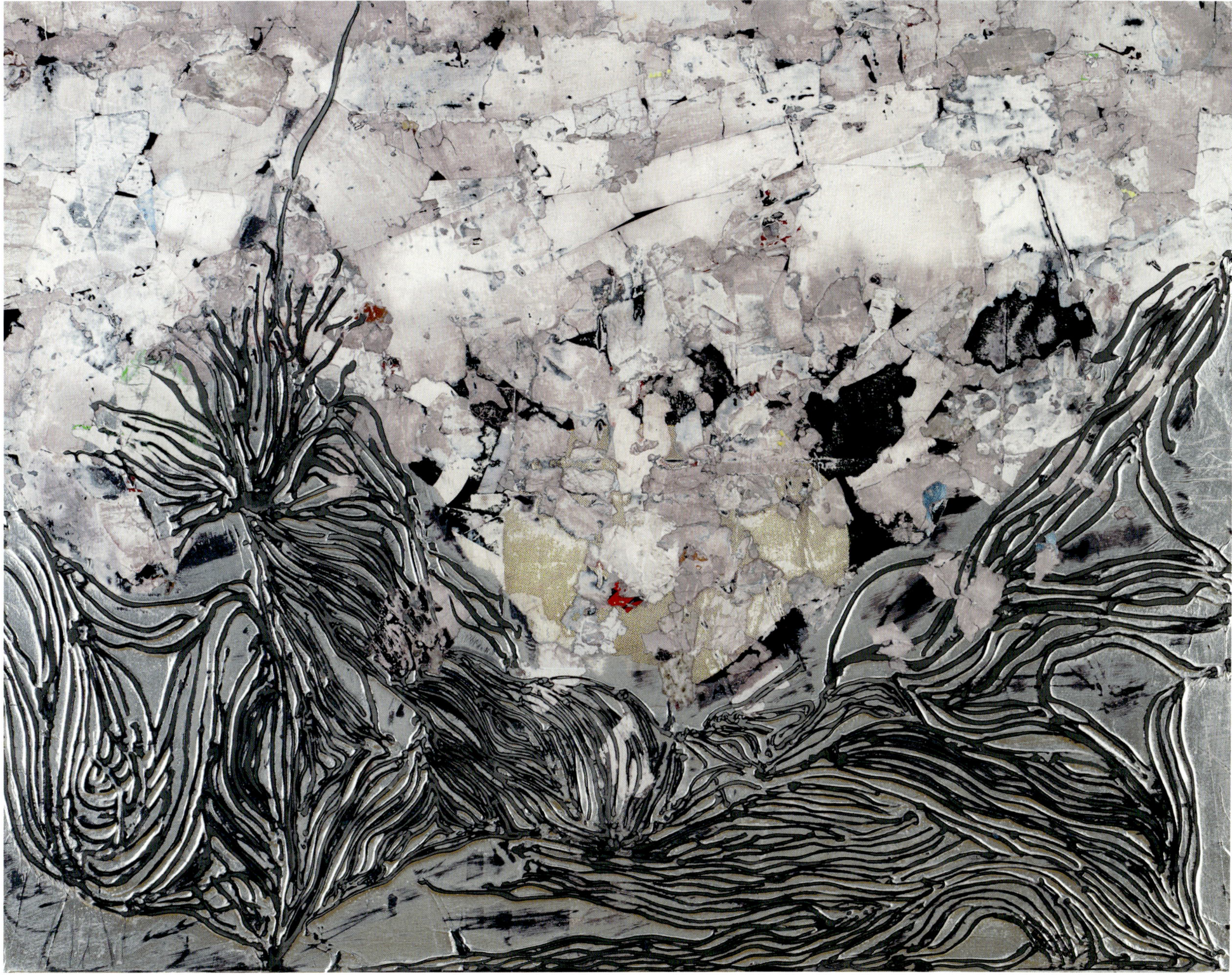

1.11

of these they have met as a result of their involvement with two institutions, the Nasher Sculpture Center in Dallas and the Nasher Museum of Art at Duke University. Jeremey Strick, director of the Nasher Sculpture Center, has introduced Nancy and David to many sculptors. Nancy and David aquired works by a number of artists—including Mark Grotjahn (pl. 12), Fernández, Katharina Grosse (pls. 10, 11), and Melvin Edwards (figs. 1.9, 1.10)—after first encountering them in Strick's exhibitions. Trevor Schoonmaker, Chief Curator and Patsy R. and Raymond D. Nasher Curator of Contemporary Art at the Nasher Museum, introduced them to the work of Mark Bradford (fig. 1.11), Kara Walker (pl. 31), Kerry James Marshall (pl. 22), and Gaines. Conner is an artist championed by Duke art historian and fellow Collection Committee member at the Nasher Museum Kristine Stiles, who gifted sixty Conners from her private collection to the museum. Raymond and Patsy were also advised by museums and curators, but Nancy and David stand apart in the amount of investment they have made in these two institutions, which have played a large role in their collecting.

Nancy and David have made it a habit to judiciously study the market, travel to all the major fairs, attend artists' lectures and openings, and frequently visit sculpture parks and projects around the world. Their collection will continue to grow, no doubt revealing new collecting patterns, habits, and interests. They have been generous to agree to the exhibition *A Material Legacy*. It is a harbinger of things to come.

FIG. 1.11
Mark Bradford, *Intimate Violence*, 2009. Mixed-media collage on canvas, 48 x 60 inches (121.9 x 152.4 cm). Image courtesy of the artist; Hauser & Wirth, London, England; and Sikkema Jenkins & Co, New York, New York. © Mark Bradford. Photo by Jason Wyche.

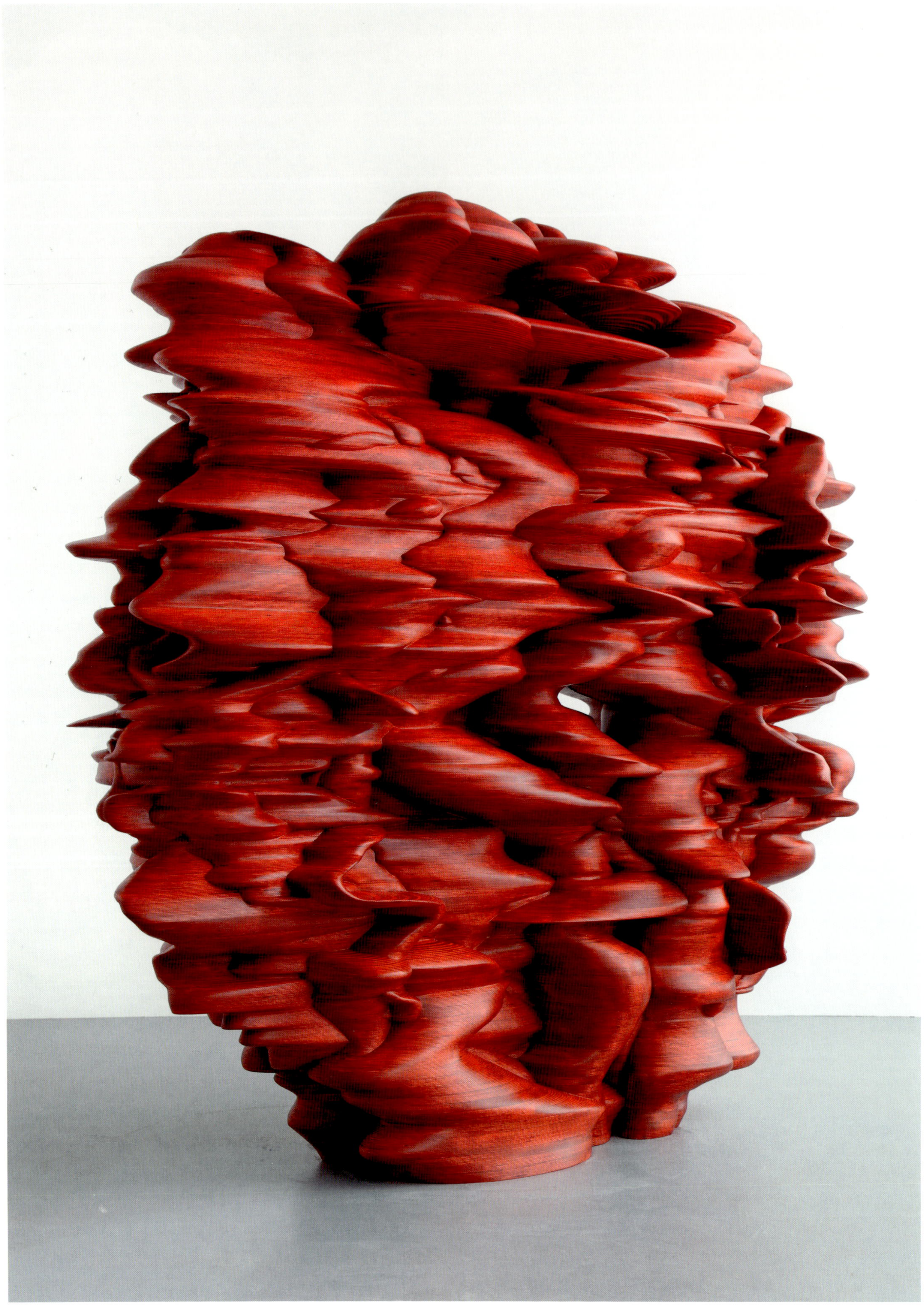

PL. 4 Tony Cragg, *Versus*, 2011. Wood, 110 1/4 x 116 x 39 1/2 inches (280 x 295 x 100.3 cm).

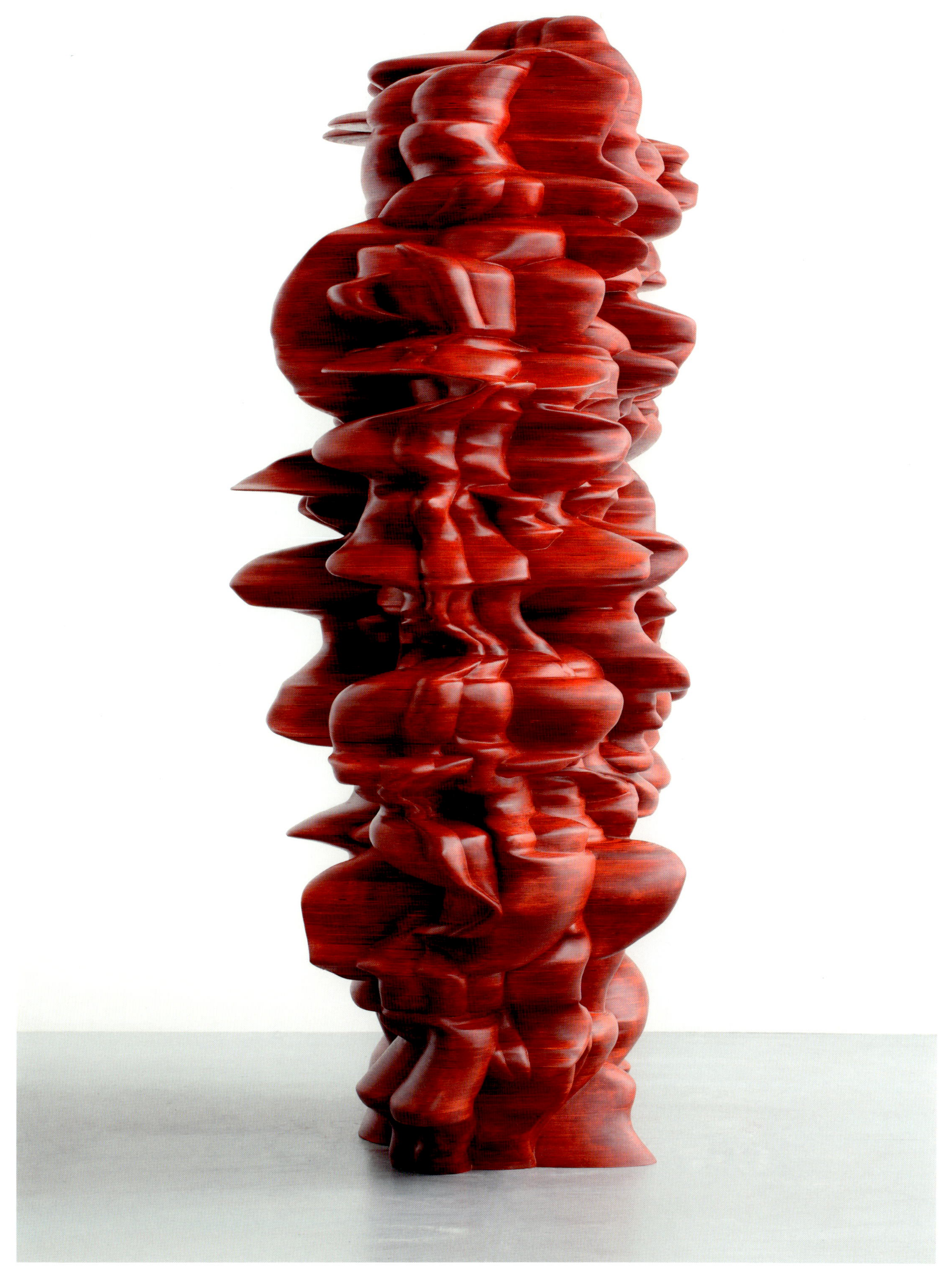

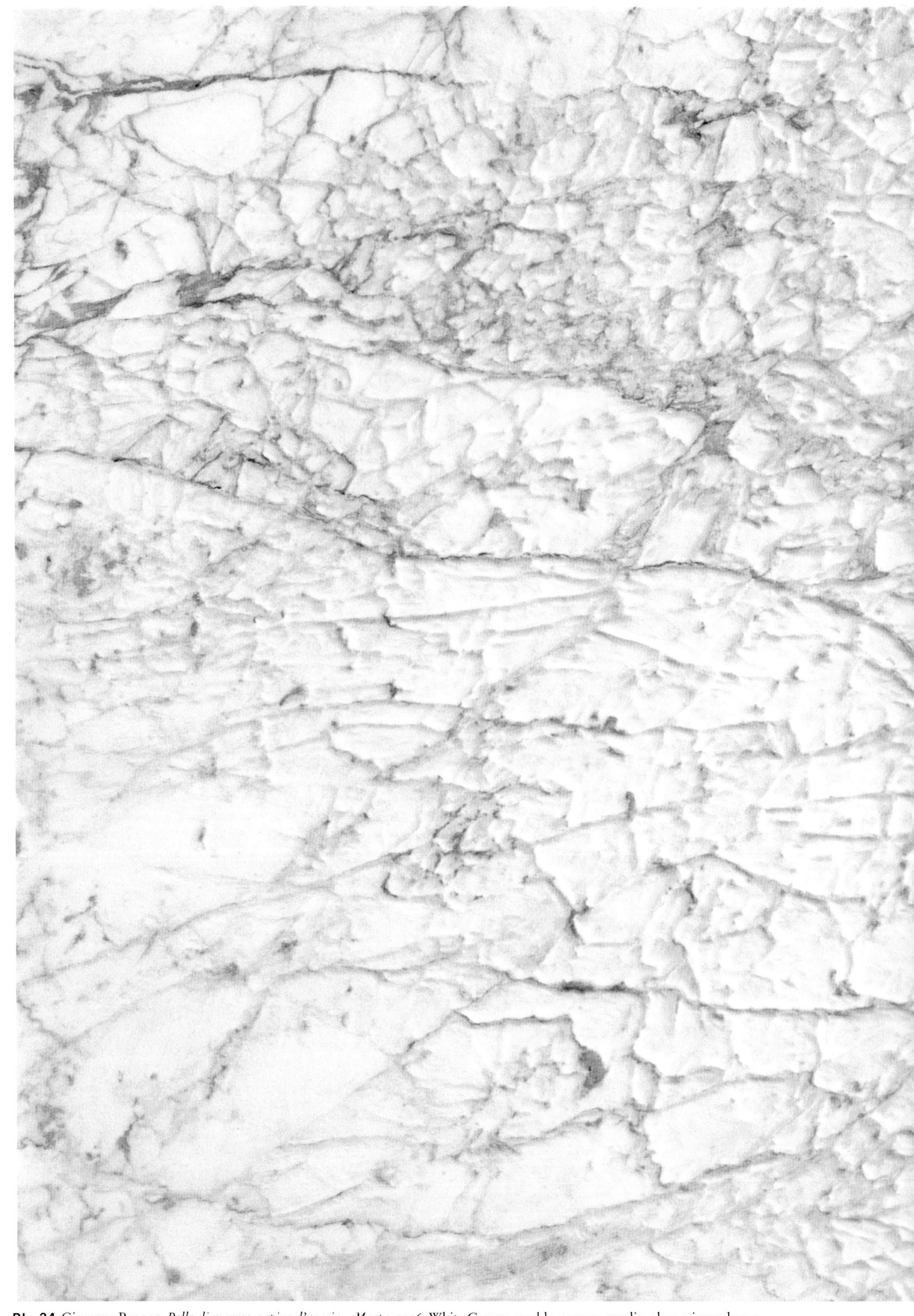

PL. 24 Giuseppe Penone, *Pelle di marmo e spine d'acacia – Marta*, 2006. White Carrara marble, canvas, acrylic, glass microspheres, and acacia thorns; 39 3/8 x 55 1/8 x 2 3/8 inches (100 x 140 x 6 cm).

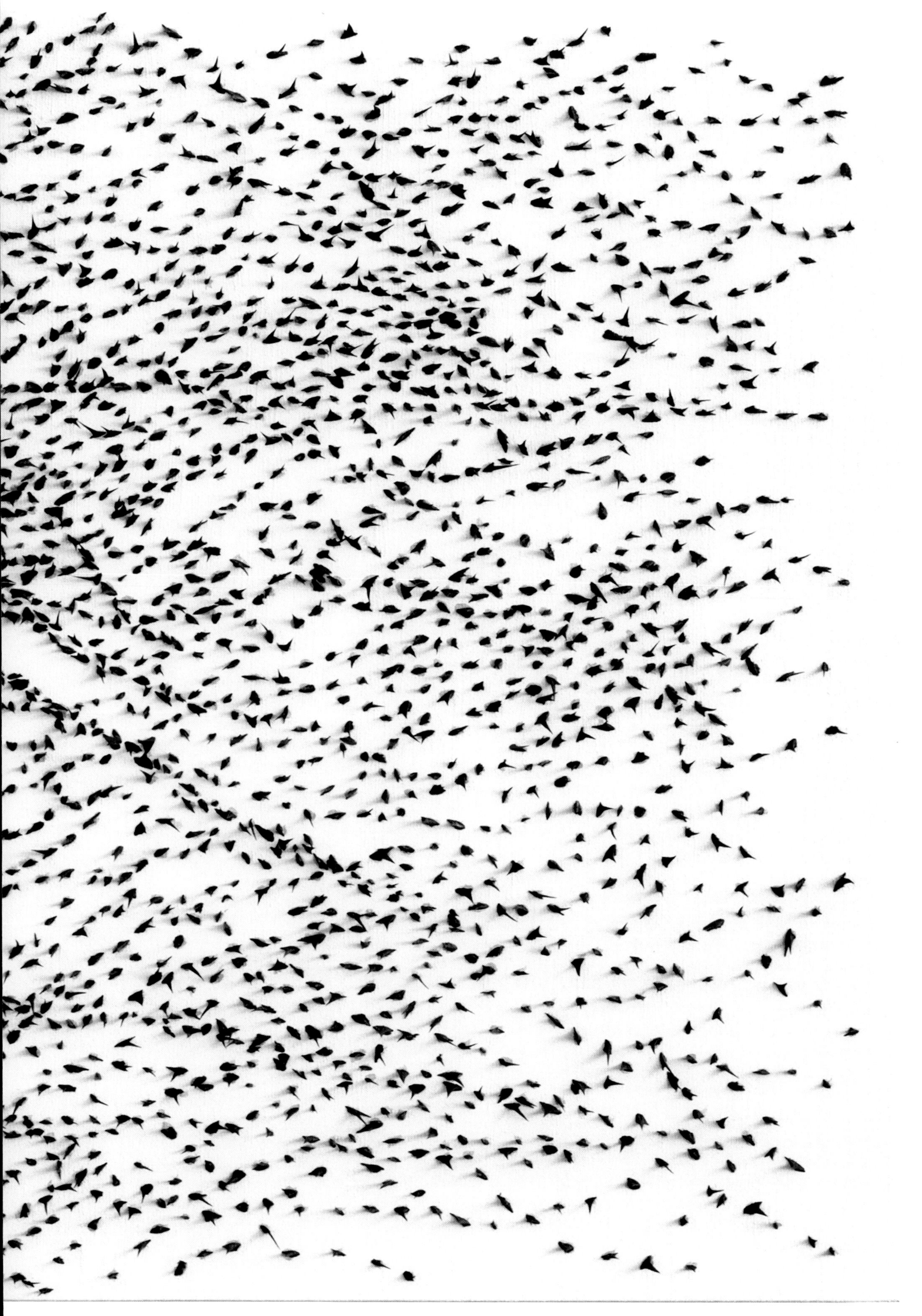

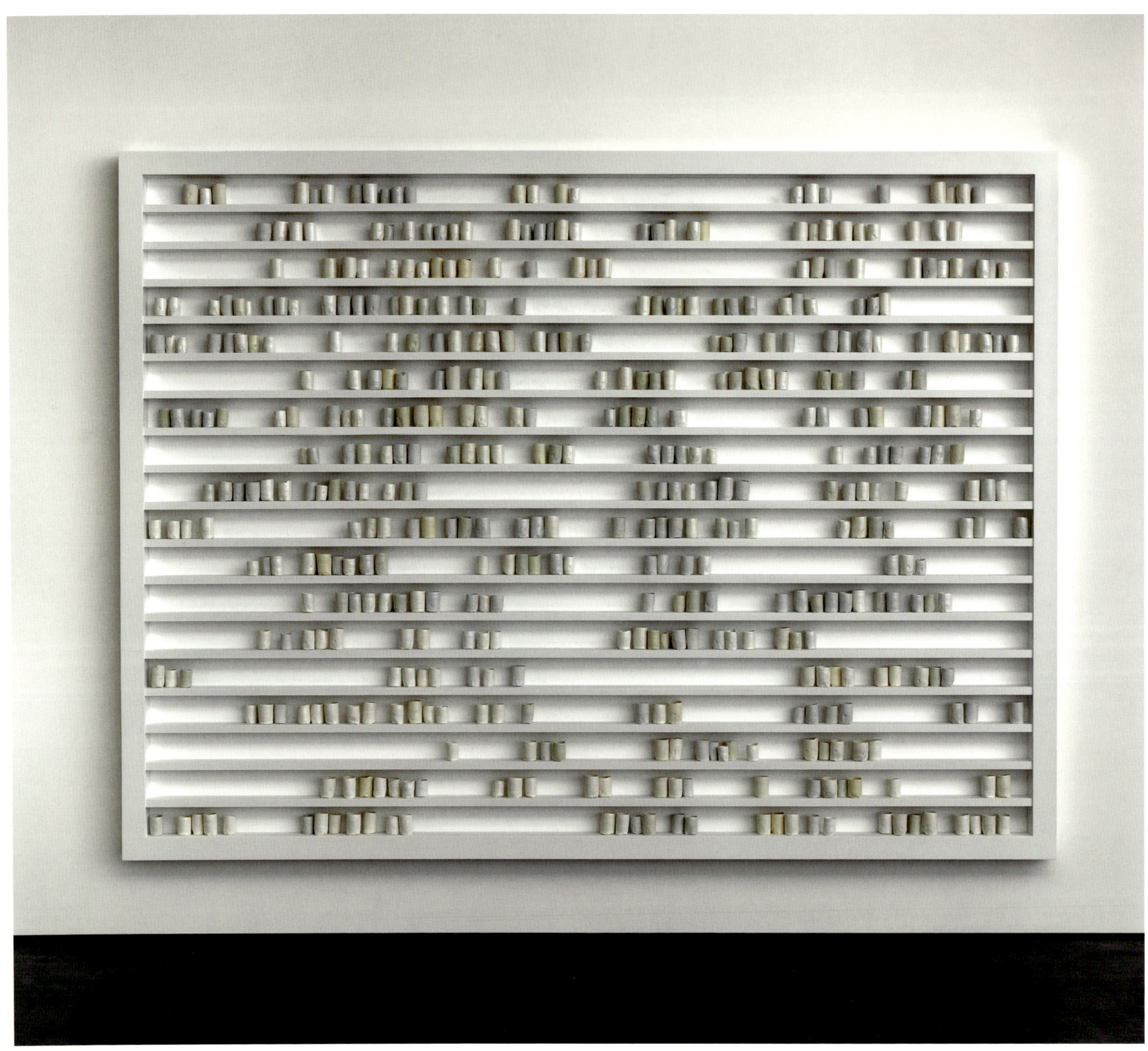

PL. 5 Edmund de Waal, *breathturn, I*, 2013. 476 porcelain vessels in aluminum and Plexiglas cabinet, 90 3/8 x 118 1/8 x 3 15/16 inches (229.6 x 300 x 10 cm).

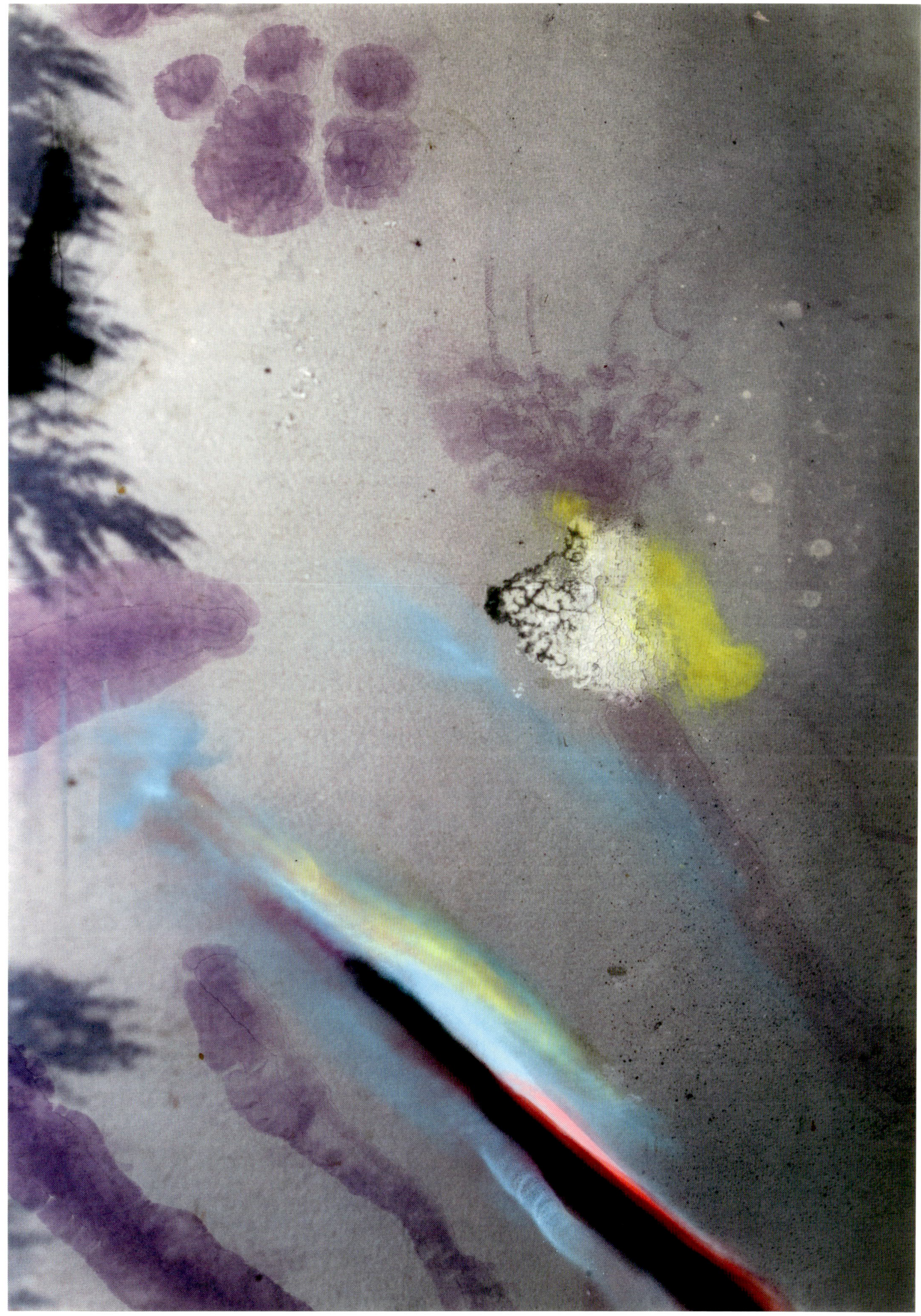

PL. 27 Julian Schnabel, *Untitled*, 2015. Ink-jet print and spray paint on polyester, 108 x 72 inches (274.3 x 182.9 cm).

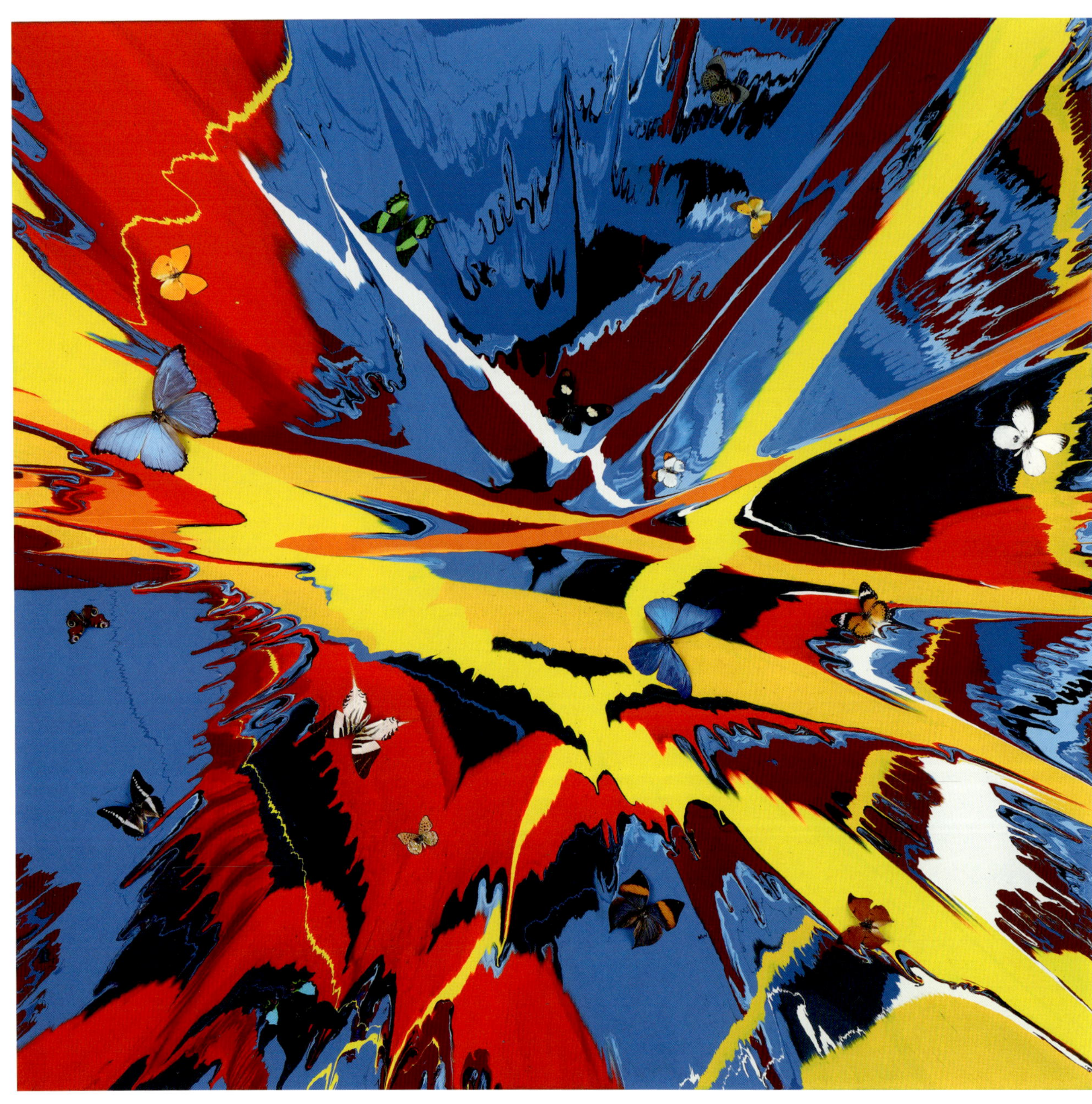

PL. 13 Damien Hirst, *Beautiful Superheroes Painting (with Butterflies)*, 2007. Butterflies and household gloss on canvas, 48 x 48 inches (122 x 122 cm).

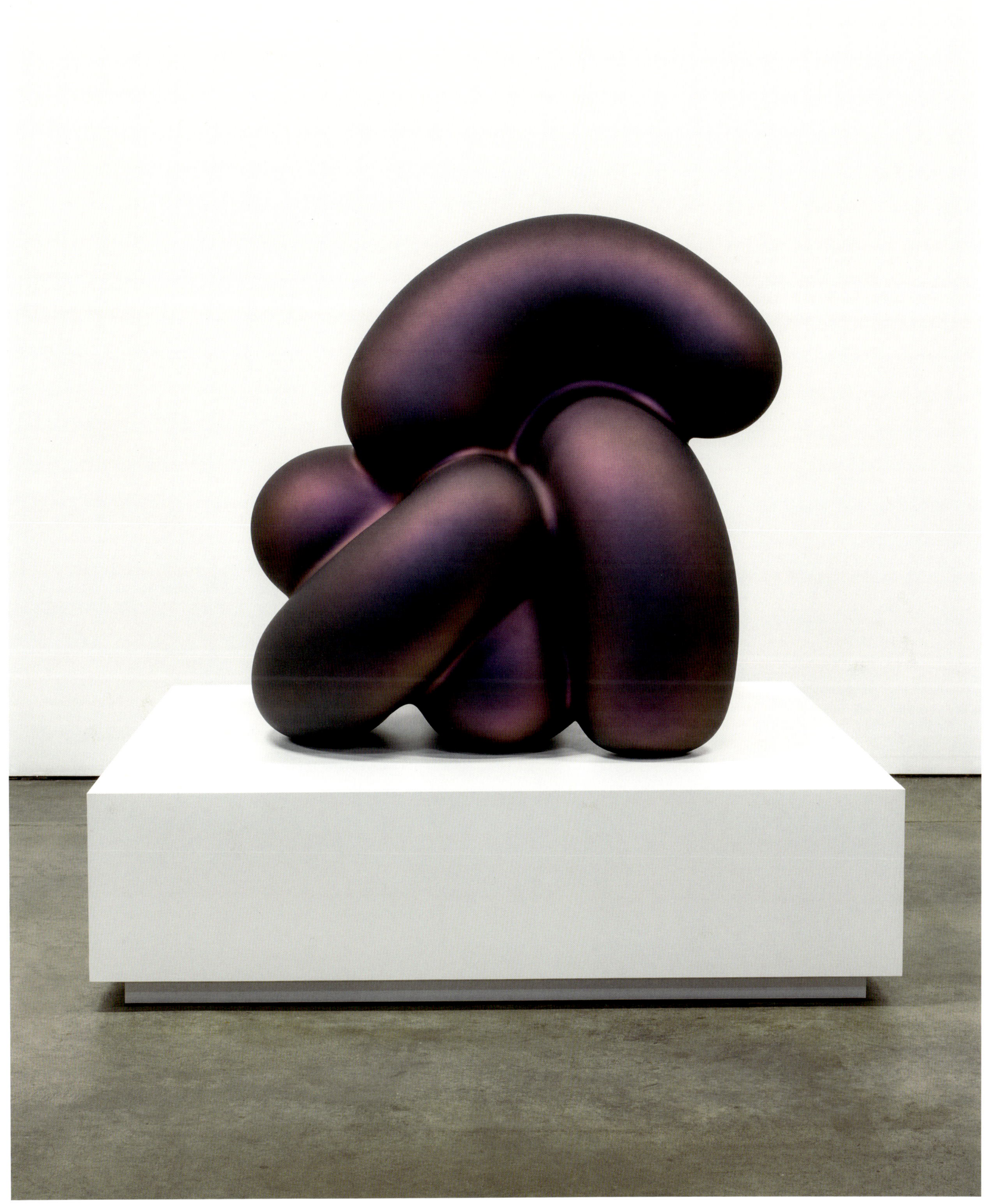

PL. 25 Ken Price, *Ceejay*, 2011. Painted bronze composite, 48 x 48 3/8 x 46 inches (121.9 x 122.9 x 116.8 cm).

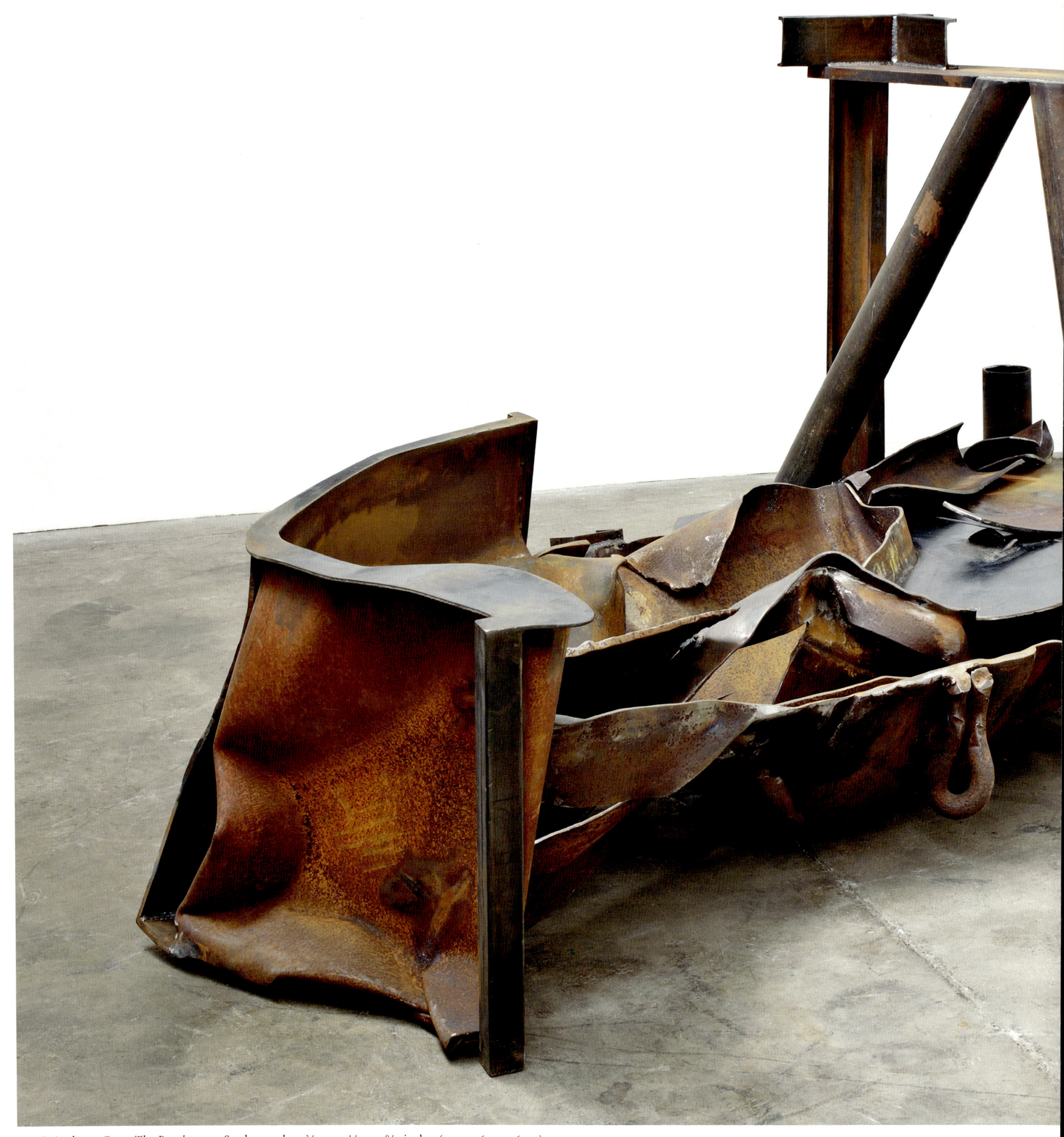

PL. 3 Anthony Caro, *The Brook*, 2012. Steel, rusted; 52 3/8 x 105 1/8 x 53 9/16 inches (133 x 267 x 136 cm).

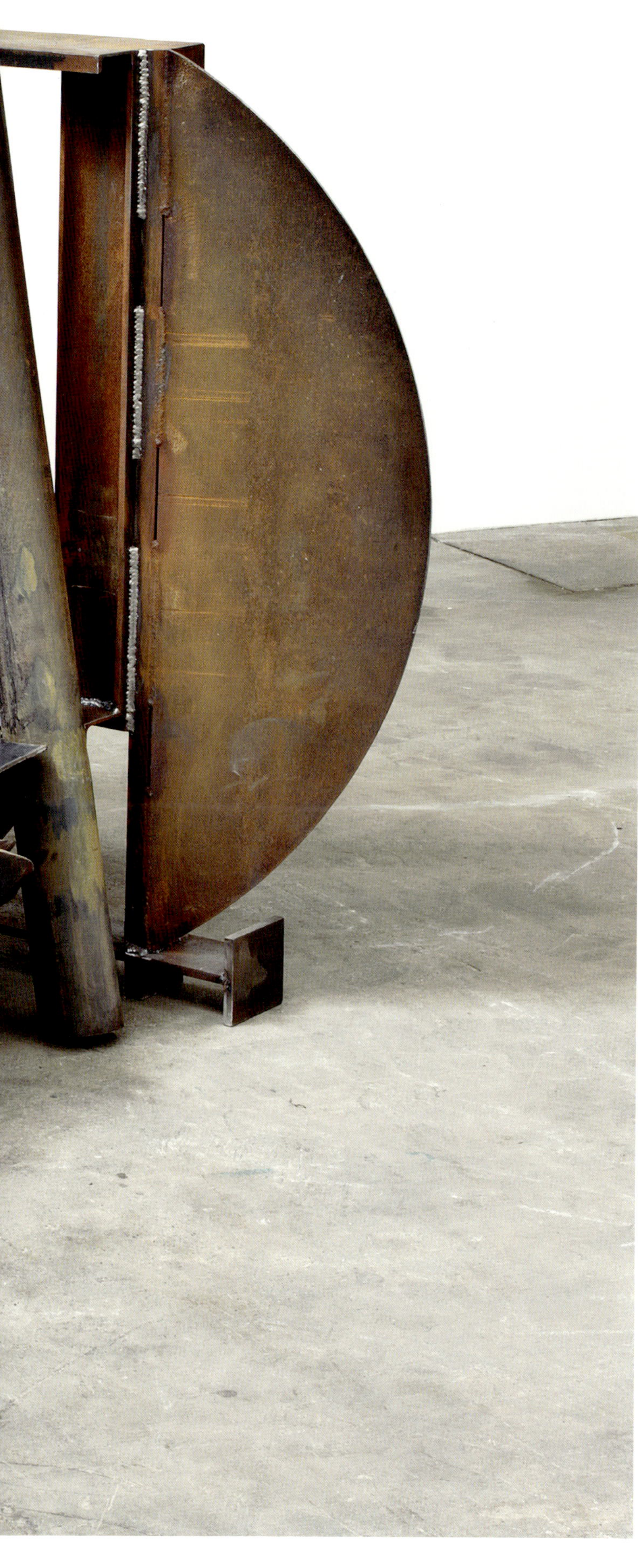

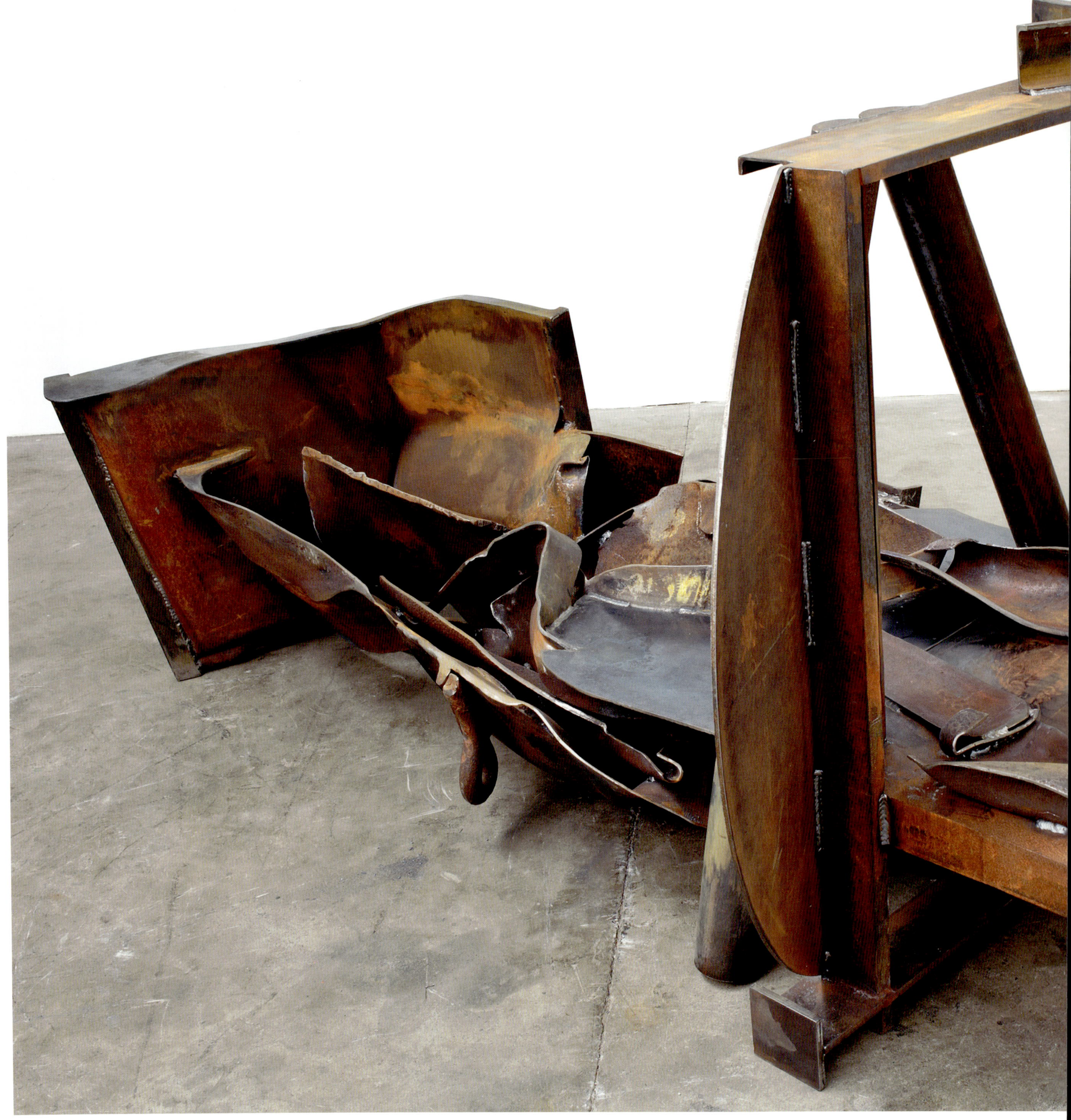

PL. 3 Anthony Caro, *The Brook*, 2012 (alternate view). Steel, rusted; 52 3/8 x 105 1/8 x 53 9/16 inches (133 x 267 x 136 cm).

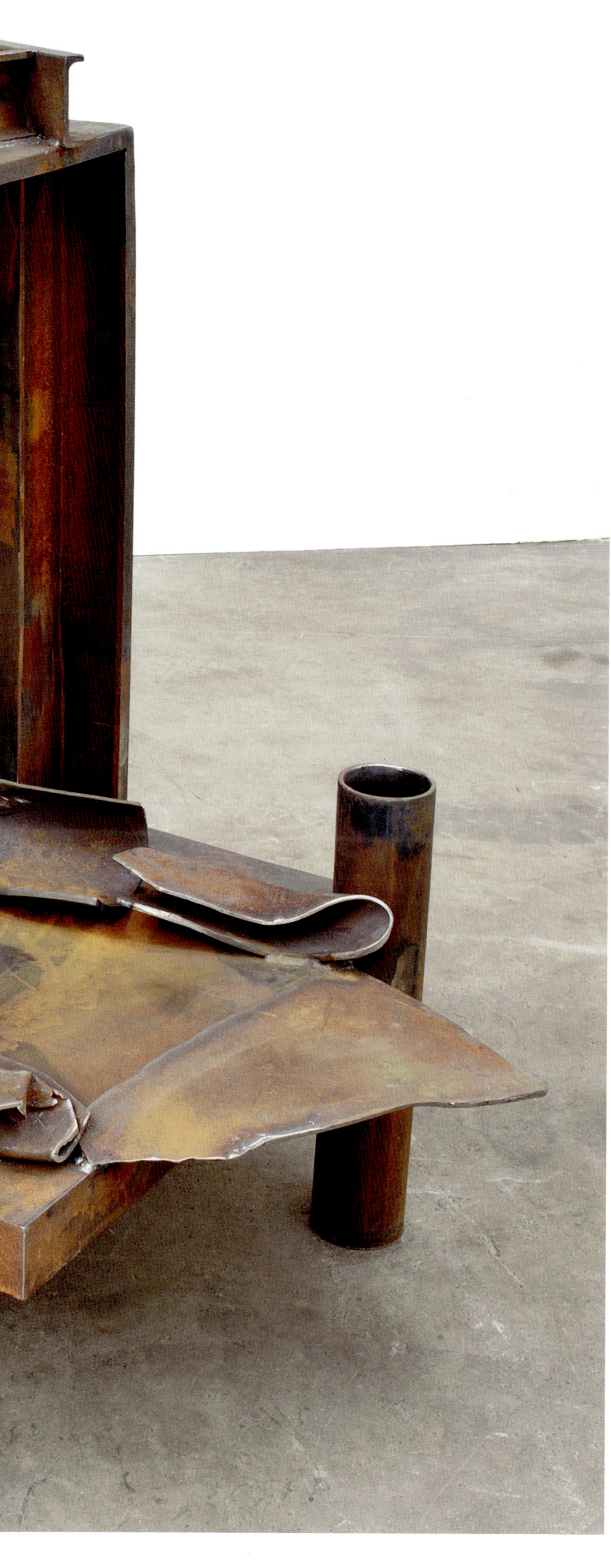

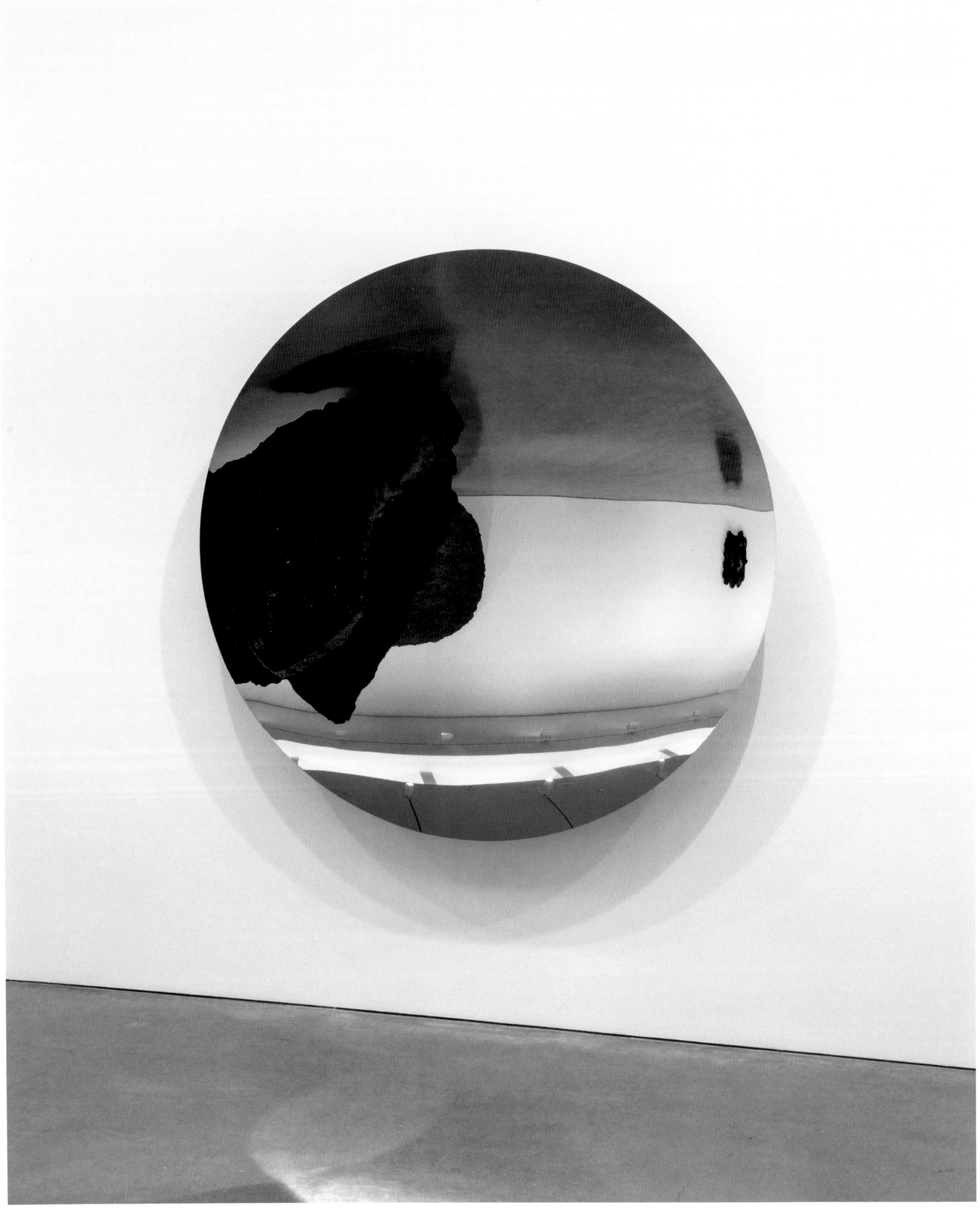

PL. 18 Anish Kapoor, *Full Moon*, 2014. Stainless steel, 70 7/8 x 70 7/8 x 10 7/8 inches (180 x 180 x 27.5 cm).

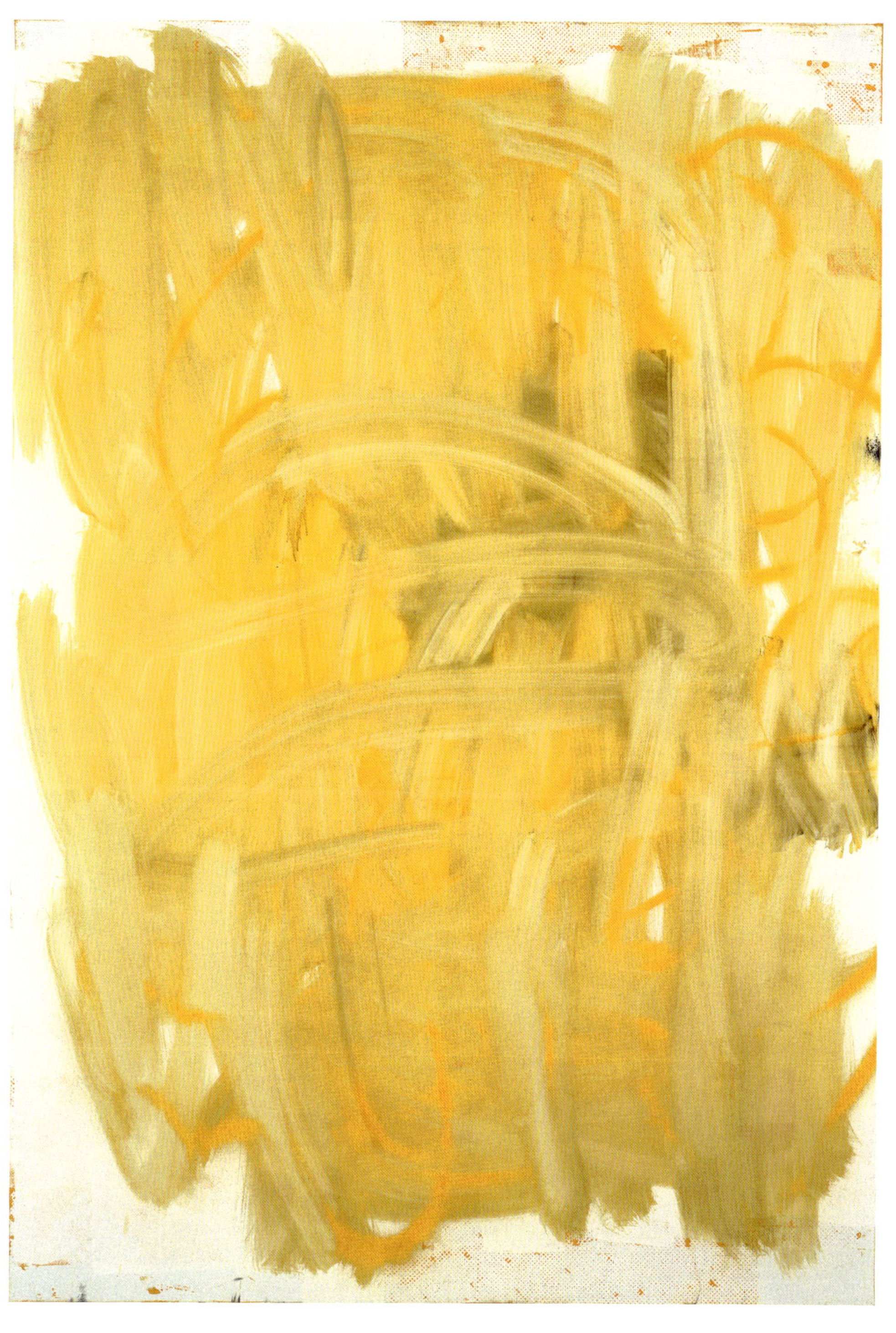

PL. 35 Christopher Wool, *Untitled*, 2000. Enamel on linen, 108 x 72 inches (274.3 x 182.9 cm).

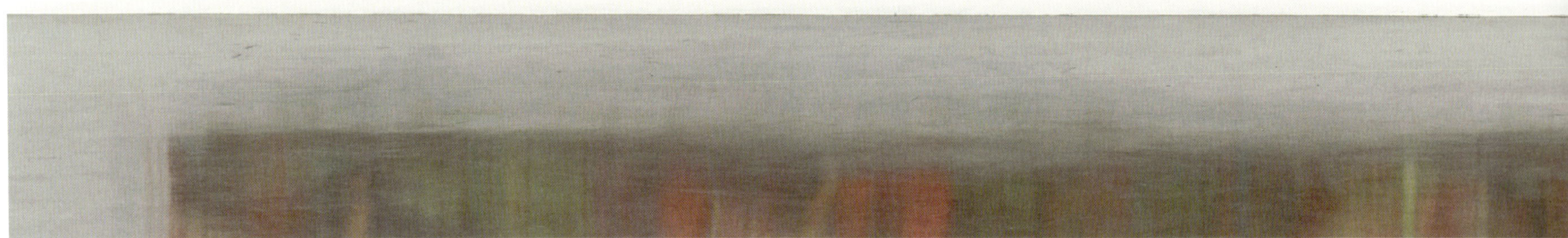

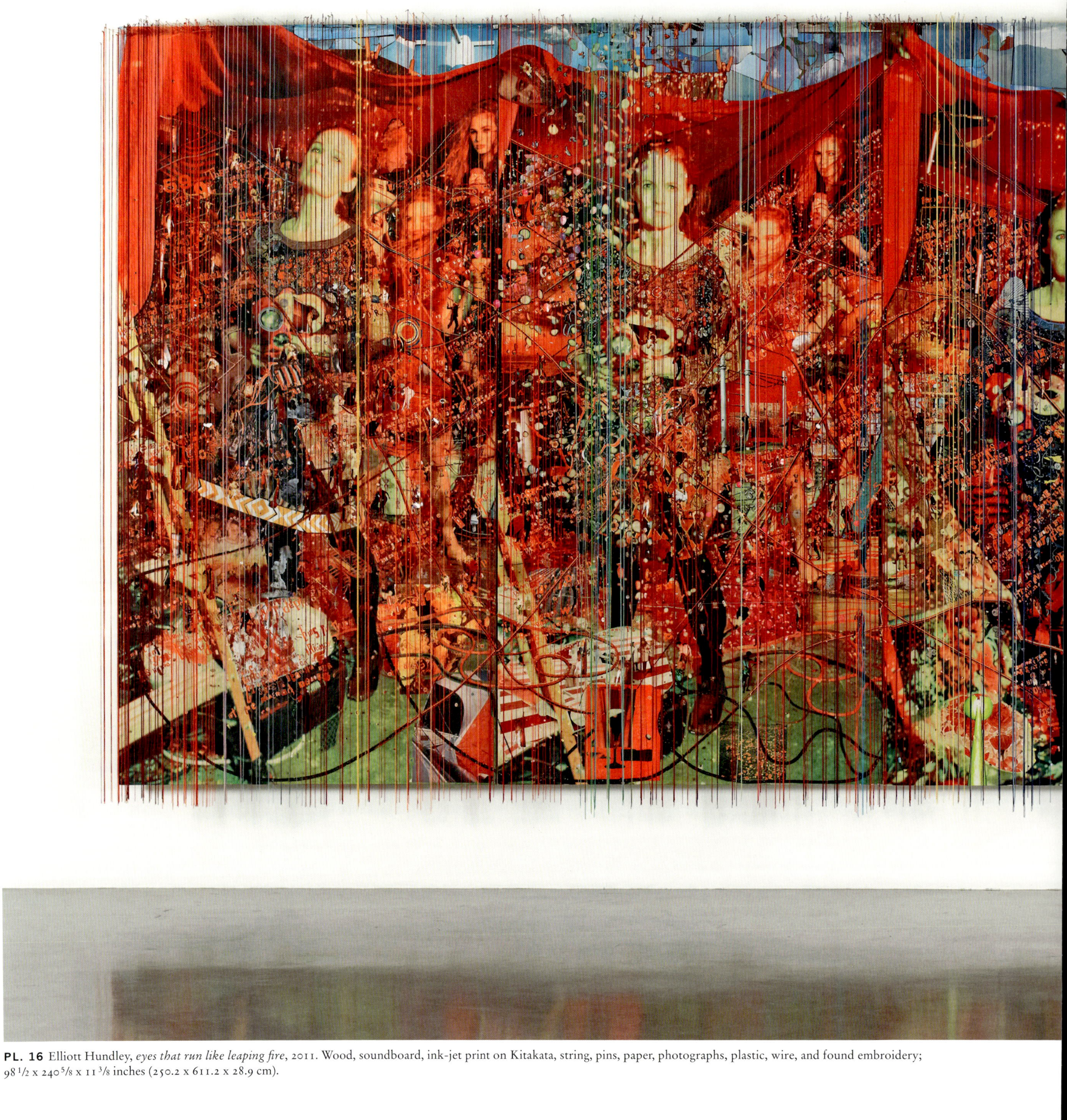

PL. 16 Elliott Hundley, *eyes that run like leaping fire*, 2011. Wood, soundboard, ink-jet print on Kitakata, string, pins, paper, photographs, plastic, wire, and found embroidery; 98 1/2 x 240 5/8 x 11 3/8 inches (250.2 x 611.2 x 28.9 cm).

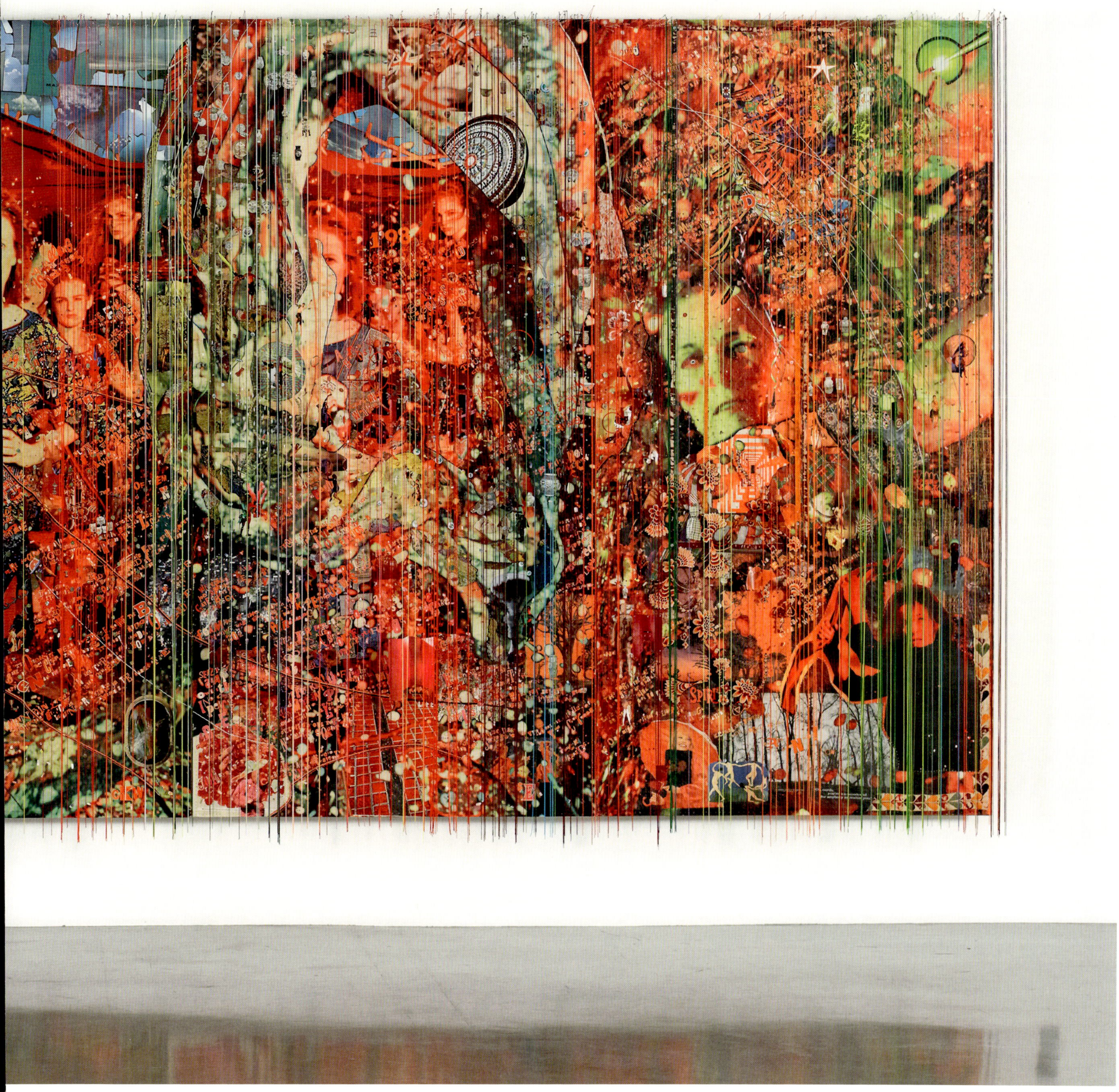

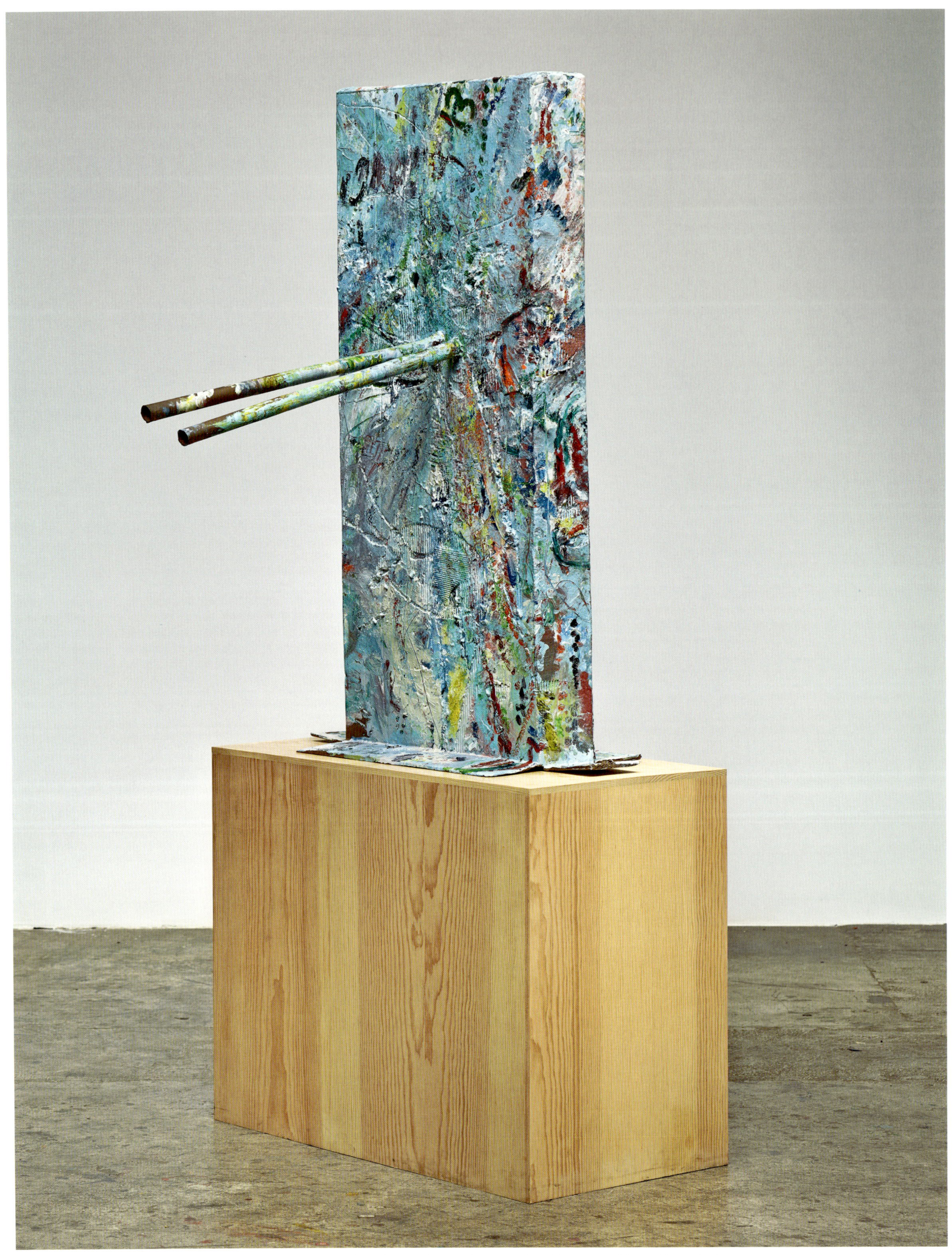

PL. 12 Mark Grotjahn, *Untitled (Pretty Lost Blue for My Girls, Italian Mask M30.b)*, 2013. Painted bronze, 52 3/4 x 33 1/2 x 38 inches (134 x 85.1 x 96.5 cm).

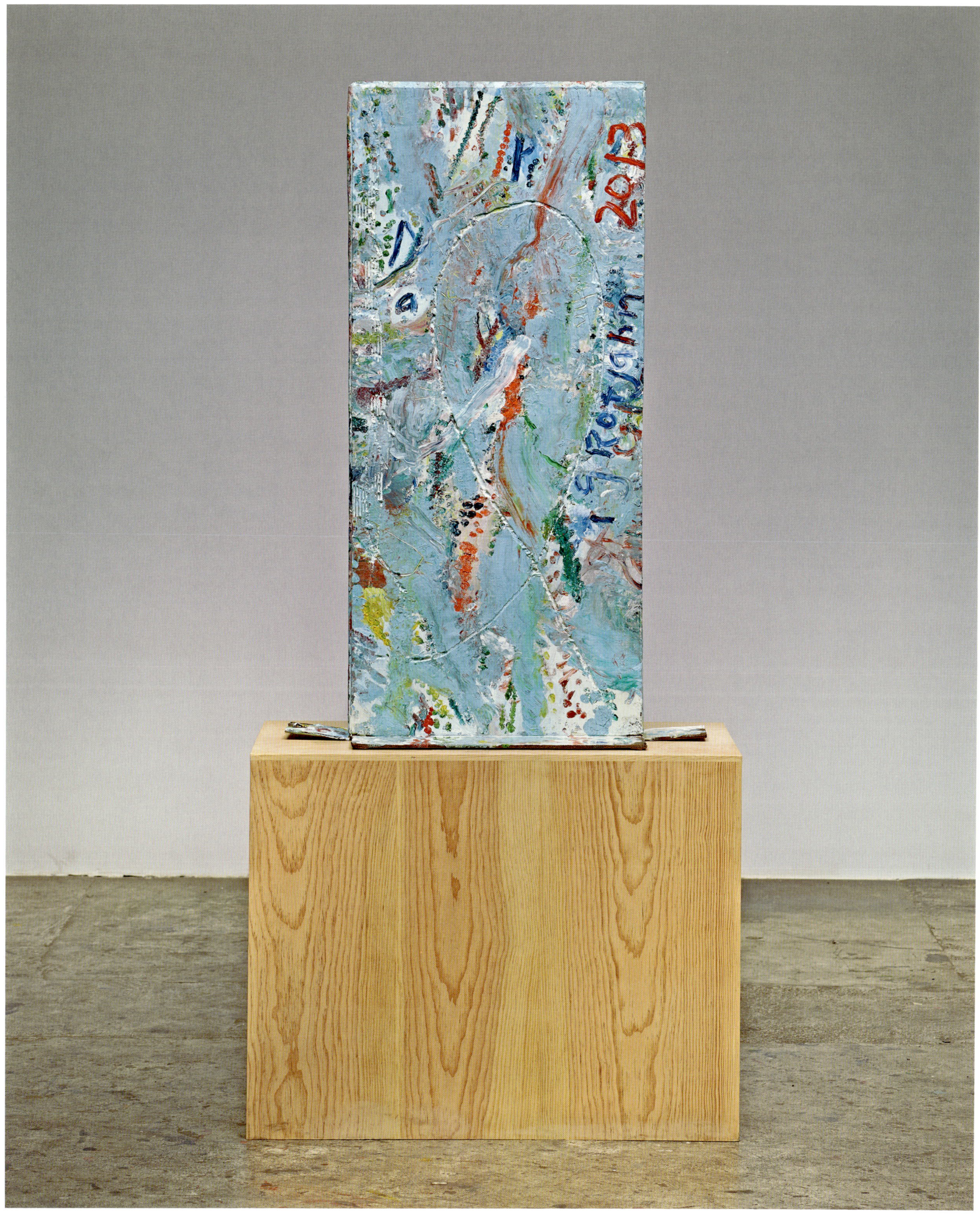
2013

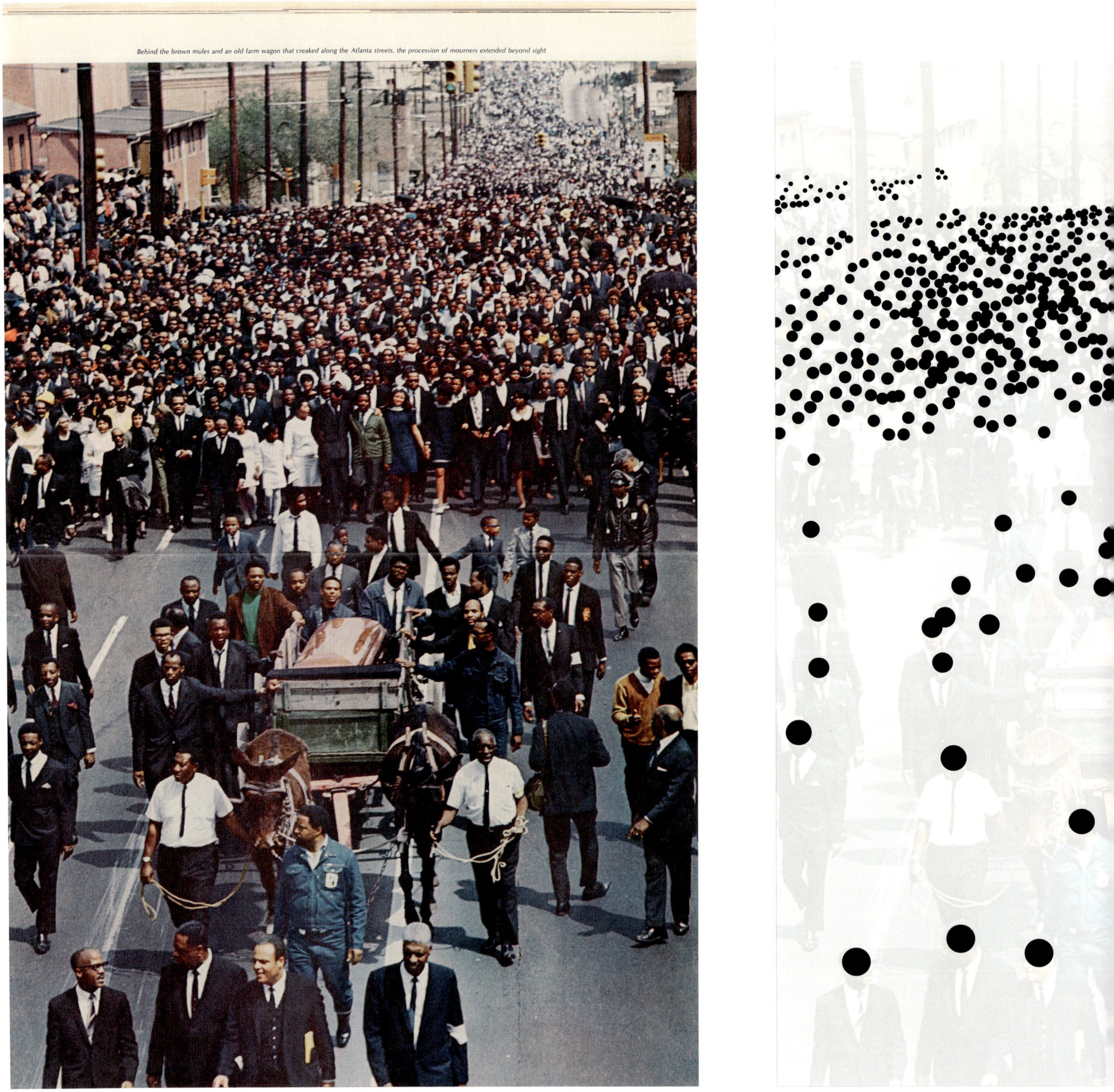

Behind the brown mules and an old farm wagon that creaked along the Atlanta streets, the procession of mourners extended beyond sight

PL. 17 Alfredo Jaar, *Life Magazine, April 19, 1968*, 1995. Three photographic prints, edition 3/3; 61 x 120 inches (154.9 x 304.8 cm) overall.

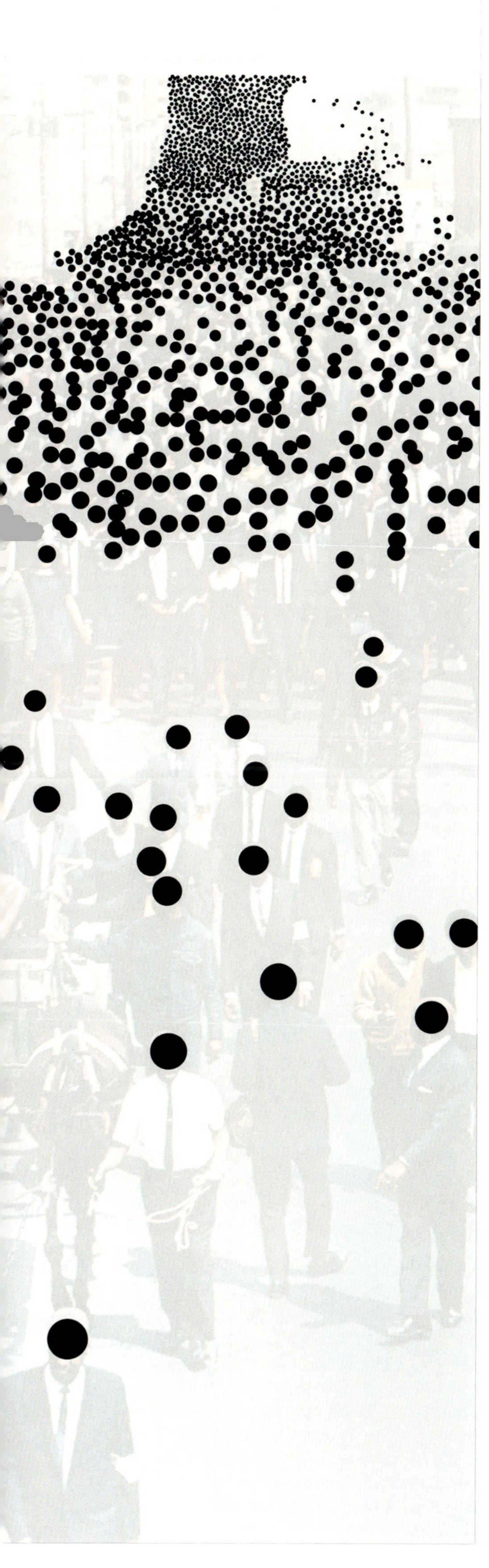

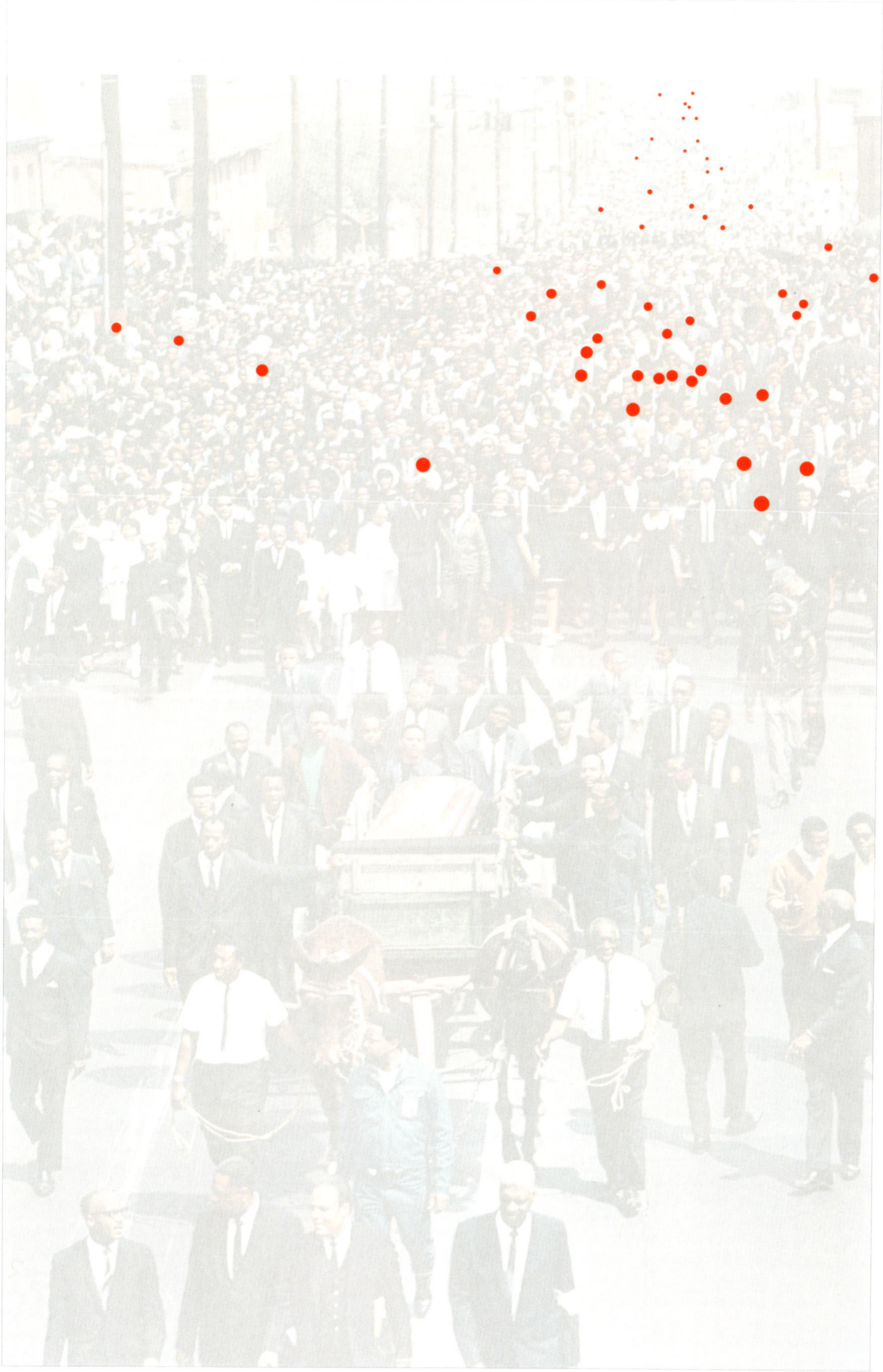

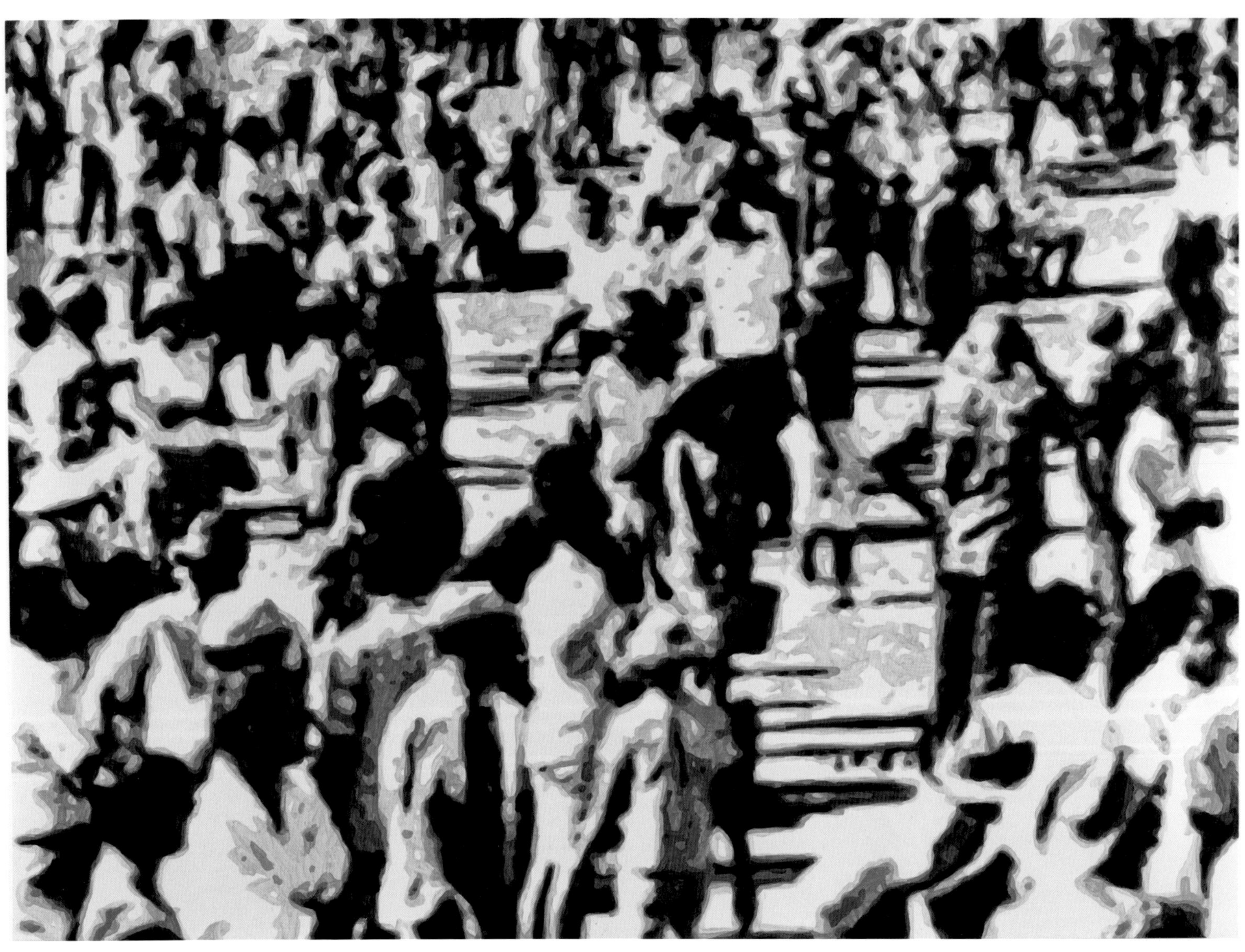

PL. 9 Wayne Gonzales, *Waiting Crowd*, 2008. Acrylic on canvas, 78 x 103 inches (198.1 x 261.6 cm).

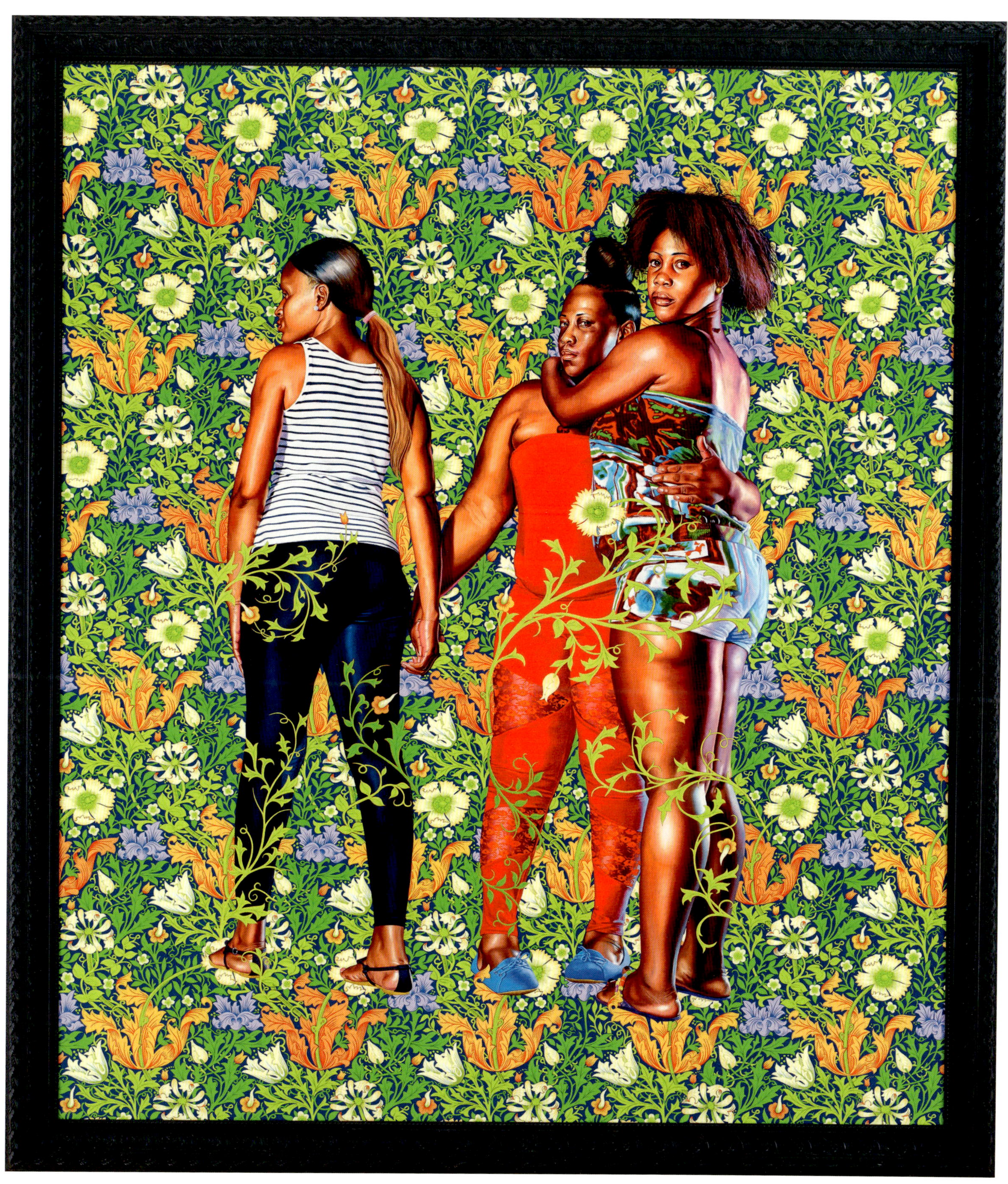

PL. 34 Kehinde Wiley, *Naomi and Her Daughters*, 2013. Oil on canvas, 180 x 90 inches (457.2 x 228.6 cm).

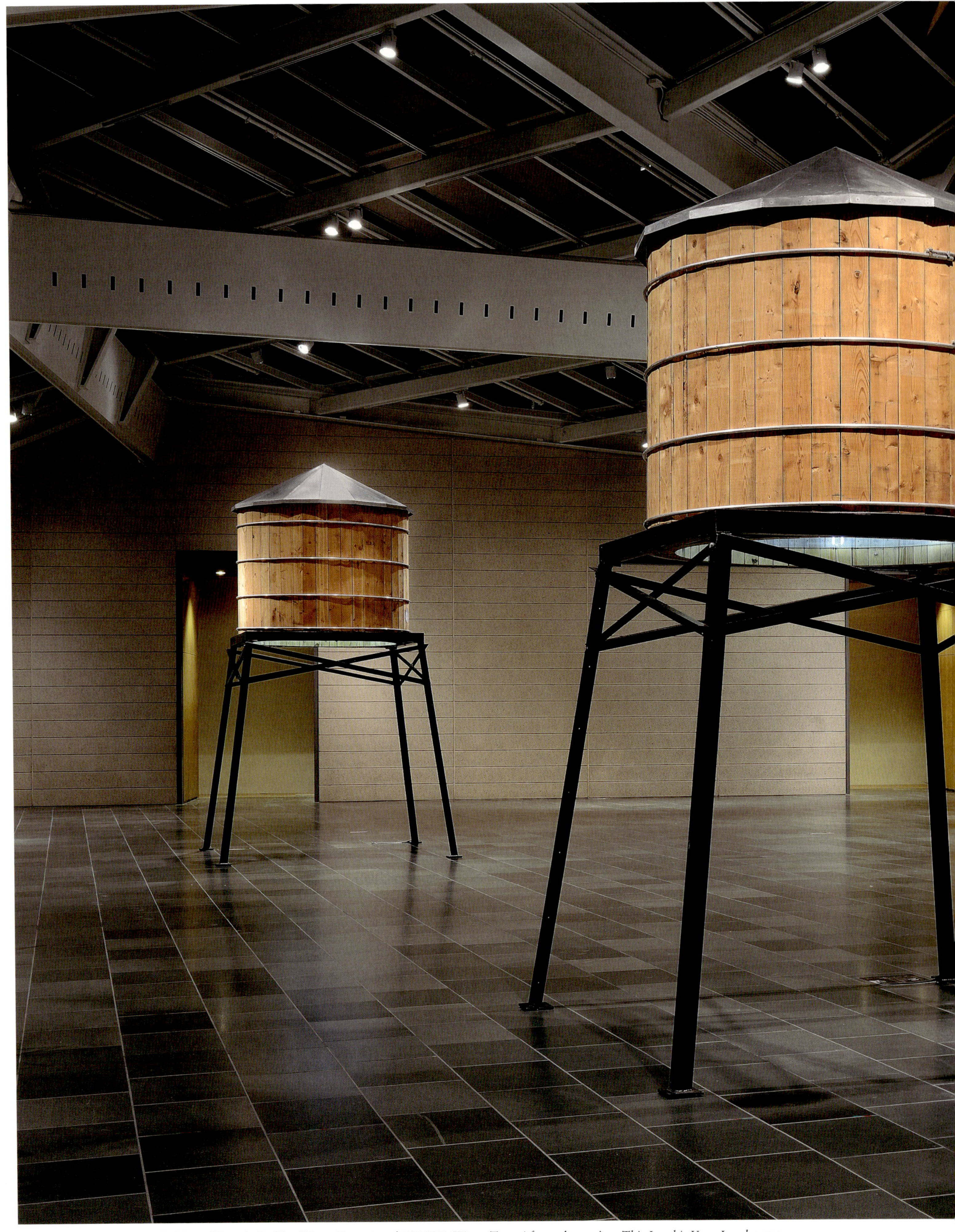

PL. 23 Iván Navarro, *BED (Water Tower)*, *Ladder (Water Tower)*, and *ME/WE (Water Tower)* from the project *This Land is Your Land*, 2014. Neon, wood, painted steel, galvanized steel, aluminum, mirror, one-way mirror, and electric energy; edition 1/3; 189 x 105 1/8 x 105 1/8 inches (480.1 x 267 x 267 cm) each.

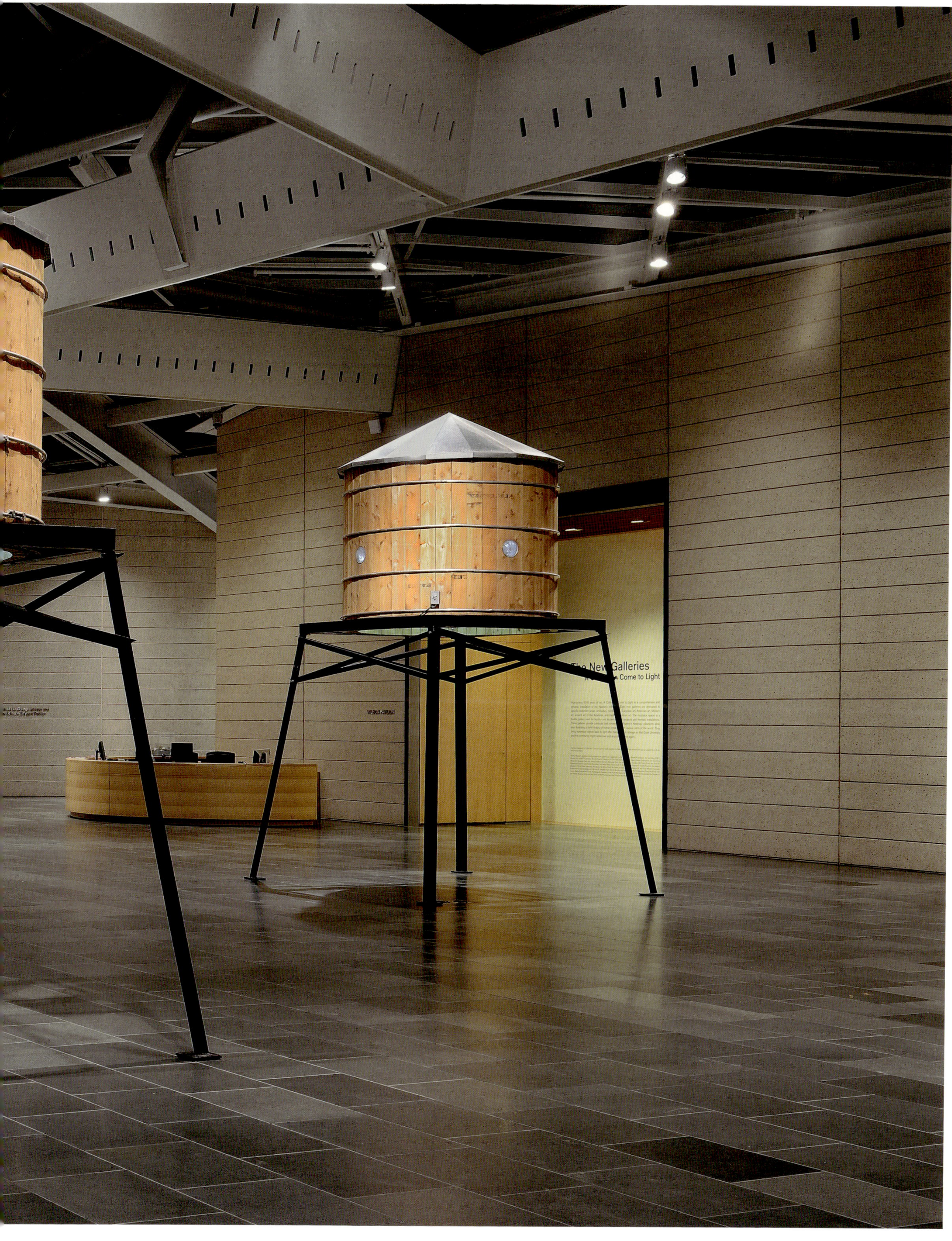
The New Galleries
Come to Light

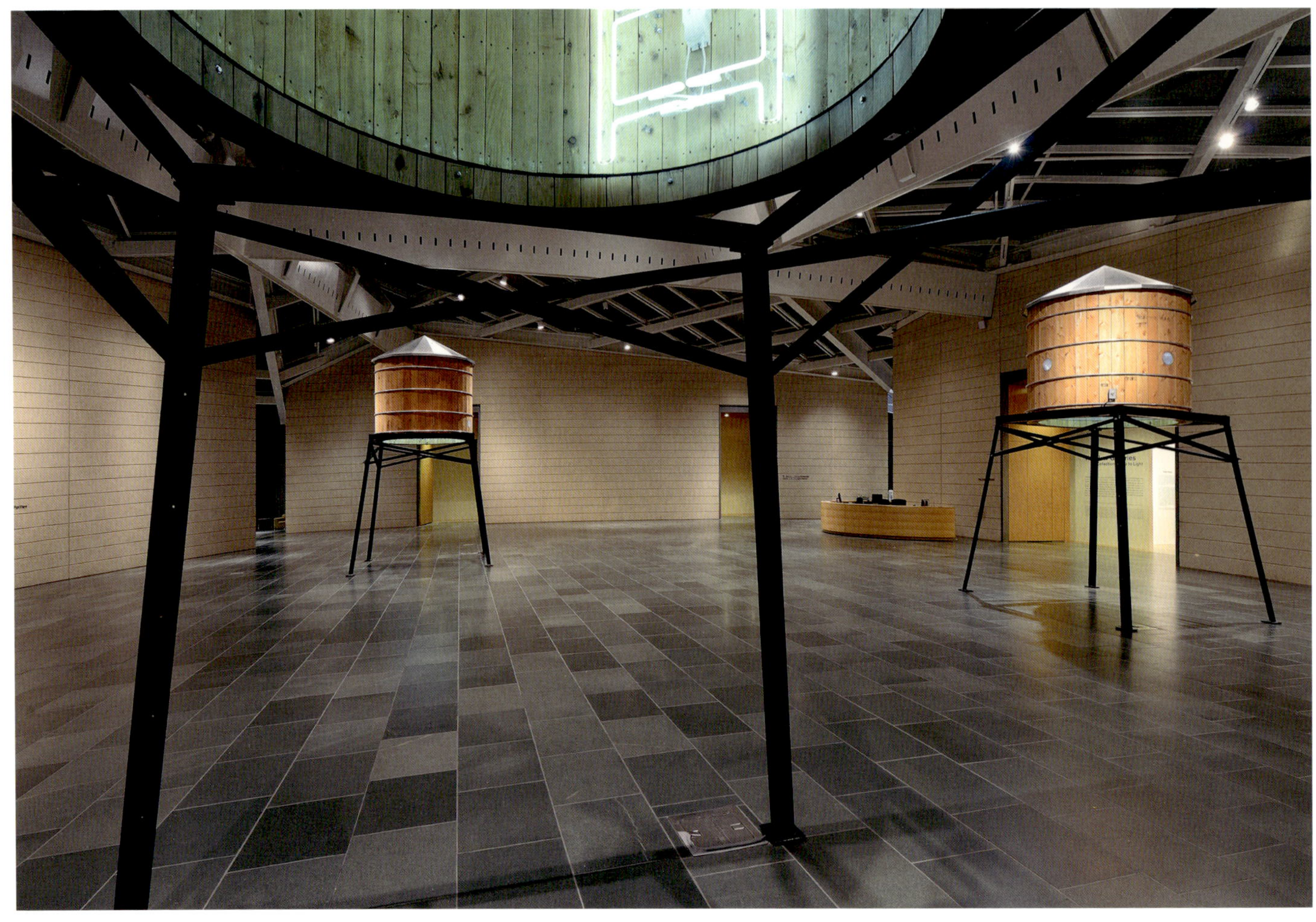

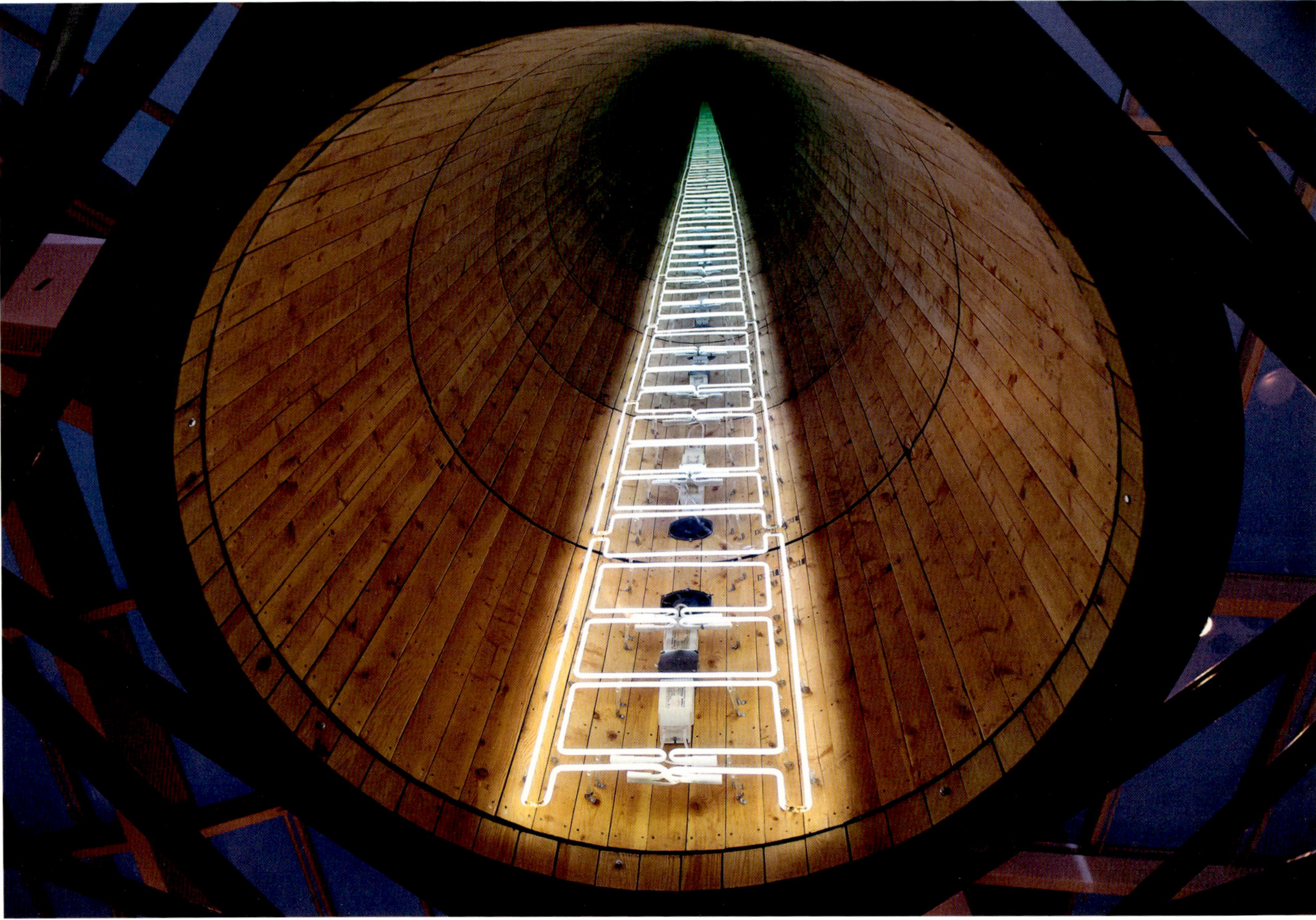

PL. 23 Iván Navarro, *BED (Water Tower)*, *Ladder (Water Tower)*, and *ME/WE (Water Tower)* from the project *This Land is Your Land*, 2014 (alternate views). Neon, wood, painted steel, galvanized steel, aluminum, mirror, one-way mirror, and electric energy; edition 1/3; 189 x 105 1/8 x 105 1/8 inches (480.1 x 267 x 267 cm) each.

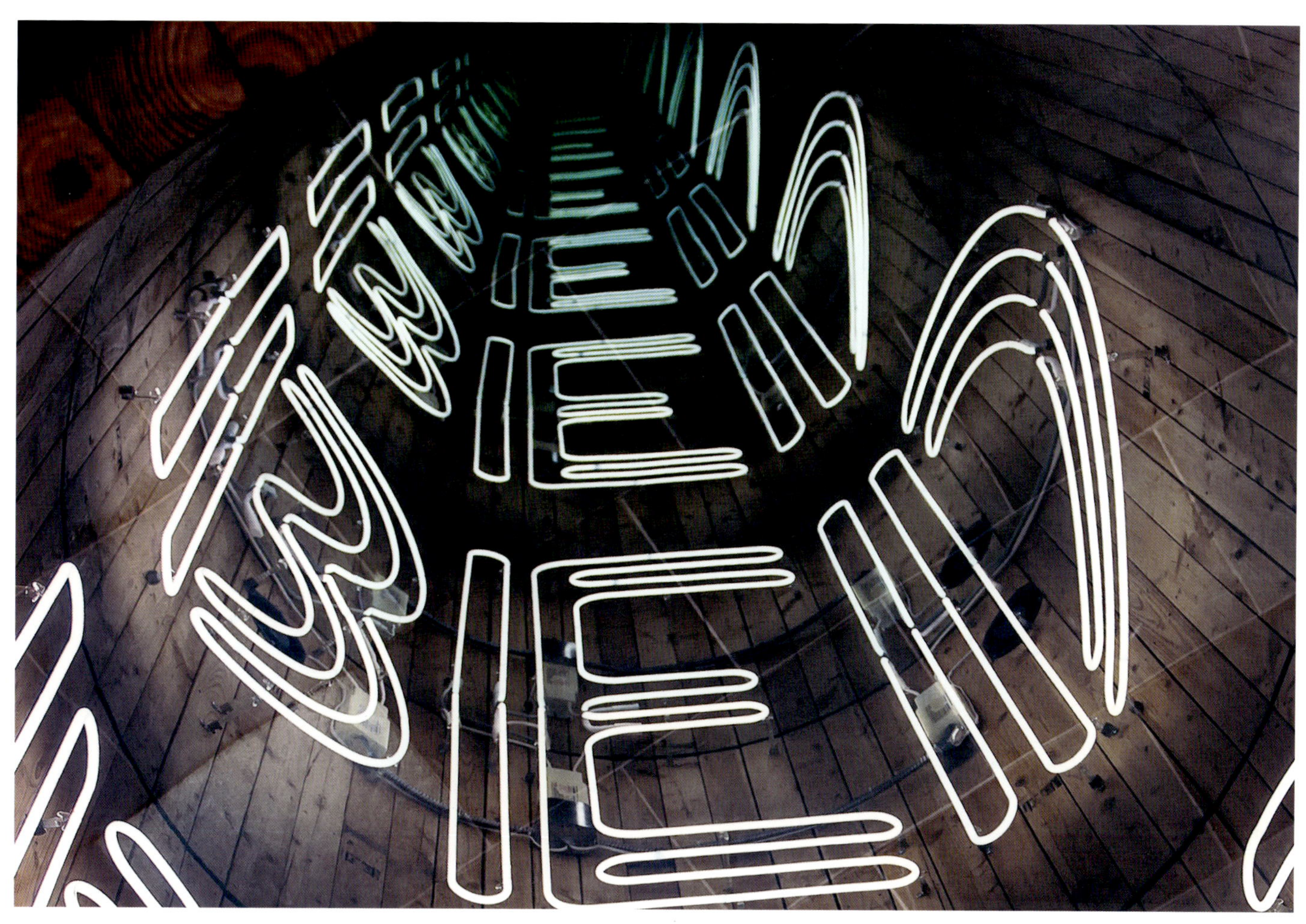

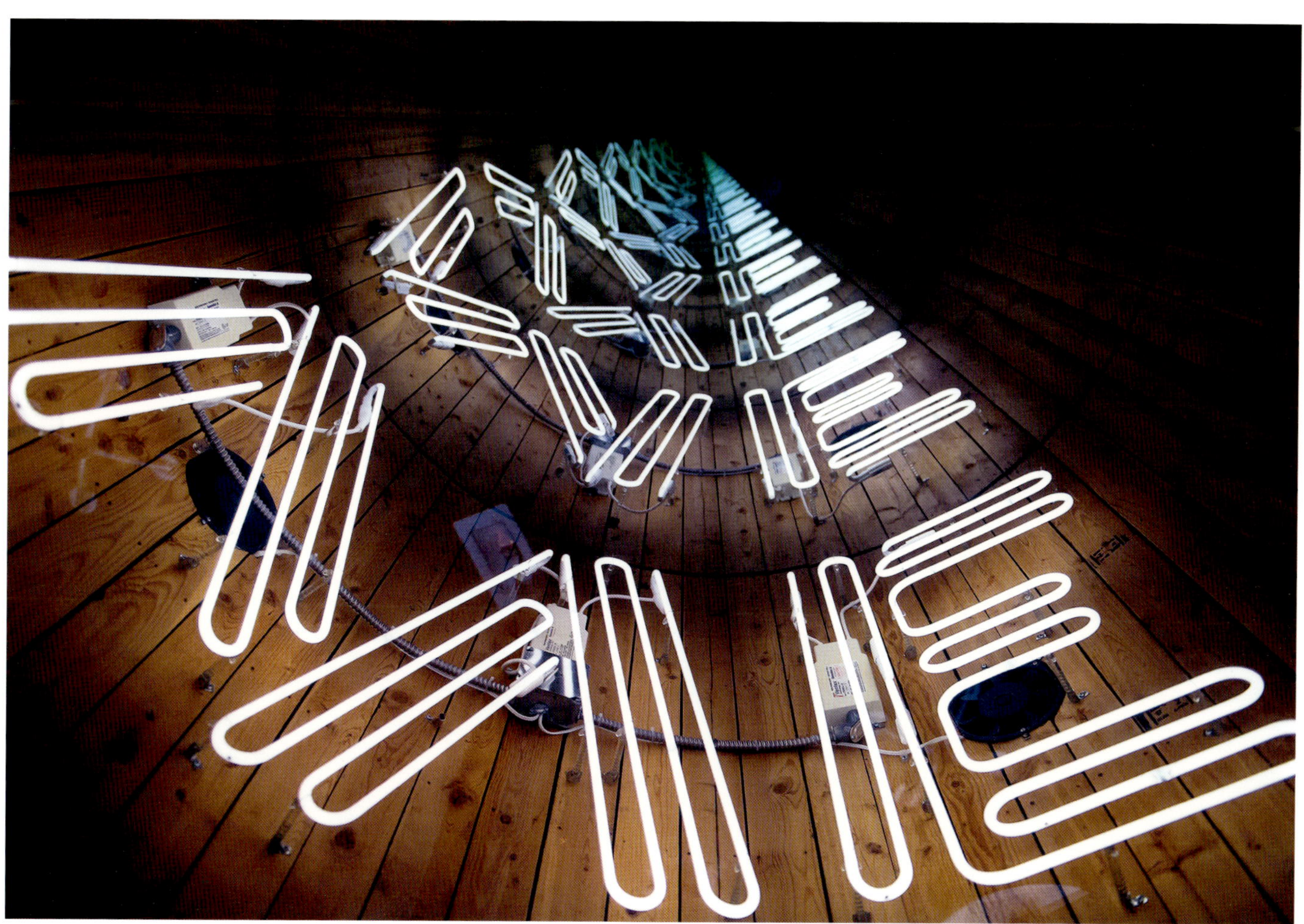

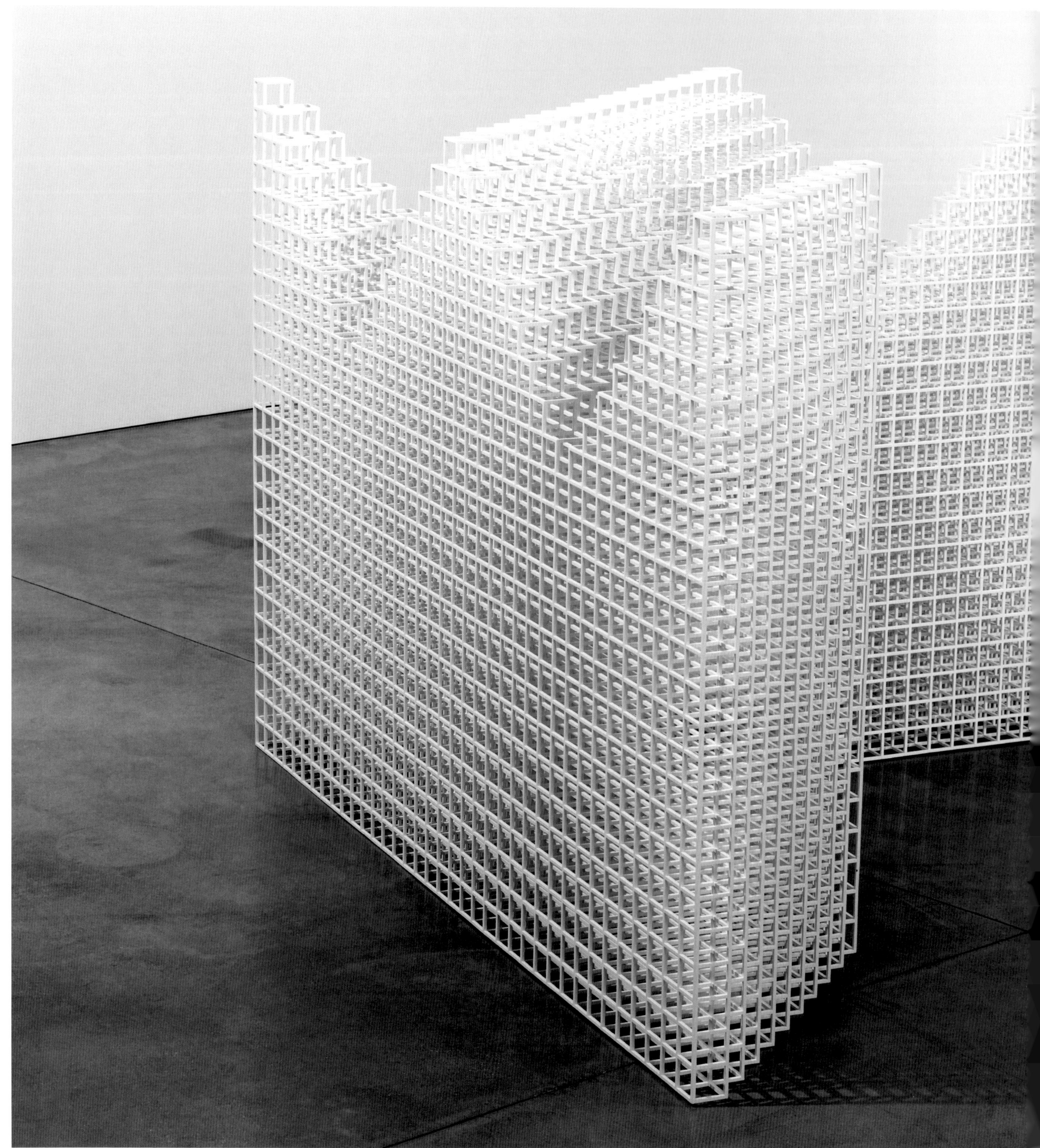

PL. 20 Sol LeWitt, *Open Cube Structure*, 2007. Painted wood, 62 x 87 x 87 inches (157.5 x 221 x 221 cm).

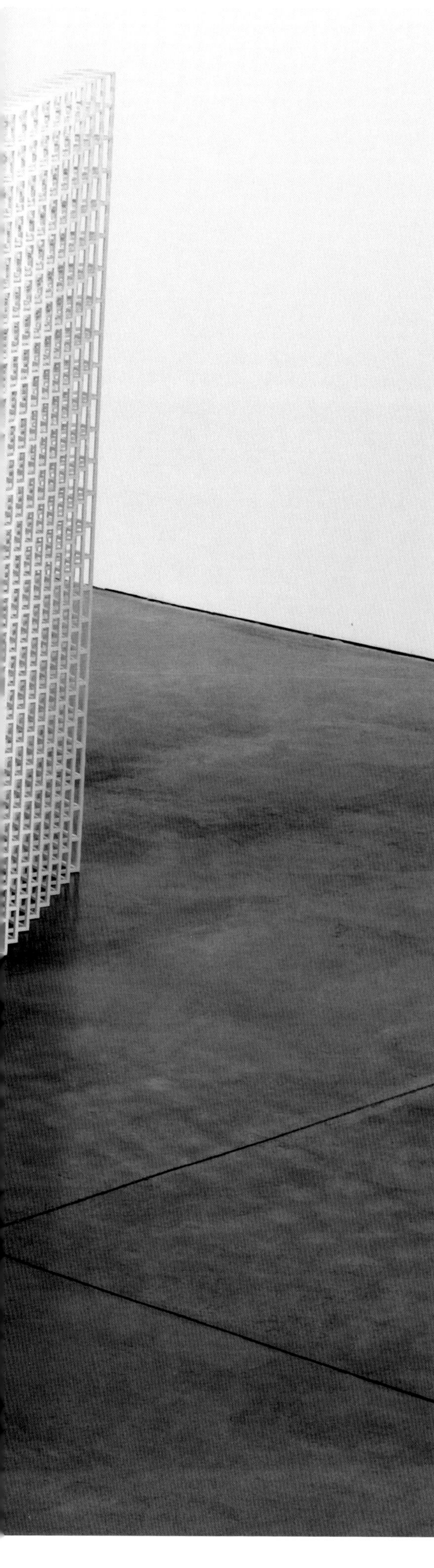

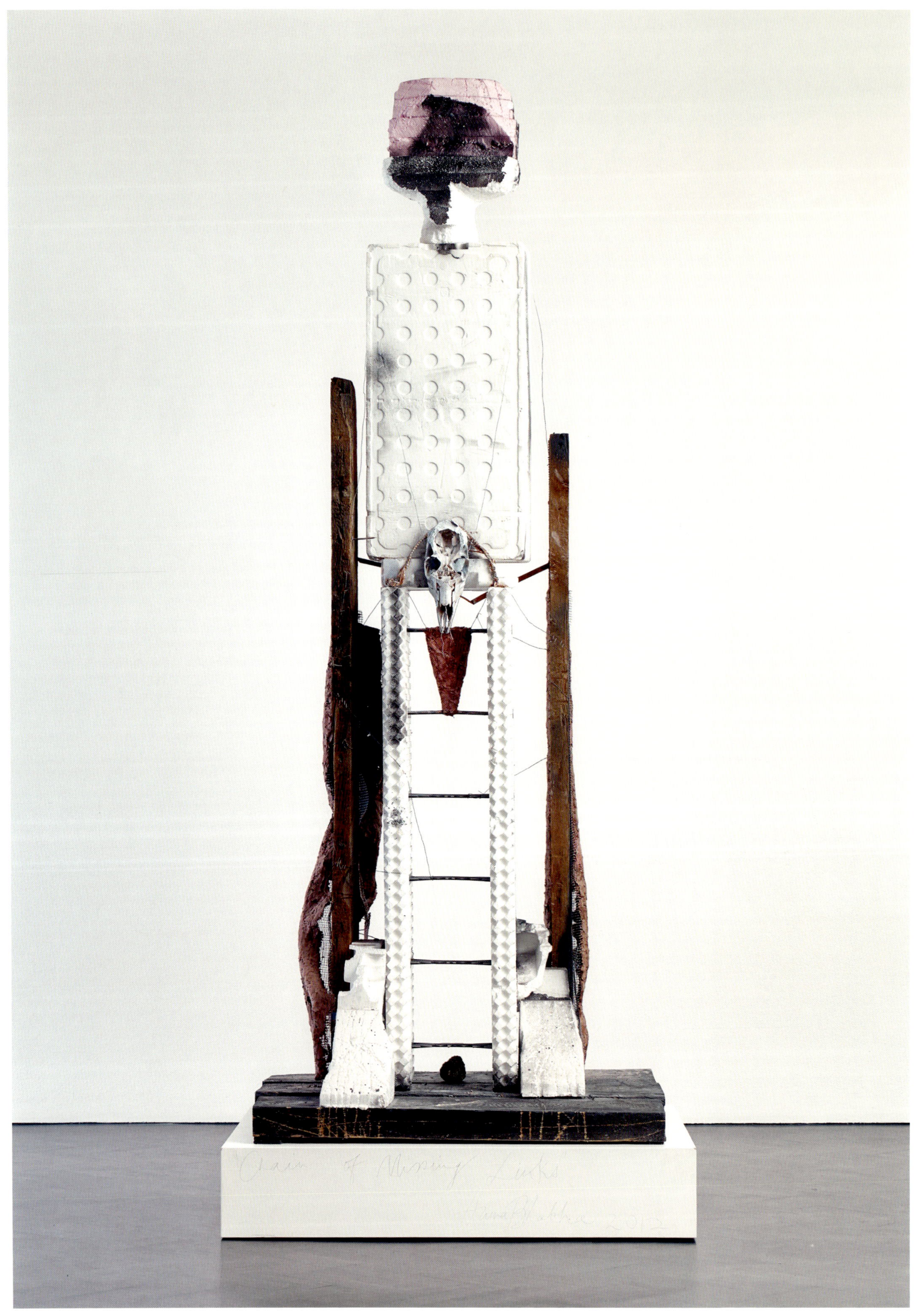

PL. 2 Huma Bhabha, *Chain of Missing Links*, 2012. Wood, styrofoam, clay, wire, Plexiglas, acrylic paint, weeds, seedpod, skull, rust, graphite, and oil stick; 101 5/8 x 38 1/4 x 29 1/8 inches (258.1 x 97.2 x 74 cm).

Material Inclinations: The Nancy A. Nasher and David J. Haemisegger Collection of Contemporary Art

Marshall N. Price

MODERN ART INTRODUCED a greatly expanded use of materials. Since antiquity, artists had sought improved paints, more permanent mediums, and better support surfaces, but significant cultural shifts in the early twentieth century were the catalyst for unprecedented inventiveness. With new materials came new directions in artistic thought. Cubism and futurism were two avant-garde movements that embraced the products of modern society: aluminum and other industrial metals, printed paper and manufactured objects, asphalt, concrete, and glass, among many others. The result was a paradigmatic transformation in the understanding and appreciation of their aesthetic potential. In 1914 Latvian-born sculptor and critic Vladimir Markov decried the ostentation of precious stones and metals in icons, declaring, "all of this destroys our contemporary conception of painting."[1] Markov was calling for a new art using new materials. Three years later, Russian art historian Nikolai Tarabukin defined constructivism by noting that *materials* dictate forms and not the reverse.[2] Marcel Duchamp (fig. 2.1), Pablo Picasso (fig. 2.2), Vladimir Tatlin, and other early pioneers responded to this call, expanding the boundaries of conventional art making and subsequently laying the foundation for the next century of artistic experimentation.

A Material Legacy: The Nancy A. Nasher and David J. Haemisegger Collection of Contemporary Art provides an opportunity for us to explore two distinct legacies: one of philanthropic collecting and another of artistic exploration of materials. Nancy Nasher and David Haemisegger continue the precedent set by Raymond and Patsy Nasher, whose legacy of sharing their collection with the public has brought about a greater understanding of modern art and touched the lives of countless people. The previous generation's patronage of artists and institutions is also continued by Nasher and Haemisegger, who have established themselves as significant collectors of contemporary art in their own right. The second aspect of this exhibition examines the legacy of material investigation that characterizes contemporary art. The artists included in this exhibition are the descendants of Duchamp, Picasso, Tatlin, and other pioneering artists who forged an uncharted path with new materials. They, like their forebears, are laying the groundwork for the next century of innovation.

The exhibition is divided into four formally based categories: black, white, and gray; color; gesture; and accumulation. Each grouping serves as an elastic descriptor of the works, not intended to be inherently fixed. Indeed, transvaluation is one of the intrinsic qualities of contemporary art, blurring the lines of distinct categorization between painted and sculpted, conceptual and performative, geometric and gestural, and so forth. It seems appropriate, therefore, to begin with a work that serves as a metaphorical entrance to the exhibition, Rachel Whiteread's sculpture *circa 1760 (II)* (pl. 33).

Since she emerged in the early 1990s, Whiteread has used a variety of building and industrial materials, such as rubber, plaster, resin, concrete, and metal. Her earliest sculptures included mundane domestic objects cast in plaster—shirts and coat hangers, hot-water bottles, mattresses. She soon began making sculptures that were casts of the negative space of furniture. In 1993 Whiteread created *House* (fig. 2.3), casting the complete interior of a multistory house in East London that had been slated for destruction.

Architectural elements have been central to Whiteread's practice since her formative years, and she continues to draw inspiration from domestic settings. The artist has investigated doors—the intrinsic threshold of a built environment—by meticulously casting historic and modern varieties in watery translucent resin. *Circa 1760* is from a series of historic doors from several different centuries that lean against the wall and do not function to delineate the transitional space between two rooms. This work is the replica of a relic from the Georgian era of Great Britain, cast from a fairly standard eighteenth-century four-plank door with a square window in the upper center, and propped against the wall, as if waiting to be discarded. The crystalline, blue-green material gives the door a ghostlike presence, underscored by the shadow it casts on the wall upon which it leans. Art historian Charlotte Mullins has described the artist's

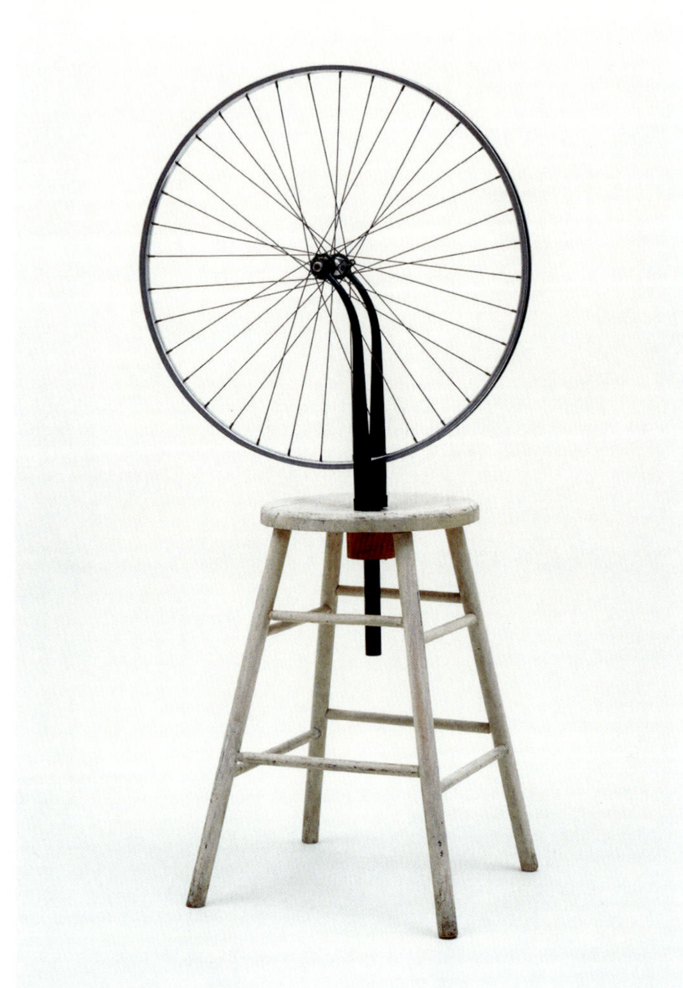
2.1

FIG. 2.1
Marcel Duchamp, *Bicycle Wheel*, 1951 (original 1913). Metal wheel mounted on painted wood stool (third version, after lost original), 51 x 25 x 16 1/2 inches (129.5 x 63.5 x 41.9 cm). The Museum of Modern Art, New York, New York. ©2015 Artists Rights Society (ARS), New York, New York / ADAGP, Paris, France / Estate of Marcel Duchamp. Digital Image ©The Museum of Modern Art / SCALA / Art Resource, New York, New York.

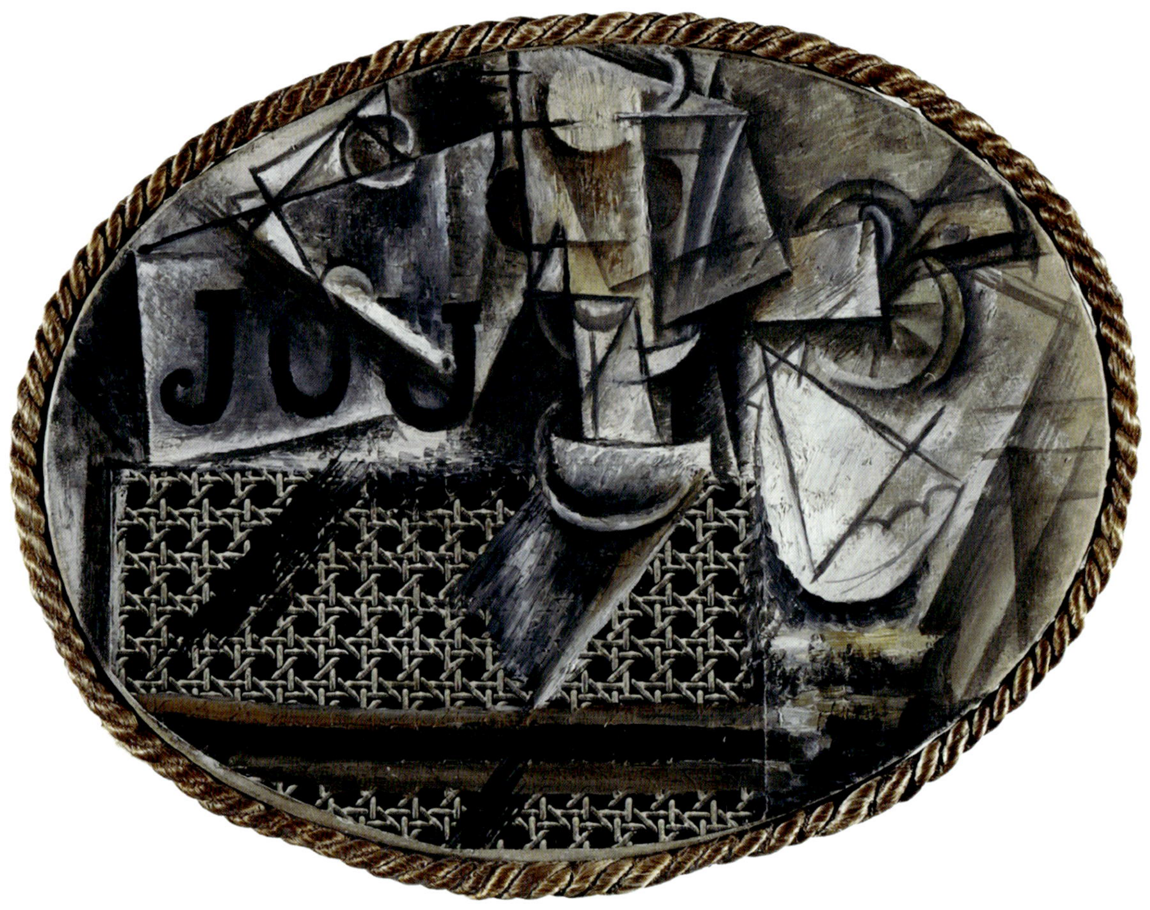

2.2

FIG. 2.2
Pablo Picasso, *Still Life with Chair Caning*, 1912. Oil on oilcloth over canvas edged with rope, 11 7/16 x 14 1/2 inches (29 x 37 cm). Musée Picasso, Paris, France. License ©2015 Estate of Pablo Picasso/Artists Rights Society (ARS), New York, New York. Digital Image ©RMN-Grand Palais, Paris, France / Art Resource, New York, New York. Photo by R.G. Ojeda.

process as excavating "memories like an archeologist, [and] continuing to hunt for traces of past human life."[3] Not intended to function as an actual door, *circa 1760* serves as a memory of the original, a poetic tribute to a commonplace object, and a vessel containing cultural fragments of a domestic past, fossilized in a contemporary material.

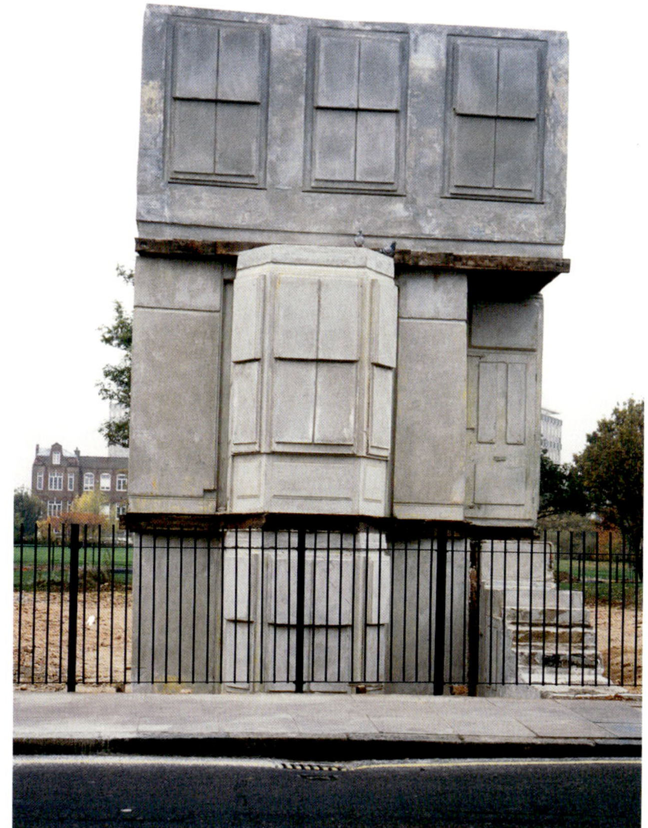

2.3

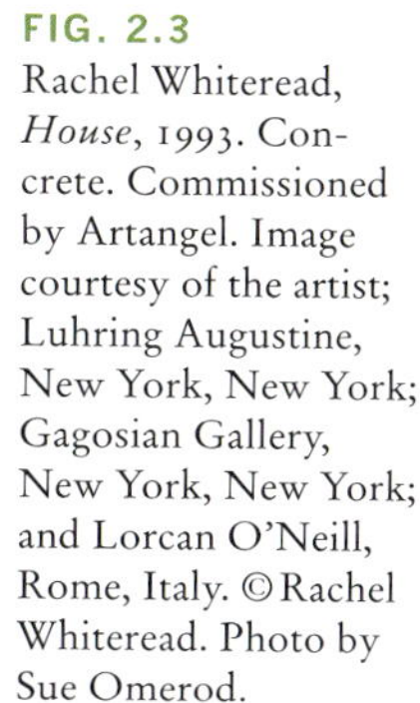

FIG. 2.3
Rachel Whiteread, *House*, 1993. Concrete. Commissioned by Artangel. Image courtesy of the artist; Luhring Augustine, New York, New York; Gagosian Gallery, New York, New York; and Lorcan O'Neill, Rome, Italy. ©Rachel Whiteread. Photo by Sue Omerod.

FIG. 2.4
Richard Serra, *Casting*, 1969. Lead, 48 x 300 x 180 inches (121.9 x 762 x 457.2 cm). Installation view of *Anti-Illusion: Procedures/Materials*, Whitney Museum of American Art, New York, New York, May 19–July 6, 1969. ©2015 Richard Serra / Artists Rights Society (ARS), New York, New York. Photo by Peter Moore.

BLACK, WHITE, AND GRAY

Materials are central to Richard Serra's work. Serra emerged as a key figure of process-based sculpture and installation in the 1960s and, like many artists of that generation, became disenchanted with the rigorous reductivism of minimal forms. One result of this was a greater interest in the process of creating a work of art as opposed to the appearance of the final product. For Serra, this was manifested in his 1967–68 *Verb List*, a series of written verbs such as "to roll, to crease, to fold . . ." that became the basis for physical works. Thus, process and performance-cum-sculpture, as in Serra's *Casting* (fig. 2.4), 1969, was not only freed from illusionism, but also liberated from the picture plane or the pedestal and shown directly on the floor. Since that time, Serra has become known as a sculptor of massive steel installations, but drawing has continued to be a critical part of his work for decades. For the artist, drawing is independent from and also part of his working, sculptural process. And, while it was not penned in his notebook, we can imagine him considering the directive "to draw" among those early written commands in the late 1960s.

One of the largest works in the exhibition, *Double Rift #10* (pl. 28) engulfs the viewer with a massive void of thickly applied oil stick punctuated by two vertically opposed slivers of exposed paper emerging from the top and bottom of the drawing. Reminiscent of his large steel structures and cleaved by two dramatic breaks, or rifts, that could easily be read as tears, the drawing recalls one of his early written instructions: "to tear." Indeed, the work has its roots in the early 1970s when his innovative process works placed him squarely in the critical eye. Its panoramic quality suggests the lingering horizontal inclination discussed by art historian Robert Pincus-Witten and found in works such as *Casting*.[4] Serra's drawings are intimately connected to all other aspects of his works and cannot be separated from his larger oeuvre. For him, drawing is a window to the mind: "If you look at artists, if you really want to understand the subtext of how they think, look at their drawings."[5]

Moving from the dense, black, void-like, horizontal work of Serra to the open, white, pyramidal structure of Sol LeWitt, we can see close contemporaries using process and materials in very different ways. Emerging in the midst of minimalism in the mid-1960s, the artist had his first solo exhibition in New York at the John Daniels Gallery with freestanding relief structures composed of plywood in right and oblique angles. In 1964 LeWitt shifted away from solid objects and toward the serially constructed, skeletal sculptures of cube shapes for which he would become known. Soon thereafter he abandoned wood (he could not seem to disguise the texture of the wood adequately to his liking) and began

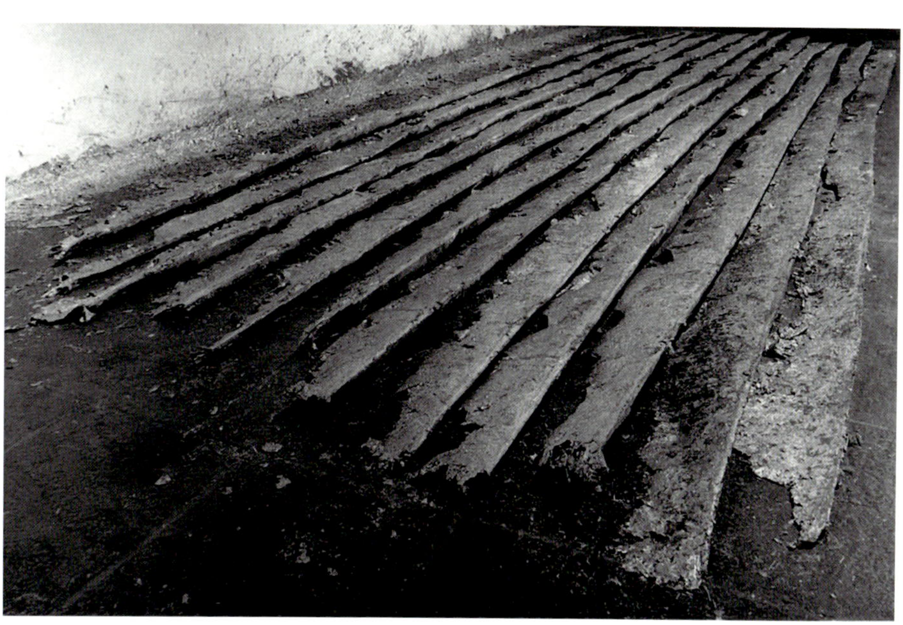

2.4

FIG. 2.5
Katharina Grosse, *Untitled*, 2013. Acrylic on fiberglass-reinforced plastic, 133 7/8 x 165 3/8 x 283 1/2 inches (340 x 420.1 x 720.1 cm). Installation view at the Nasher Sculpture Center, Dallas, Texas. Photo by Kevin Todova.

working in metal, painting the objects white. LeWitt's systemic sculptures inherently related to minimalism but also hewed closely to the ideas of the emergent conceptual practices of the time. Instrumental in expanding the field of sculpture, LeWitt challenged the hegemony of minimalism.

Ideas were LeWitt's primary medium, and he believed that the appearance of a work was secondary to its concept.[6] In this way, many of his white cube sculptures are built on an internal logic. LeWitt's *Open Cube Structure* (pl. 20) from 2007 is one of the last sculptures completed by the artist before his death. Constructed from his signature repeating, small, open cubes, *Open Cube Structure* contains several chevron shapes in various orientations. The entire piece is composed of a large V-shape turned on its side with two arms radiating out from a central point. The top of the sculpture is comprised of a series of lateral pyramid shapes. His recurring, methodical vocabulary is inherently architectural in nature and yet, at the same time, suggests a mathematical equation waiting to be solved. However, the artist famously stated in the late 1960s, "The logic of a piece or series of pieces is a device that is used at times, only to be ruined. Logic may be used to camouflage the real intent of the artist, to lull the viewer into the belief that he understands the work, or to infer a paradoxical situation (such as logic vs. illogic)."[7]

The grounding of LeWitt's sculpture on the floor contrasts with Teresita Fernández's celestial *Nocturnal (Cinematic Sky)* (pl. 7). Known for her large-scale installations of accumulated unconventional materials, such as pulp paper, silk yarn, polycarbonate, and gold thread, Fernández investigates the phenomenological aspects of landscape. Scale is important to the artist and even modestly sized works (by Fernández's standards), such as *Nocturnal*, present a sense of vastness, space, volume, and the infinite. Fernández often explores the relationship between the celestial and earthly: "Historically, we've always had this instinct to look up for information, to the night sky especially, for orientation and information. We use it for navigation. It's the first clock and it's the first calendar. It's the first everything. The sky is what orients us in the world."[8]

While Fernández's use of materials is eclectic and wide-ranging, graphite has been a principal medium for her for many years. The artist became interested in graphite after researching its history and discovering that this crystalline form of carbon was first mined in England in the sixteenth century. Fernández uses it in *Nocturnal* to make an obsidian and vast rendering of the sky. Thus, by using an earthly material in the imagining of a celestial realm, the artist further explores the correlation between earth and sky. Made from a solid piece of graphite that is then adhered to a wooden panel,

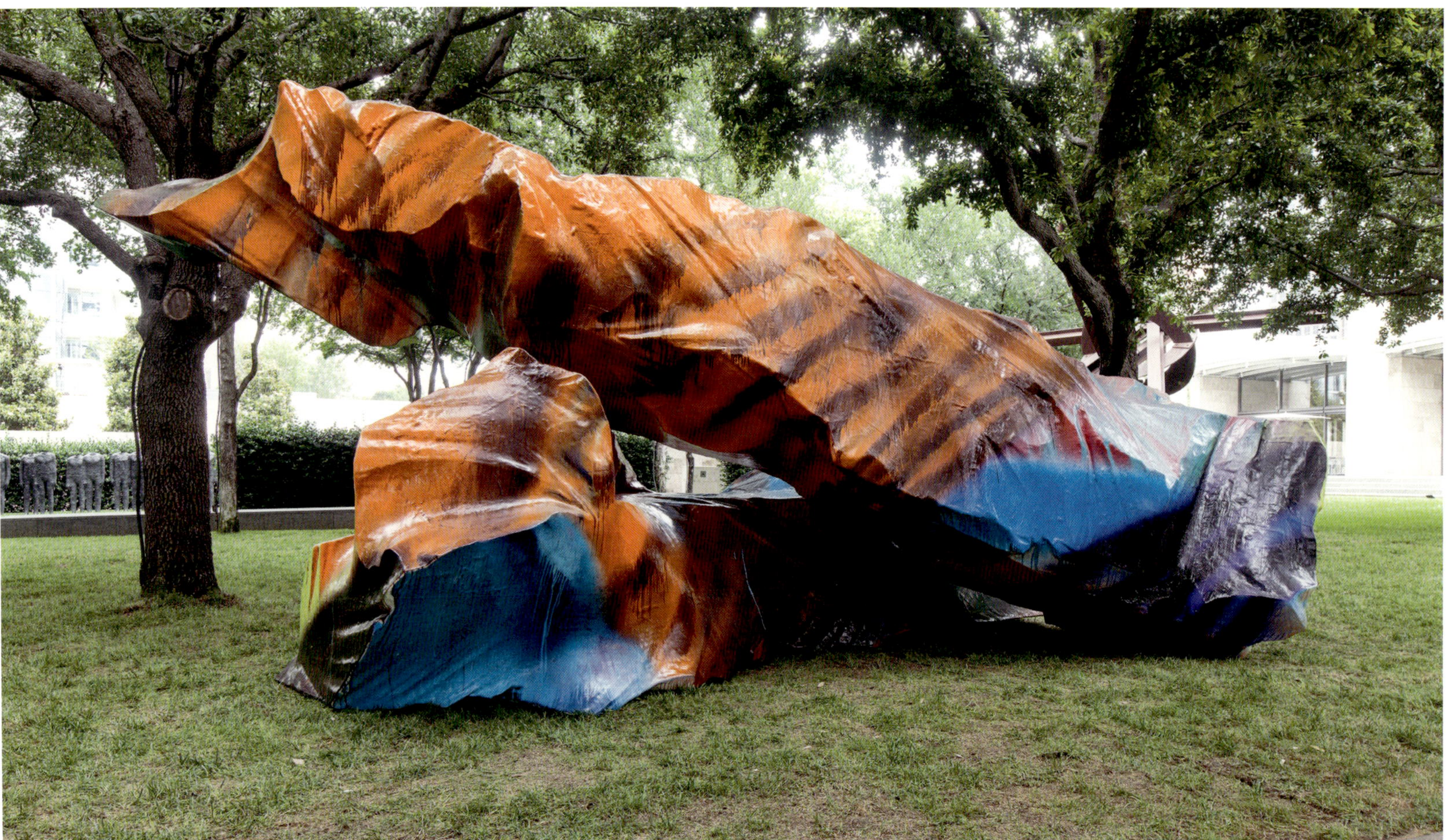

2.5

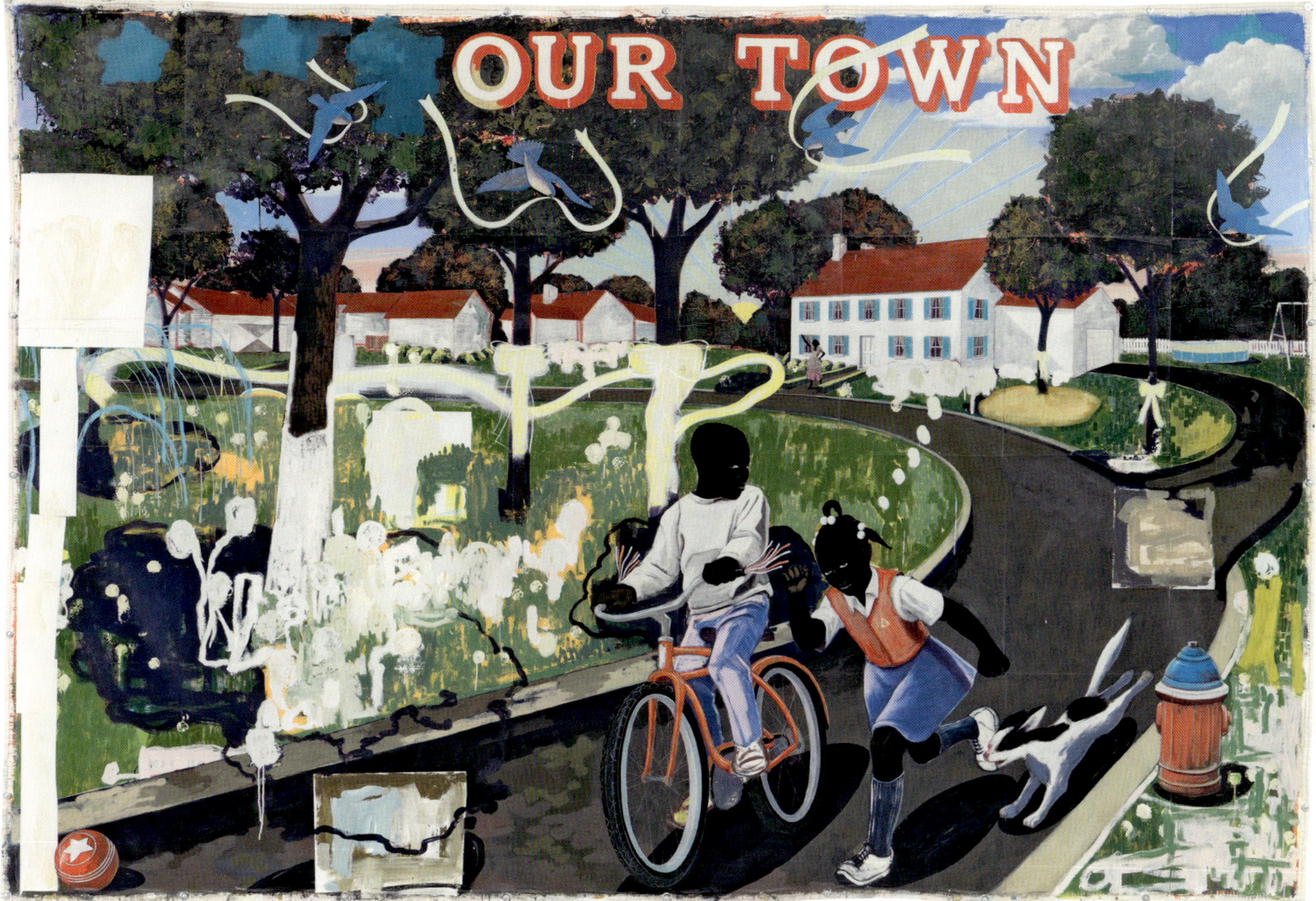

2.6

FIG. 2.6
Kerry James Marshall, *Our Town*, 1995. Acrylic and collage on canvas, 101 x 143 inches (256.5 x 363.2 cm). Collection of the Crystal Bridges Museum of American Art, Bentonville, Arkansas. Courtesy of the artist and David Zwirner, New York, New York, and London, England. © Kerry James Marshall. Photo by Vancouver Art Gallery.

Nocturnal is a subtle piece with repeated horizontal striations alternating between the dark gray of the graphite and a deep purple found in the nocturnal world. The earth is articulated with a rugged topography, contrasting against the smooth upper portion of the night sky. The nature of the material lends both a geological gravity to the work as well as an infinite celestial dimension.

COLOR

The visceral, playful, and perhaps even aggressive chromatic explosions of Katharina Grosse are, in many ways, the antithesis of the works previously described. While she has created many large-scale installations and massive, craggy sculptures (fig. 2.5), Grosse is first and foremost a painter. Her work in other mediums grows out of her painting practice, which comes from a long lineage of gestural abstract painting rooted in the abstract expressionism of artists like Jackson Pollock and Willem de Kooning. However, Grosse's work also encompasses other types of historical and contemporary painting, such as color field, neo-Expressionism, and graffiti. Her work is painterly in the extreme, and deliberately so, as the artist noted, "Using paint in such a generous way is also, in a sense, absurd. It's overdone. And I think that's a fantastic artistic strategy, to over do. . . . It's not just about being a big, beautiful, sensual experience. It does talk a lot about other things. Like anarchy and doing things you're not supposed to do in a funny and amusing way. What you would love to do as a kid: take the felt pen and paint the most beautiful furniture your parents have."[9]

Grosse's colossal painting *Untitled* (pl. 11), like much of her work, is a veritable patchwork of gestural bravado. The artist's use of color in such an exuberant way borders on unbridled chromophilia, suggesting that she operates at the limits of physical control while also embracing those chance effects of unintentionally dripped, spilled, or sprayed paint. It is a kaleidoscopic composition seemingly set into motion by infinite color shifts overlaid on a white ground that occasionally peers through the chromatic cacophony. Broad areas of blues and reds fill the painting and are punctuated by looping skeins of blue in the lower left and several horizontal passages of dripped paint in the upper right. The work's overlapping areas of color, along with the apparently haphazard nature of their application, is reminiscent of graffiti or tagging. Grosse is interested in these urban traditions, and incorporating aspects of them into her practice is simply another way for her to expand notions of what it means to make a painting today.

Color—in many different forms—is important to Kerry James Marshall. He works with a wide chromatic range to create figure-based, narrative paintings that address serious issues of racial and social inequality.

FIG. 2.7
Mark di Suvero, *Hankchampion*, 1960. Wood, steel hardware, and chains; 77 1/2 x 152 x 109 3/16 inches (196.9 x 386.1 x 277.3 cm) overall. Collection of the Whitney Museum of American Art, New York, New York. Gift of Mr. and Mrs. Robert C. Scull, 73.85 a-i. Courtesy of the artist and Spacetime CC, Long Island City, New York. ©Mark di Suvero. Photo by Jerry L. Thompson.

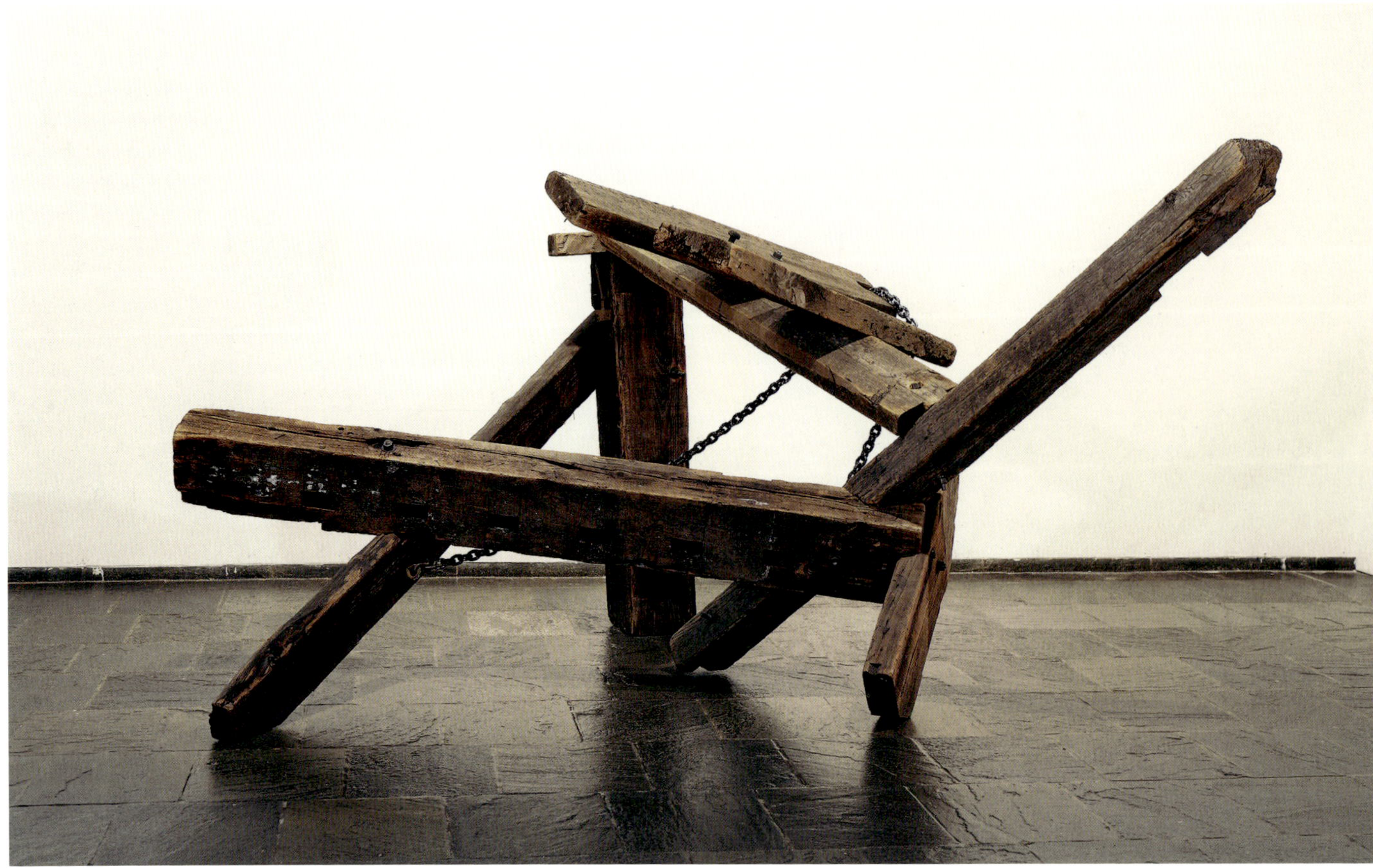

2.7

Born in Birmingham, Alabama, and coming of age during the civil rights movement, Marshall was deeply affected by these historical events. As a child, he had the opportunity to study at Otis Art Institute in Los Angeles, where he met the artist Charles White, whose large paintings and drawings of African American figures captivated the younger artist. White would later become Marshall's mentor and a great inspiration to him. Since he began exhibiting in the early 1980s, Marshall has been making visually astute, socially aware critiques of the perception of African Americans. They are a response, a rebuttal, and a rebuke to stereotypical representations of black people in society. In large paintings, such as *Our Town* (fig. 2.6), the artist confronts difficult topics by questioning how much these dynamics have actually changed.

Rendering black bodies has been an important part of Marshall's work for the better part of three decades. The artist himself noted that "since the overwhelming majority of the bodies on display in art and advertising are white, producing images of black bodies was important to offset the impression that beauty is synonymous with whiteness."[10] A new direction for Marshall, *Untitled (Blot)* (pl. 22) is one of several recent works by the artist that eliminate any overt references to the figure in an abstract, Rorschach-like composition of chromatic symmetry. That does not mean that figures are entirely absent. In *Untitled (Blot)*, red, green, pink, and black organic forms could easily be read in a corporeal way. Shown for the first time in London at an exhibition titled *Look See*, the artist described them as "a representation of a Rorschach. It's an invitation to see what you can see, really."[11]

Primarily known as a sculptor of large-scale steel works, Mark di Suvero's wide-ranging practice includes painting, drawing, and printmaking. Di Suvero was born in China to Italian parents with whom he immigrated to the United States when he was a child. After attending the University of California, first at Santa Barbara and later at Berkley, the artist moved to New York in 1957. Three years later he had his first exhibition at the Green Gallery in New York with large-scale, abstract sculptures made from wood salvaged from demolished buildings, such as *Hankchampion* (fig. 2.7). This early work was strongly connected to late abstract expressionism and shared an affinity with the vocabularies of Franz Kline, Willem de Kooning, and other painters at the time. Not long after that, di Suvero began working in steel, and his sculptures took on a decidedly more constructivist character. He exhibited them at the seminal Park Place Gallery in SoHo, New York, to early critical acclaim. Color also took a place of greater importance in his work at this time, as he painted the steel with solid, and often saturated, colors.

Not easily categorized, di Suvero's mature work fell somewhere between the heroic character of abstract expressionism, the hard-edged reductive forms of minimalism, and the exuberance of assemblage and welded "junk" sculpture. The artist's paintings, such as *Untitled* (pl. 6), have a much different sensibility than the sculptures but share di Suvero's great interest in color. As a lesser-known but equally important part of his practice, painting offers the artist an opportunity to experiment and the freedom to improvise, something that is essentially precluded when working with large steel beams. *Untitled* is divided into three vertical areas of small, striated brushstrokes of red, orange, and yellow over a ground of royal blue. Calligraphic in nature, these marks cluster on the left and right sides of the painting, suggesting microscopic organisms viewed at great magnification. *Untitled* is more organic in nature than di Suvero's rigorous and angular geometric sculpture.

GESTURE

One of the most skillful collagists of his generation in any medium, Christian Marclay is a transdisciplinary artist who often incorporates visual and auditory elements into his works. Born in California, Marclay grew up in Switzerland and attended college at the Cooper Union for the Advancement of Science and Art in New York and the Massachusetts College of Art, where he received a BFA in 1980. Marclay performed as a DJ around that time and began incorporating samples, short clips of sound or music, into his art. He is a master of appropriation, using it in performance, film and video, painting, collage, and sound pieces. He works concurrently as a musician/performer and a visual artist, frequently blurring the boundaries between these disciplines. *Actions: Flopppp Sllurp Spaloosh Whoomph (No. 3)* (pl. 21) is from a series of screenprints with painting in which the artist has articulated onomatopoeias of the physical action of painting. Appropriating from several different historical sources in the creation of these works, he presents an amusing and perhaps absurdist look at the experience of painting.

Marclay began to use the screenprint process in 2006 for a body of work based on Andy Warhol's *Electric Chair* painting. His *Actions* paintings are playful nods to pop art icons such as Warhol and Roy Lichtenstein, while also referring to the famous dictum by art critic Harold Rosenberg, who in 1952 coined the term "action painting" to describe abstract expressionism. As an artist who combines performance with other creative practices, Marclay must have been instinctively drawn to Rosenberg's famous declaration that "at a certain moment the canvas began to appear to one American painter after another as an arena in which to act—rather than as a space in which to reproduce, re-design, analyze or 'express' an object, actual or imagined. What was to go on the canvas was not a picture but an *event*."[12] The

FIG. 2.8
Kara Walker, *Burning African Village Play Set with Big House and Lynching*, 2006. Painted laser-cut steel, edition 13/20; 24 x 38 1/4 x 90 inches (61 x 97.2 x 228.6 cm). Image courtesy of the artist and Sikkema Jenkins & Co, New York, New York. © Kara Walker. Photo by Luciano Fileti.

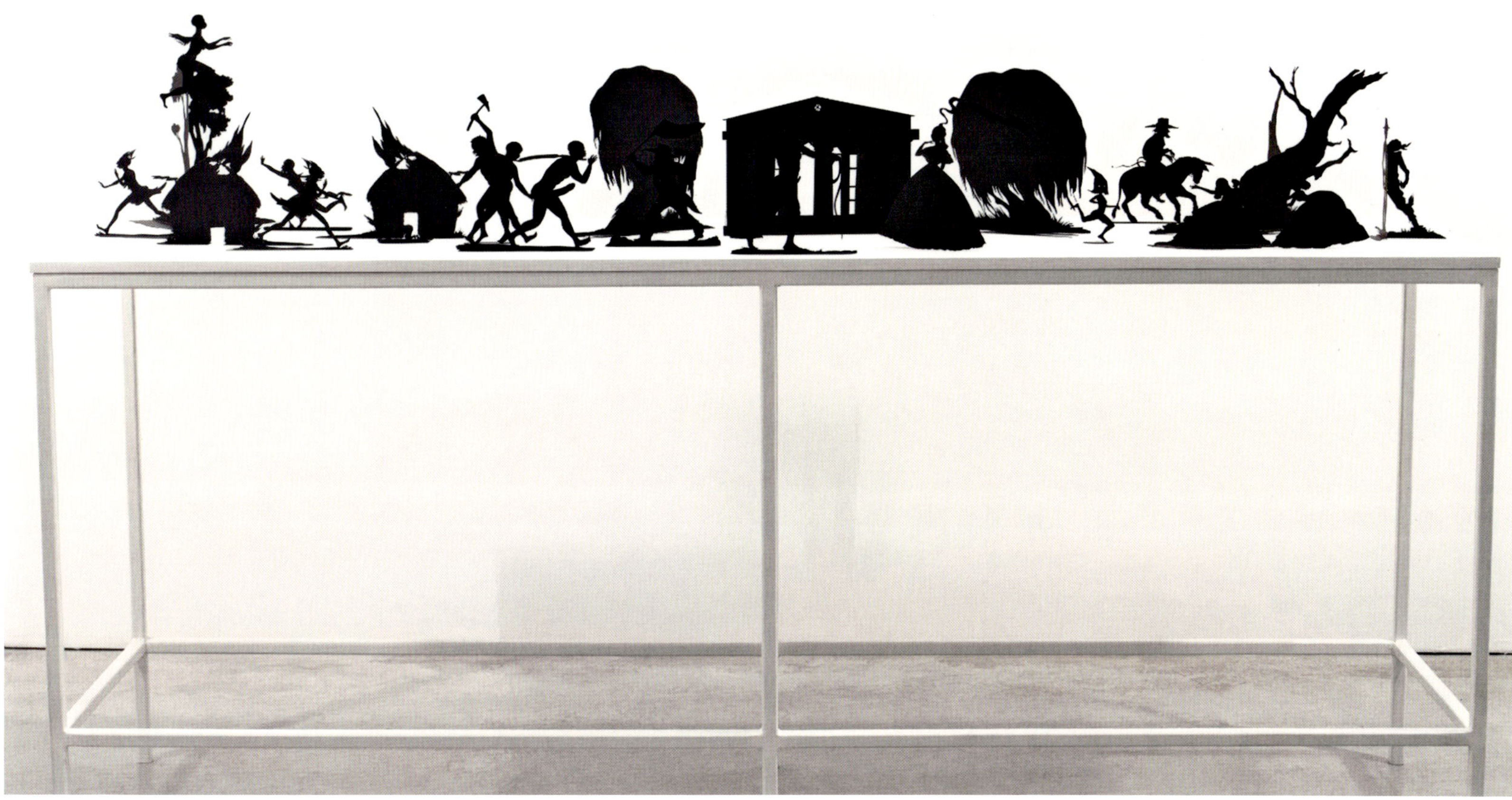

2.8

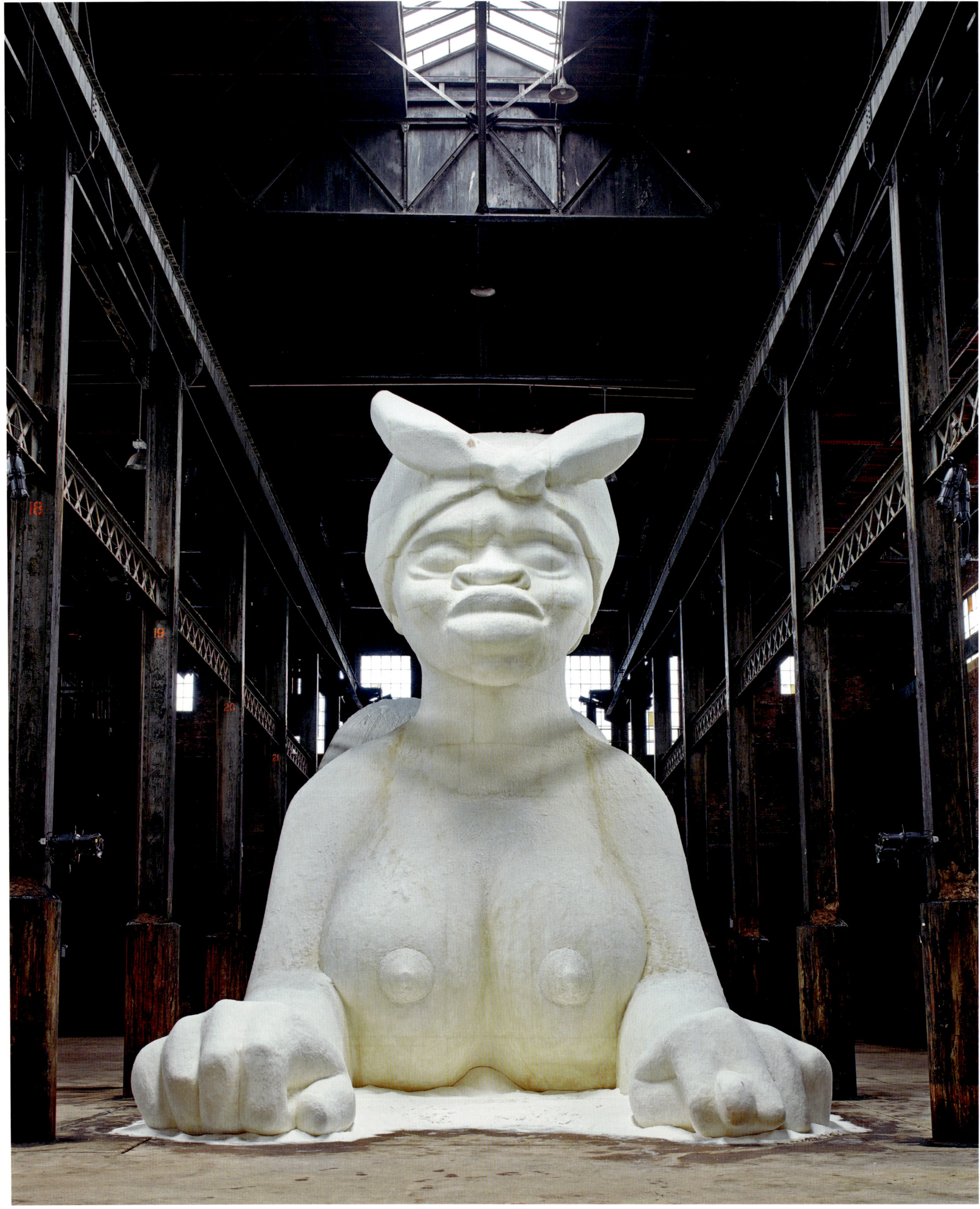

FIG. 2.9 Kara Walker, *A Subtlety, or the Marvelous Sugar Baby*, 2014. Sugar subtlety. Installation view at Domino Sugar Refinery, Brooklyn, New York, May 10–July 6, 2014. Commissioned by Creative Time, New York, New York. Image courtesy of the artist and Sikkema Jenkins & Co, New York, New York. © Kara Walker. Photo by Jason Wyche.

irony in Marclay's *Actions* paintings (something of an art historical inside joke), including *Flopppp Sllurp Spaloosh Whoomph (No. 3)*, is found in the use of screenprinting, a process closely associated with pop art from the 1960s, to spell out grand-gesture sounds associated with painting of the 1950s. It is a clever and deliberately campy conflation of two very different painting generations.

Kara Walker makes grand gestures of a different sort. Emerging in the mid-1990s, Walker was on the front line of so-called identity politics with a series of silhouette cutouts that combined the nineteenth-century technique with racially charged scenes, such as *Cottonhead, a Mouthfull of Teeth and Spitting Seeds*, 1994. Since that time she has unapologetically confronted ongoing issues of racial and cultural stereotyping in her work. Walker's practice evolved from cutout silhouettes into large-scale wall drawings, laser-cut three-dimensional metal versions (fig. 2.8), and most recently, large, site-specific sculpture, as in *A Subtlety, or the Marvelous Sugar Baby* (fig. 2.9). Installed in 2014 in the former Domino Sugar factory in Williamsburg, Brooklyn, which was once used to store raw sugar cane as it arrived from the Caribbean, it was Walker's grandest gesture to date.

Walker's large drawing *Object Lesson in Empire Building* (pl. 31) comes from the group of works made in preparation for and concurrently with *A Subtlety*. Like the massive sculpture, the drawing depicts a sphinxlike, African American female figure, crouching and naked, her head wrapped in a kerchief. Unlike Walker's earlier cleanly cut, hard-edge silhouette works, this drawing has the immediacy and looseness of a study. The artist's hand is clearly visible in the sweeping, gestural outlines of the figure in graphite and charcoal. The sphinx figure here, like the sculpture in the Domino Sugar factory, is a conflation of several historical ideas: the Egyptian figure of the Sphinx; a stereotyped African American woman; and a subtlety, an elaborate confection accompanying a dinner to amuse as a decoration and sometimes be consumed. Walker's figure, in sculptural and drawn form, serves as both a historical critique of the nefarious sugar trade, as well as an indictment on current social attitudes and inclinations. *A Subtlety* and its related works not only reinforce and reinvigorate discussion of racial dynamics, but also examine the infinitely complex issues of spectatorship, health, and how these issues are tied to socioeconomic standing within the community.

Matthew Ritchie's painting *Link of Nature* (pl. 26), 2014, epitomizes a generative and analytical approach to gestural painting. For many years, Ritchie's two- and

FIG. 2.10
Matthew Ritchie, *Command and Control*, 2014. Oil and ink on canvas, 84 x 112 x 2 1/2 inches (213.4 x 284.5 x 6.4 cm). Image courtesy of the artist and Andrea Rosen Gallery, New York, New York. © Matthew Ritchie. Photo by Lance Brewer.

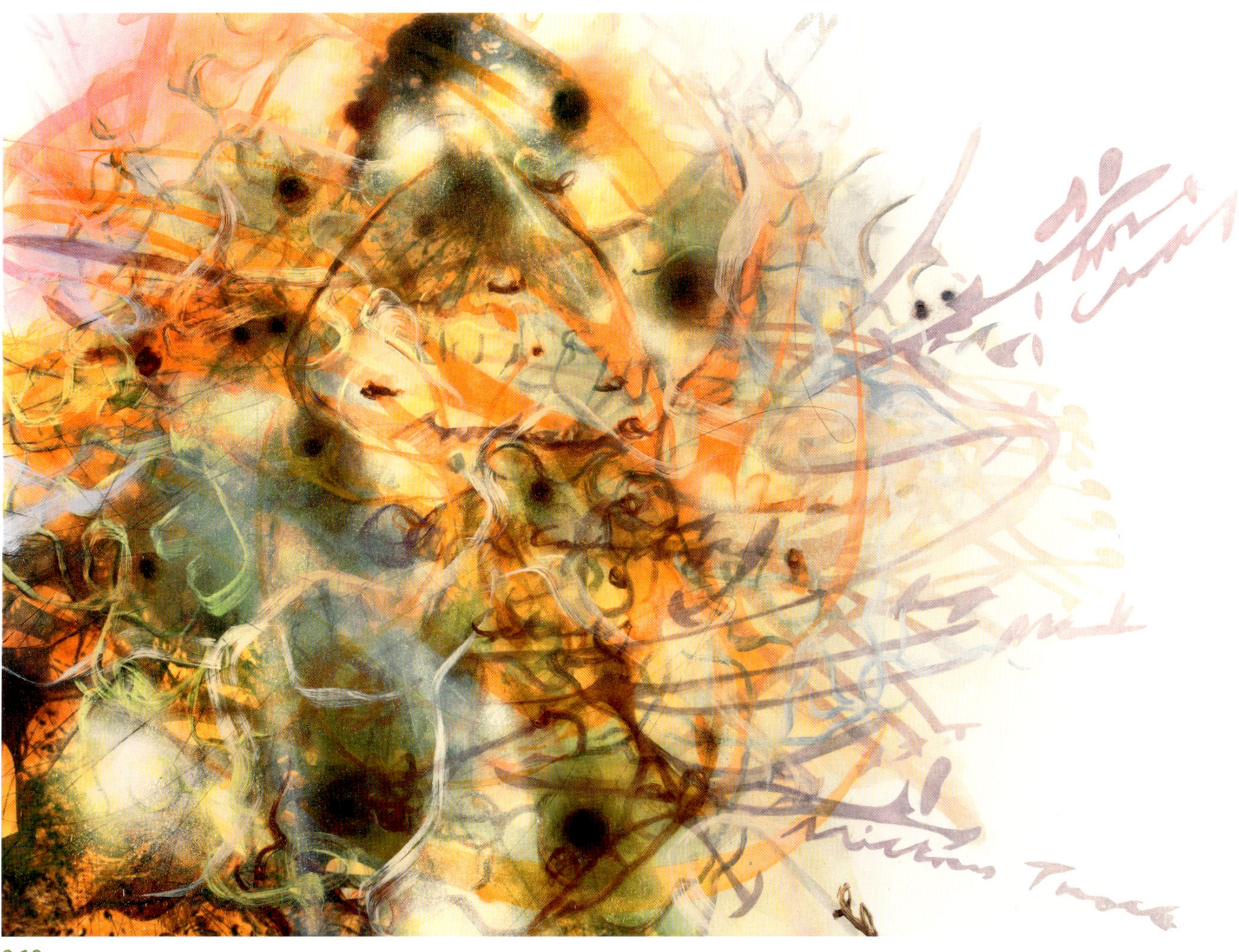

2.10

FIG. 2.11
David Smith, *Hudson River Landscape*, 1951. Welded painted steel and stainless steel, 48 3/4 x 72 1/8 x 17 5/16 inches (123.8 x 183.2 x 44 cm). Collection of the Whitney Museum of American Art, New York, New York. Purchase, 54.14. Art © Estate of David Smith / Licensed by VAGA, New York, New York. Digital image © Whitney Museum of American Art.

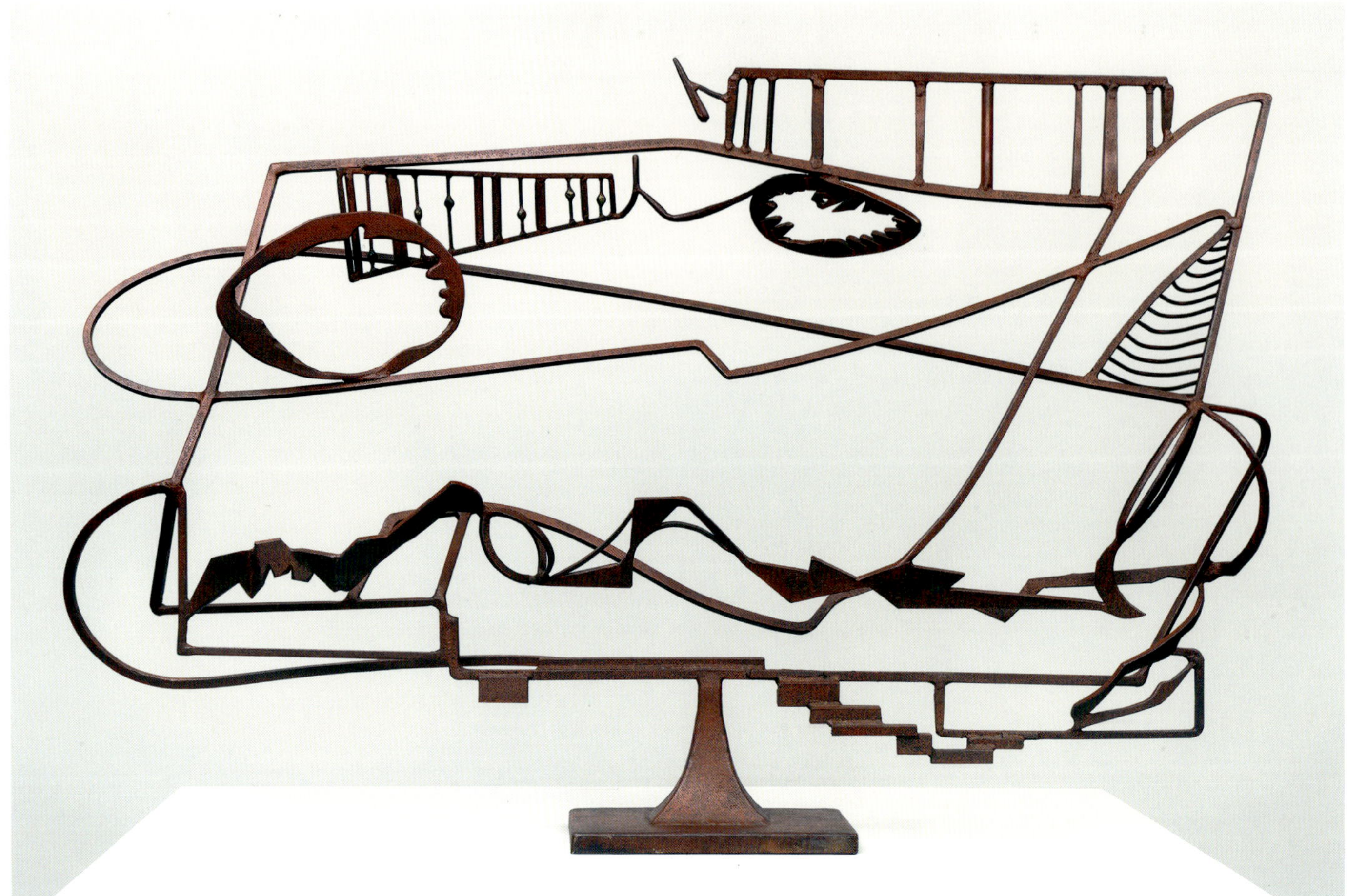

2.11

three-dimensional works have charted the human experience as abstract and extremely complex blueprints. However, like Walker, his work is inextricably rooted in drawing, which manifests as a generative type of mark making epitomized in *Link of Nature*. In much of his work, the artist seeks to plot the flow of thought and information by picturing their complex interactions. In doing so, he creates abstract works filled with an "internal ecology of meaning."[13] Ritchie is interested in charting the development of human knowledge, a Herculean task. Instead of declaring this as a futile endeavor, the artist embraces it as a reason for investigation, and he has developed a visual language expressing these relationships in a diagrammatic way.

Ritchie's work is extremely cerebral. At the heart of it, he is suggesting that as a result of mapping every aspect of our world along with society's digital inclination to live at an increasing remove from reality, perhaps humanity is becoming disconnected from itself. *Link of Nature* is from a series of works that was inspired by Ritchie's exhaustive two-volume compendium *The Temptation of the Diagram*. The artist combines a search for a meaningful topology of the diagram with the language of abstract painting-drawing (as his practice seems to walk a fine line between the two). *Link of Nature* and other accompanying works in the series, such as the related *Command and Control* (fig. 2.10), were described by Corina Larkin in *The Brooklyn Rail* as "a relatively rational analysis of how diagrams convey information combined with an overwhelming sense of chaos; there are the living, breathing clusters of disaggregated information that seems [sic] to harbor an answer to one of the uncountable mysteries of life; and there's an uncomfortable human narrative that is somehow absolved through visual flights of fancy."[14] Indeed, Ritchie transforms these into elegant, gestural abstractions.

ACCUMULATION

Anthony Caro's accumulative impulse was the culmination of an immense career as one of the most important sculptors of the twentieth century. At the urging of his parents, Caro initially studied engineering at Cambridge University, but after several years he left to enroll at the Royal Academy to study art. This was a formative experience for him, but his true education came after university, while working as an assistant to Henry Moore in the 1950s. Caro visited the United States in 1959 and met many American artists, including sculptor David Smith, whose large, welded sculptures would have a tremendous impact on him. After his return to England, Caro took up the welding torch to make large-scale steel sculptures in a more constructivist way. In the 1960s he became part of the so-called "New Generation" of British sculptors, which included his peers Phillip King,

William Tucker, and many others. The New Generation was a response to high modernism and part of a larger sculptural renaissance in England that dated back to just after World War II. Stylistically, their work existed somewhere between the severe forms of minimalism and the bright colors of pop art. While it may seem unremarkable today, Caro caused something of a sensation at the time by removing the sculpture from the pedestal and showing it directly on the floor.

Landscape has been a theme in Caro's sculpture since the early 1960s, perhaps inspired by Smith's works, such as *Hudson River Landscape* (fig. 2.11), 1951. He continued to work on this subject into the 1970s with horizontally oriented sculptures such as *Larry's Land* (fig. 2.12), 1970. The artist revisited this landscape theme in *The Brook* (pl. 3) and other sculptures from the *Park Avenue Series*, a group of works based on an unrealized project intended to be installed along the eponymous thoroughfare in New York. *The Brook* is a low, horizontal conglomeration of welded steel pieces, but unlike *Larry's Land* and other 1970s sculptures, it is much more densely accumulated. The cresting side of *The Brook* is punctuated by a conspicuous chevron shape and framed by a rectangle, which is bound on one side by a large semicircle. Undulating steel-as-water flows across the length of the piece before being abruptly interrupted by a crumpled barricade. Caro's marriage of materials and composition in the creation of this series led critic and art historian Michael Fried to write of the *Park Avenue Series* that "all the sculptures make a certain show of their materiality. . . . More precisely, all the sculptures foreground the material specificity of the various elements that went into their making."[15]

Employing a figurative vocabulary, Huma Bhabha accumulates a broad range of seemingly disposable materials to make works that have the permanence of antique sculpture. Born in Karachi, Pakistan, Bhabha came to the United States in 1981 to attend art school at the Rhode Island School of Design. She completed her BFA there, received an MFA from Columbia University, and by the early 1990s was exhibiting her sculpture. A decade later, Bhabha was incorporating Styrofoam, rebar, clay, and other various materials in works that appeared to be a cross between fragmentary Greek

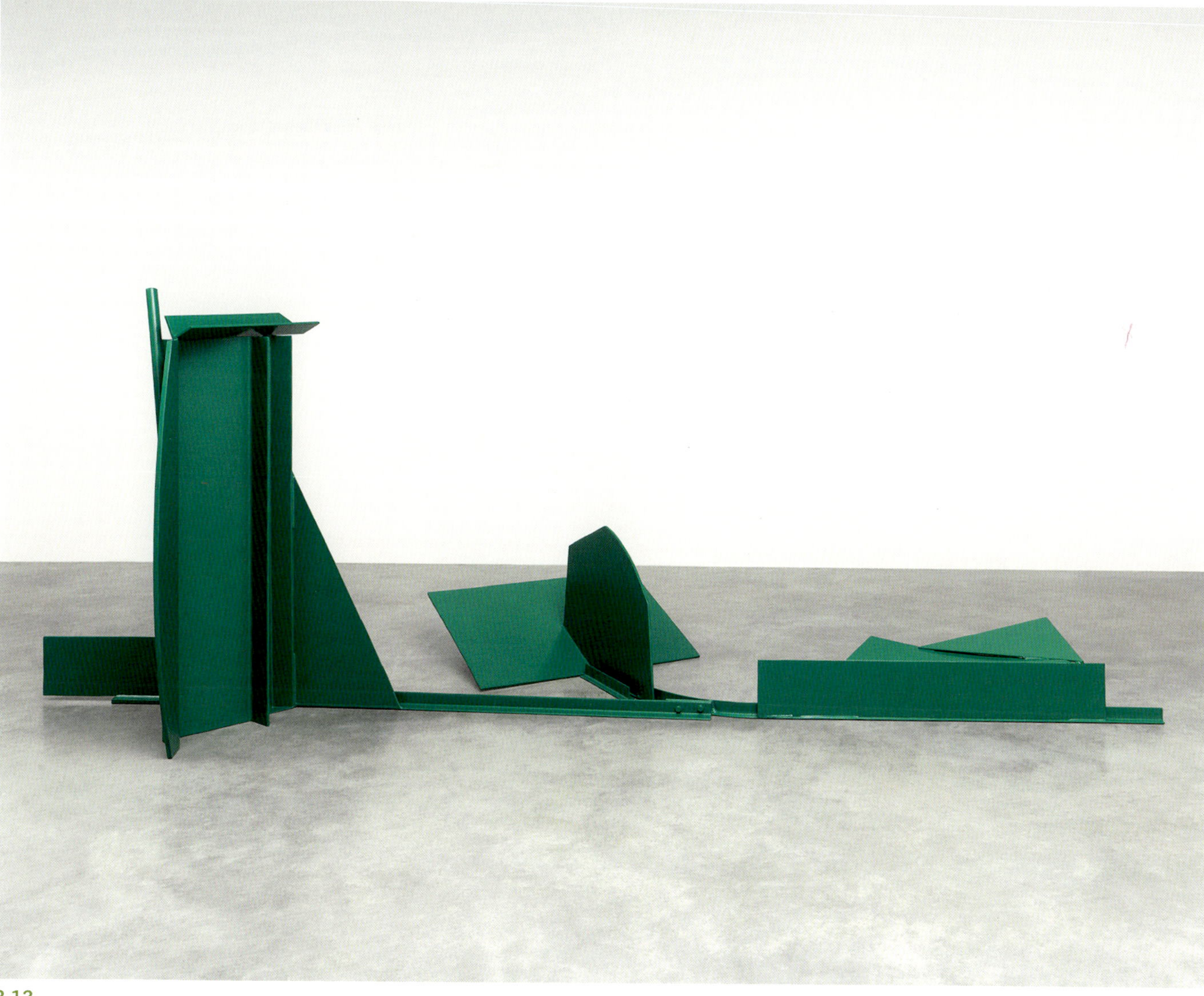

2.12

FIG. 2.12
Anthony Caro, *Larry's Land*, 1971. Steel and paint, 67 x 236 x 120 inches (170 x 600 x 305 cm). Private collection. Image courtesy of the artist, Barford Sculptures Ltd., and Gagosian Gallery, New York, New York. © Anthony Caro. Photo by Mike Bruce.

kouros figures and grotesque inventions of science fiction. The artist made these figures at a moment when US foreign policy engaged the country in several calamitous military conflicts in the Middle East. While her work is not overtly political, Bhabha has acknowledged that those events indirectly provided inspiration for her work. The ongoing war and destruction of cultural artifacts in that region has given Bhabha an inexhaustible pool upon which to draw.

Chain of Missing Links (pl. 2) from 2012 stands resolutely upright, a totemic sentinel on watch. Like many of Bhabha's sculptures, the skeletal nature of the figure suggests a postapocalyptic narrative that could have emanated from the war-ravaged lands of the Middle East. Bhabha's work is characterized by her creative marriage of industrial materials and detritus. In many cases, including *Chain of Missing Links*, the figures appear to be nomadic or wandering in an enigmatic existential drama, while the materials serve to underscore a narrative of destruction and resurrection. The artist has said, "In many ways my work is quite traditional. Art has always been a response to circumstances, whether in one's own situation or in the world as a whole. These days, the global is local—and globalization is the new colonialism."[16] When considered in light of the destruction of antiquities and the ongoing threat to ancient sites by militant groups and military conflict, Bhabha's work takes on a greater cultural resonance and urgency and may serve as an admonishing talisman.

Accumulation is at the heart of Elliott Hundley's creative process and, like many artists of his generation, he combines painting, photography, sculpture, collage, and installation into a seamlessly transdisciplinary practice. Hundley attended the Rhode Island School of Design and, after finishing his BFA, spent several years living in Rome, where he was deeply inspired by the surrounding remnants of antiquity. He returned to the States, received an MFA from the University of California, Los Angeles, and exhibited a series of multimedia works inspired by the fifth-century Athenian tragedian Euripides's *Hekabe*. Hundley's work is frequently compared to that of Robert Rauschenberg in its inventive combinations of materials and to that of Cy Twombly in its references to ancient Greece. His combination of the modern and the antique using the tessellated language of collage results in densely layered visual excavations.

Hundley employs an "all-over" effect in many of his works, including the monumental *eyes that run like leaping fire* (pl. 16). Reminiscent of abstract expressionism (fig. 2.13), the entire picture plane of Hundley's works are covered with mosaic bits of photographs, found paper, string, beads, sequins, or any other objects at his disposal. For Hundley, this *horror vaccui* is the sine qua non of these large-scale works. *Eyes that run like leaping fire* is from a series of works that the artist based on *The Bacchae*, a play by Euripides. The title for Hundley's work is taken from the moment in the play

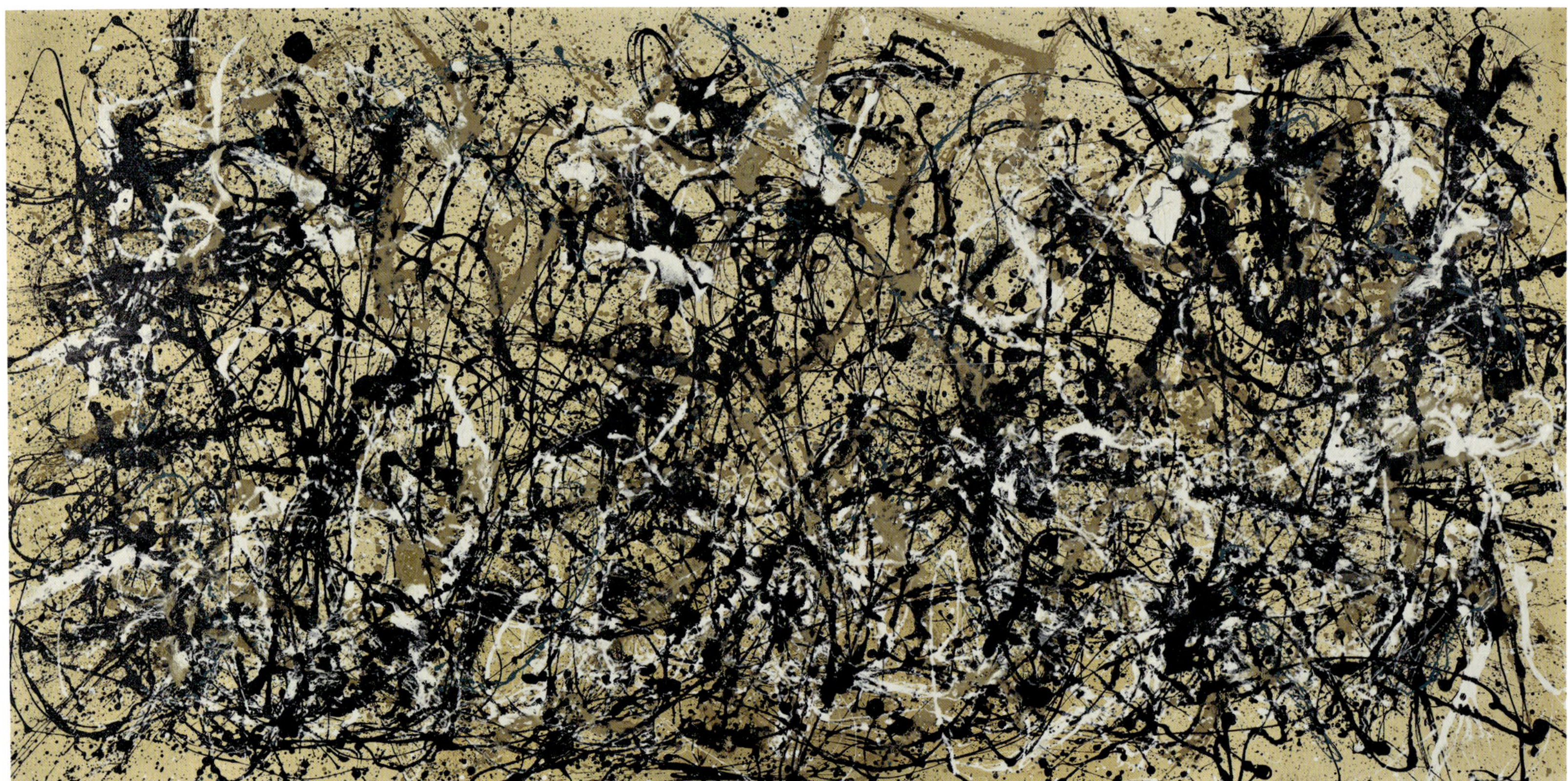

2.13

FIG. 2.13
Jackson Pollock, *Autumn Rhythm (Number 30)*, 1950. Enamel on canvas, 105 x 207 inches (266.7 x 525.8 cm). The Metropolitan Museum of Art, New York, New York. George A. Hearn Fund, 1957; 57.92. © 2014 The Pollock-Krasner Foundation / Artists Rights Society (ARS), New York, New York. Digital Image © The Metropolitan Museum of Art / Art Resource, New York, New York.

when Agavê, King Pentheus's mother, is devastated by the recognition of her son, who she had mistaken for a wild beast and, in her madness, slaughtered. The scale and architecture of *eyes that run like leaping fire* gives it an intrinsic theatrical and set-like quality—a backdrop upon which this tragedy unfolds. It is not necessary to know this Greek tale to appreciate Hundley's complex and panoramic theatre-cum-collage masterpiece.

CONCLUSION

A Material Legacy presents a selection of works from the Nasher Haemisegger Collection by artists who have expanded the use and understanding of materials. Seen through the lens of this considerable and judicious private collection, these works tell us more than simply the collectors' aesthetic preferences; they provide a snapshot of contemporary artists' material inclinations. The artists in this exhibition build on the legacy of those pioneering painters and sculptors of the early twentieth century and capitalize on the new resources available to them. Their works are made with an array of conventional and unconventional materials such as acrylic paint, porcelain, wood, welded steel, cut paper, visually articulated onomatopoeia, and the penultimate immaterial material: ideas. Nasher and Haemisegger continue to build on their family legacy while resolutely forging their own. It will be a welcome affair to watch this collection continue to grow, ultimately providing an extremely rich, intrinsically fertile, and undeniably material legacy for generations to come.

NOTES

1 Vladimir Markov quoted in Jeremy Howard, Irēa Bužinska, and Z. S. Strother, *Vladimir Markov and Russian Primitivism* (Farnham, Surrey, and Burlington, VT: Ashgate Publishing Company, 2015), 207.

2 Hal Foster, Rosalind Krauss, Yve-Alain Bois, Benjamin H. D. Buchloh, *Art Since 1900: Modernism, Anitmodernism, Postmodernism*, vol. 1 (New York: Thames & Hudson, Inc., 2004), 126. Emphasis mine.

3 Charlotte Mullins, *Rachel Whiteread* (London: Tate Publishing, 2004), 7.

4 Robert Pincus-Witten, *Post-minimalism* (New York: Out of London Press, 1977), 29.

5 Charlie Rose, "Richard Serra," charlierose.com, 54:12, April 20, 2011, http://www.charlierose.com/watch/50142616.

6 Saul Ostrow, "Sol LeWitt," *Bomb Magazine* 85 (2003), accessed September 2, 2015, http://bombmagazine.org/article/2583/sol-lewitt.

7 Sol LeWitt, "Paragraphs on Conceptual Art," in *Art in Theory 1900-1990: An Anthology of Changing Ideas*, eds. Charles Harrison and Paul Wood (Oxford: Blackwell, 1992), 834.

8 Lale Arikoglu, "Creative Space: Artist Teresita Fernández," *Whitewall* (February 1, 2013), accessed August 9, 2015, http://www.whitewallmag.com/art/creative-space-artist-teresita-fernandez.

9 Quoted in Catherine Craft, "Setting the Surface Free," in *Katharina Grosse: Wunderblock* (Dallas: Nasher Sculpture Center, 2013), 10.

10 "An Argument for Something Else: Dieter Roelstraete in Conversation with Kerry James Marshall" in *Aesthetic Justice: Intersecting Artistic and Moral Perspectives*, eds. Pascal Gielen and Niels van Tomme (Amsterdam: Valiz, 2015), 133.

11 Martin Coomer, "Kerry James Marshall interview: 'When have you ever seen a painting of a black person that seems self-satisfied?'" *Time Out London*, October 23, 2014, accessed September 4, 2015, http://www.timeout.com/london/art/kerry-james-marshall-interview-when-have-you-ever-seen-a-painting-of-a-black-person-that-seems-self-satisfied.

12 Harold Rosenberg, "The American Action Painters" from *Tradition of the New*, originally in *Art News* 51 (1952): 22. Emphasis mine.

13 Matthew Ritchie, e-mail message to author, August 20, 2015.

14 Corina Larkin, "Matthew Ritchie: Ten Possible Links," *The Brooklyn Rail*, October 3, 2014, accessed August 22, 2015, http://www.brooklynrail.org/2014/10/artseen/matthew-ritchie-ten-possible-links.

15 Michael Fried, "Anthony Caro's *Park Avenue Series*," in *Caro: Park Avenue Series* exh. cat. (London: Gagosian Gallery), 12.

16 "In the Studio: Huma Bhabha with Steel Stillman," *Art in America* 98 (2010): 92.

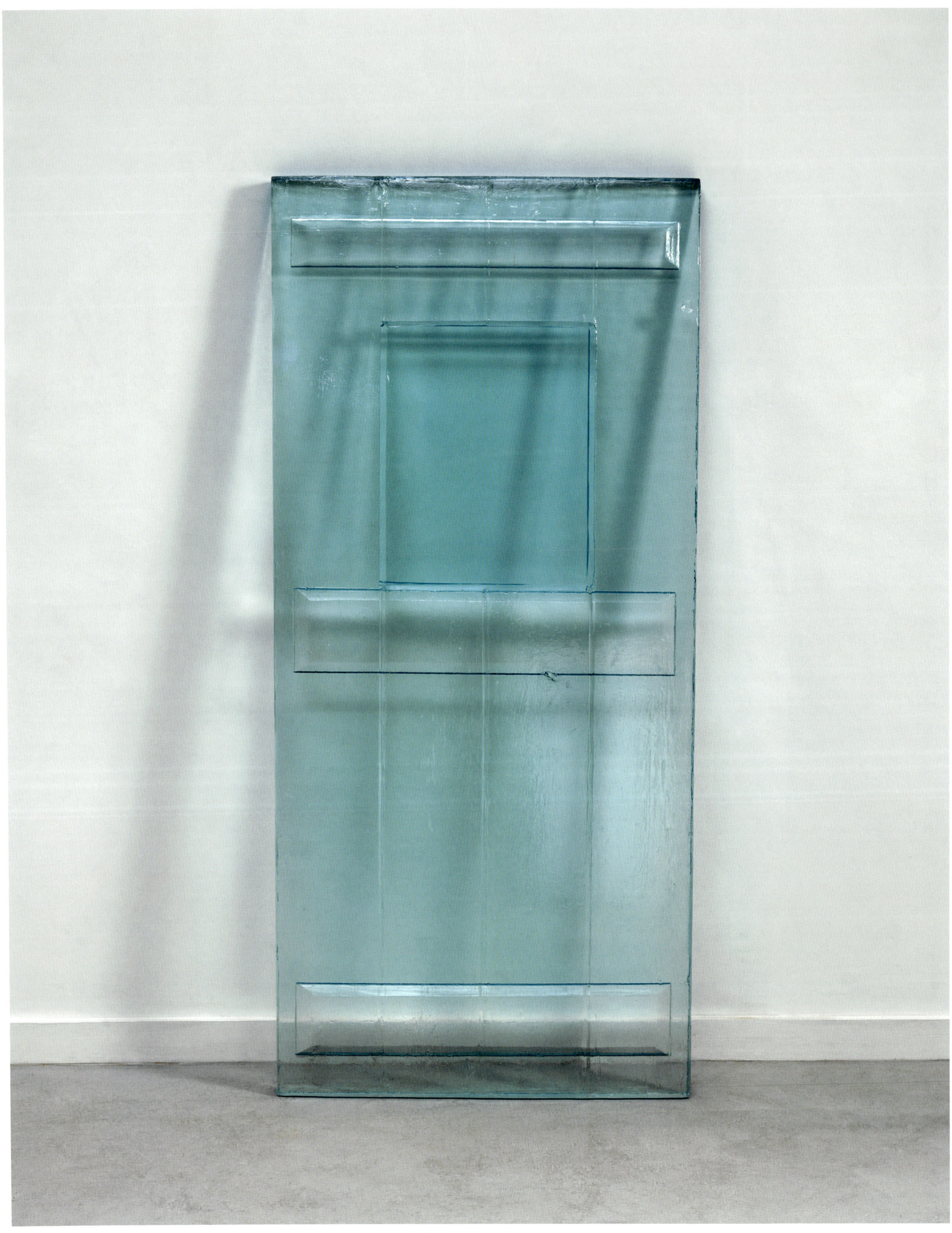

PL. 33 Rachel Whiteread, *circa 1760 (II)*, 2012. Resin, 73 1/4 x 33 7/16 x 2 9/16 inches (186.1 x 84.9 x 6.5 cm).

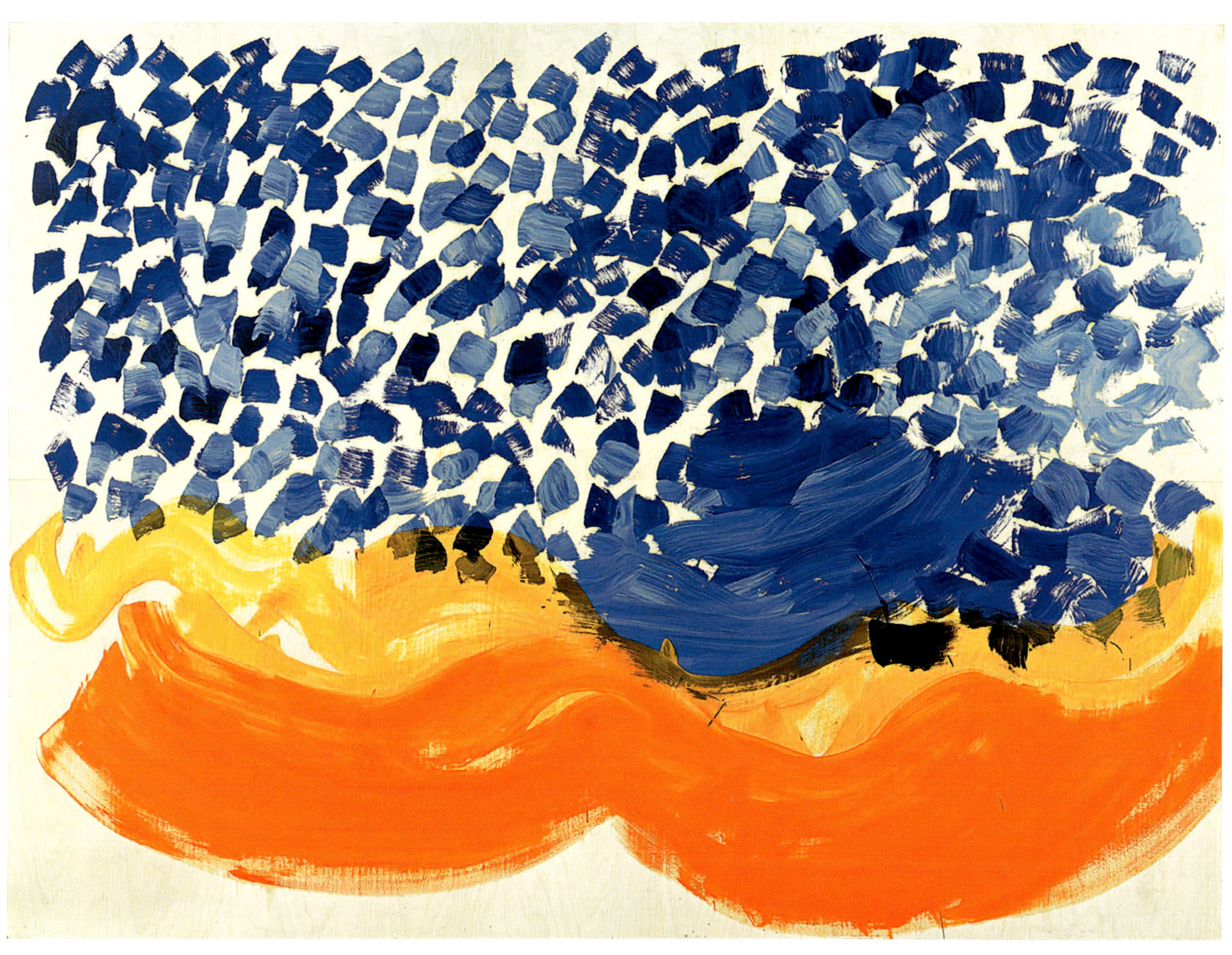

PL. 14 Howard Hodgkin, *Where Seldom Is Heard a Discouraging Word*, 2007–08. Oil on wood, 80 1/8 x 105 inches (203.5 x 266.7 cm).

PL. 28 Richard Serra, *Double Rift #10*, 2013. Paint stick on handmade paper, 84 x 240 3/8 x 3 3/4 inches (213.4 x 610.6 x 9.5 cm).

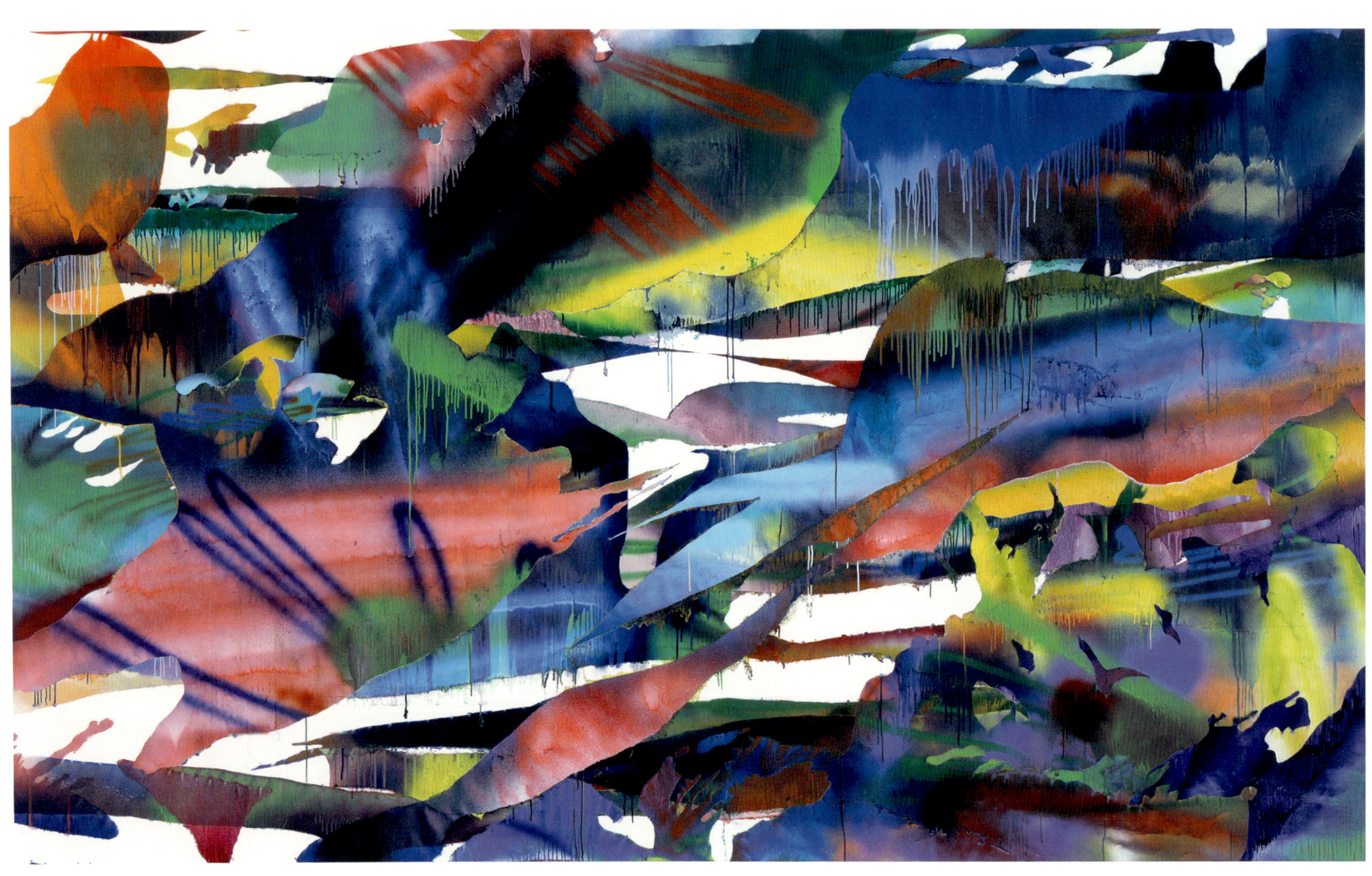

PL. 11 Katharina Grosse, *Untitled*, 2013. Acrylic on canvas, 94 1/2 x 152 3/4 inches (240 x 388 cm).

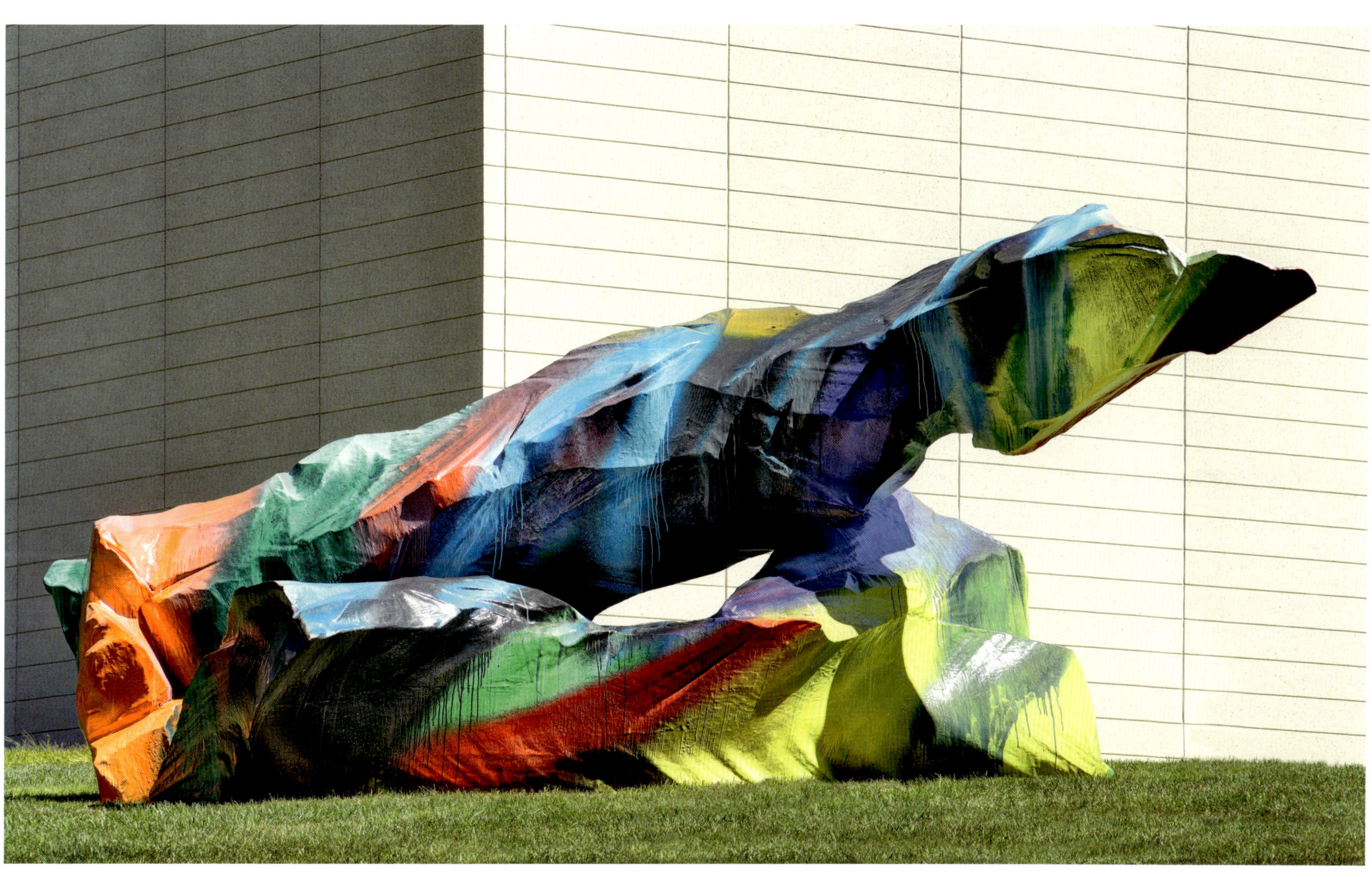

PL. 10 Katharina Grosse, *Untitled*, 2013. Acrylic on fiberglass-reinforced plastic, 133 7/8 x 165 3/8 x 283 1/2 inches (340 x 420.1 x 720.1 cm).

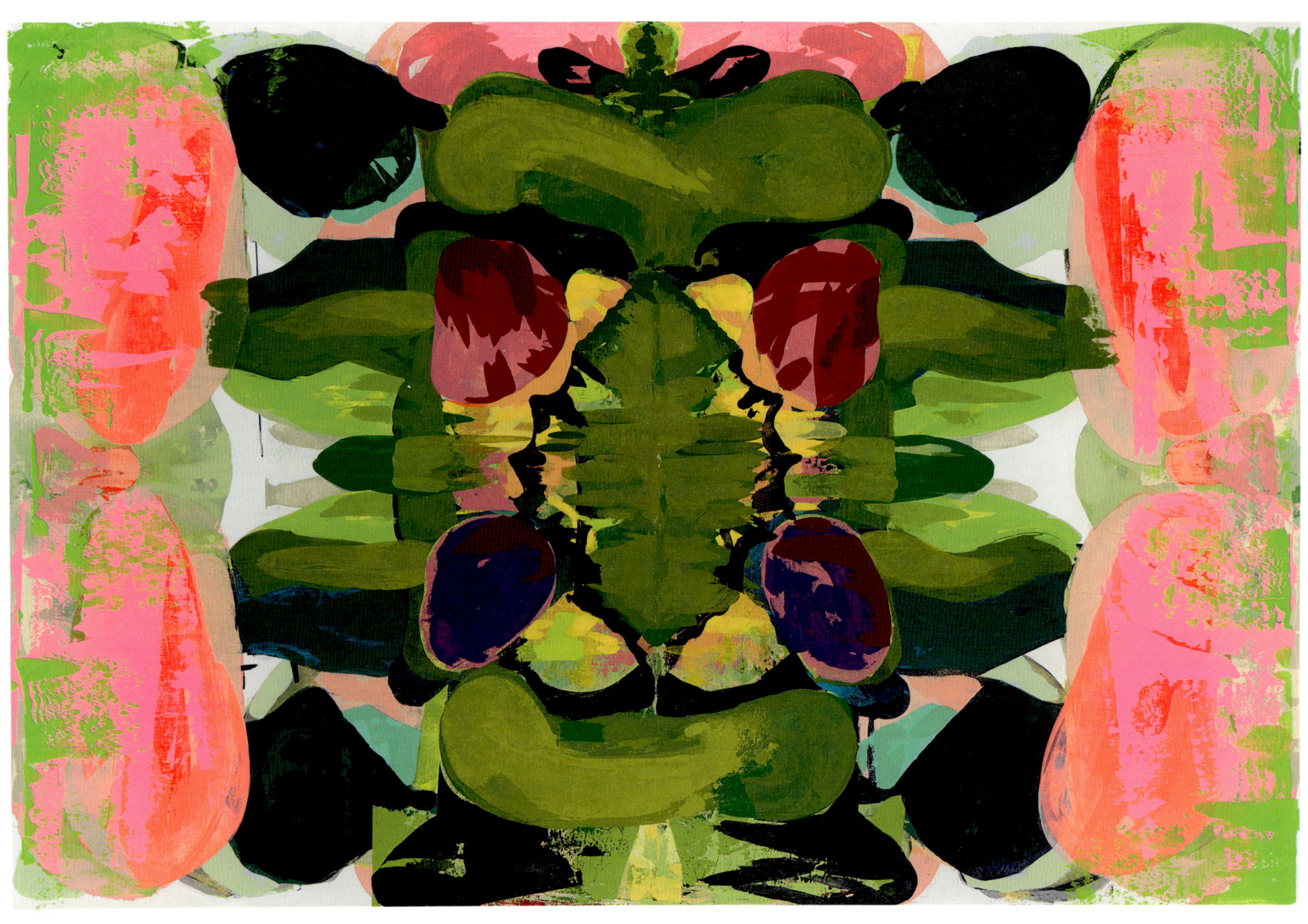

PL. 22 Kerry James Marshall, *Untitled (Blot)*, 2014. Acrylic on PVC panel, 84 x 119 inches (213.4 x 302.3 cm).

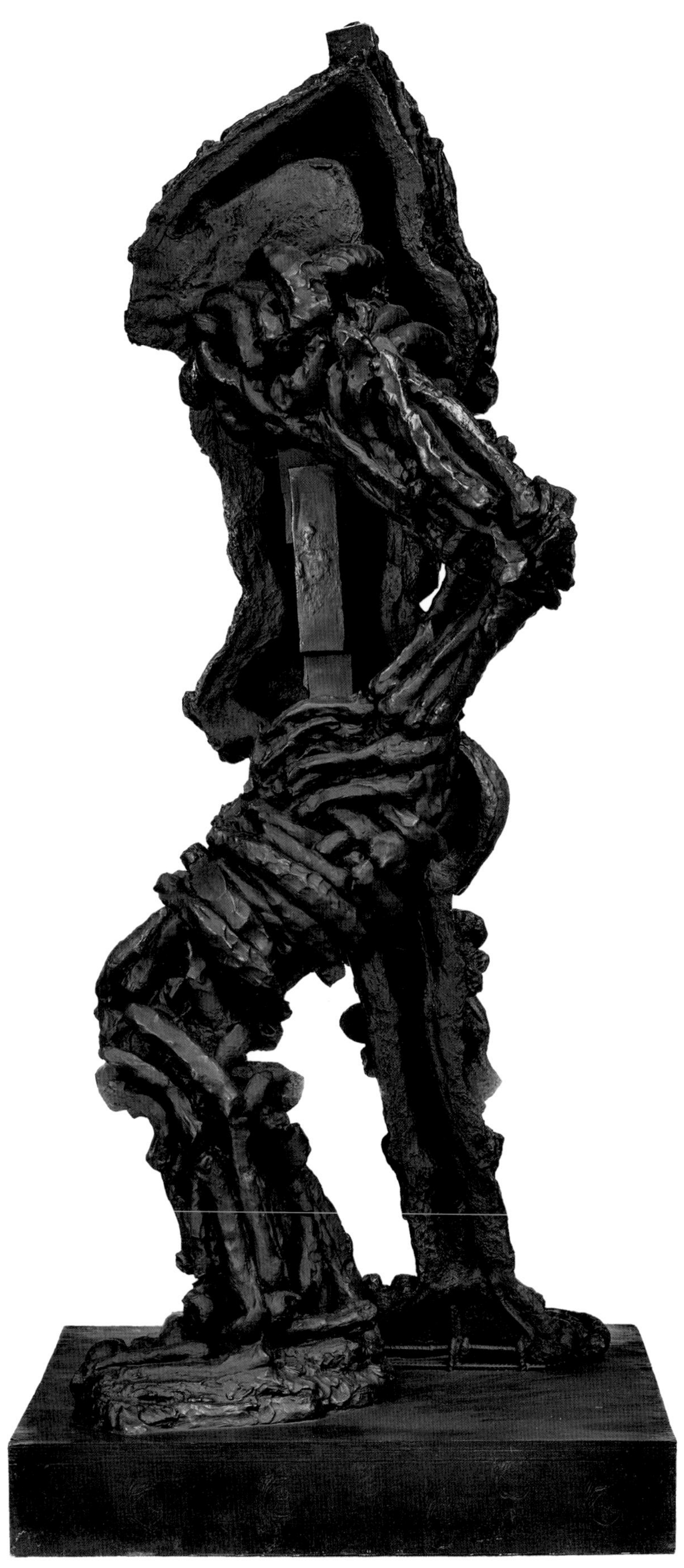

PL. 15 Thomas Houseago, *Yet to be titled*, 2012. Bronze, edition 2/3; 110 x 46 x 44 inches (279.4 x 116.8 x 111.8 cm).

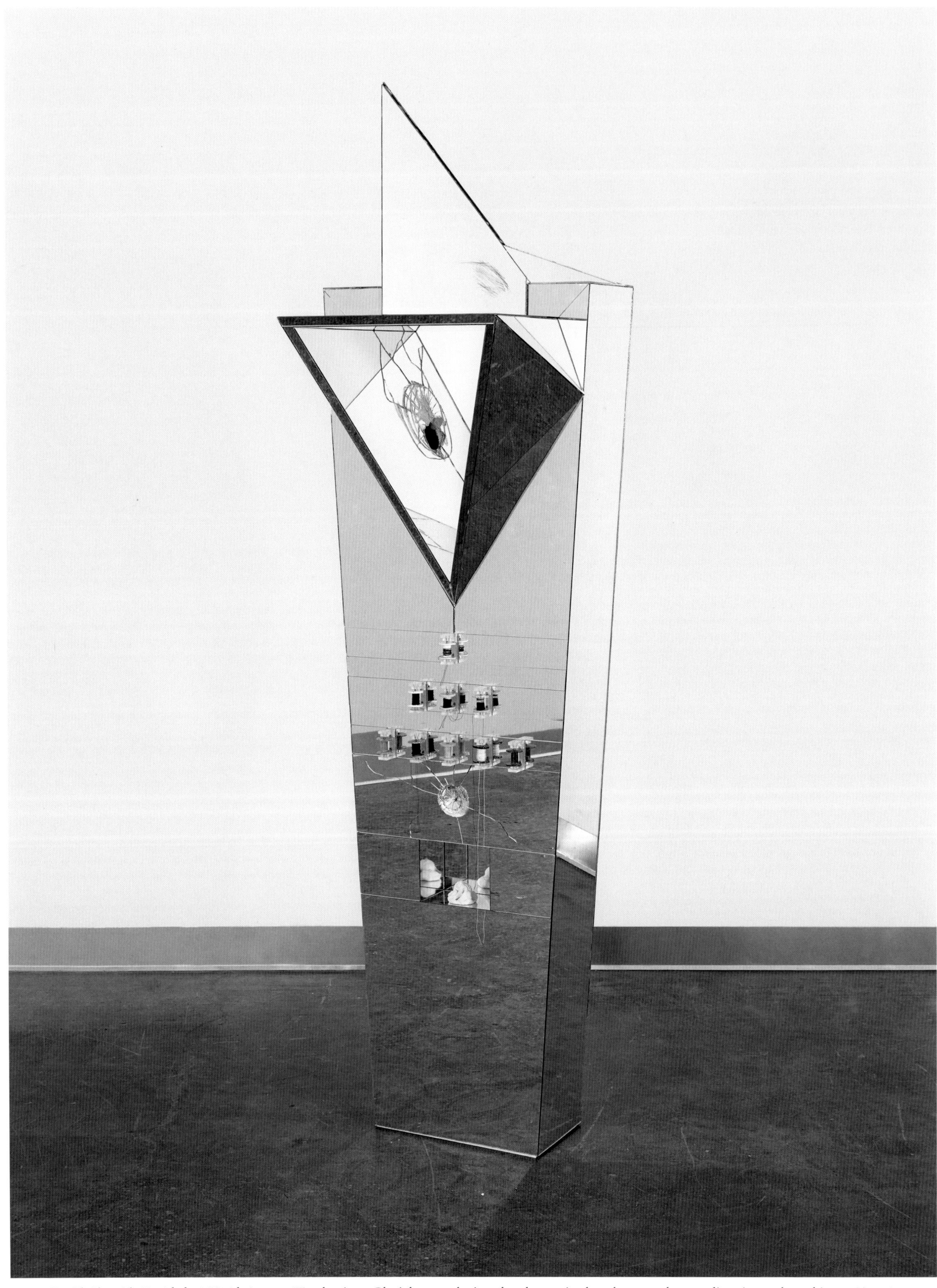

PL. 1 David Altmejd, *Untitled 16 (Guides)*, 2013. Wood, mirror, Plexiglas, metal wire, glazed ceramic, thread, epoxy clay, acrylic paint, and graphite; 79 1/2 x 28 x 21 inches (201.9 x 71.1 x 53.3 cm).

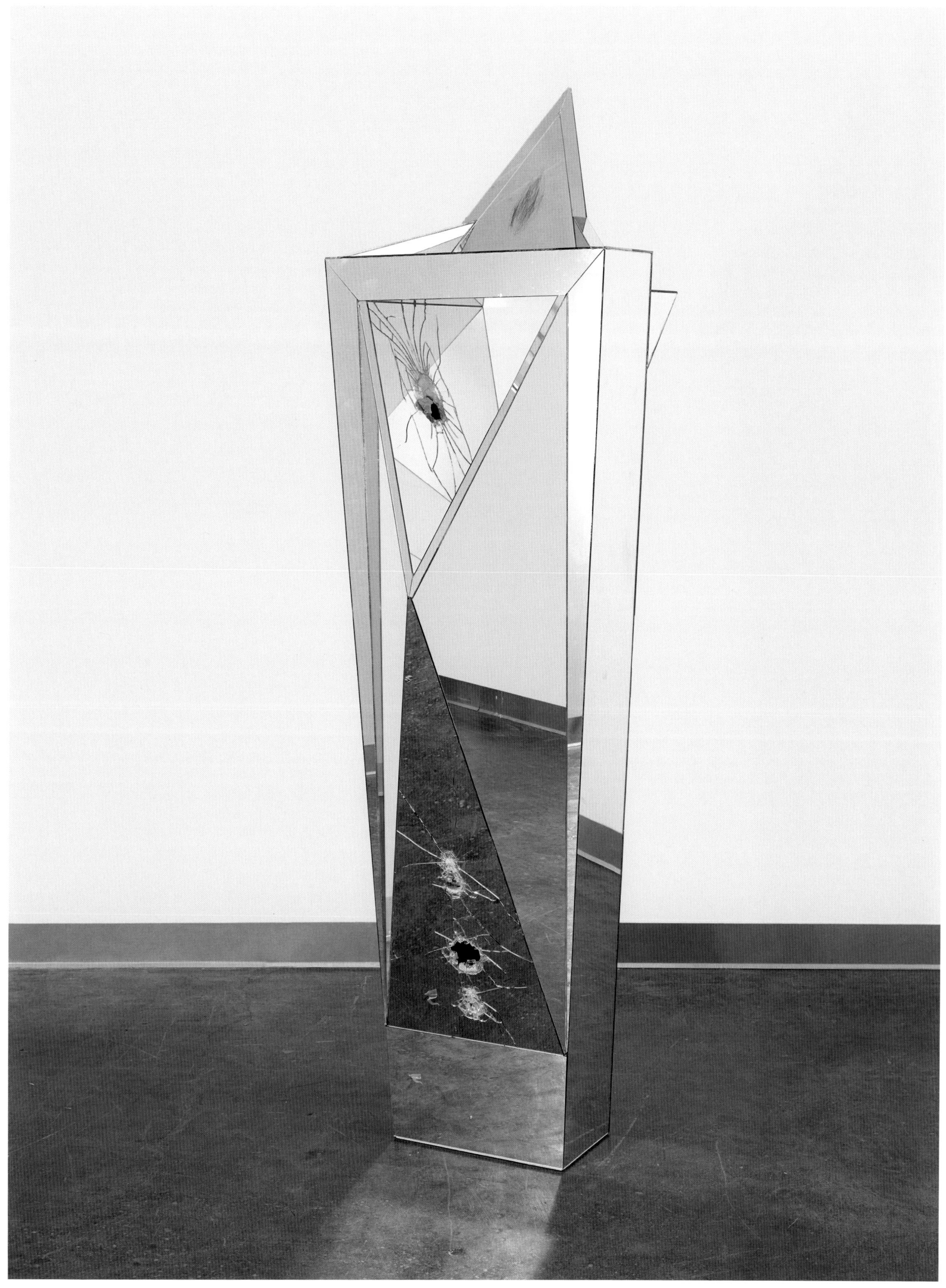

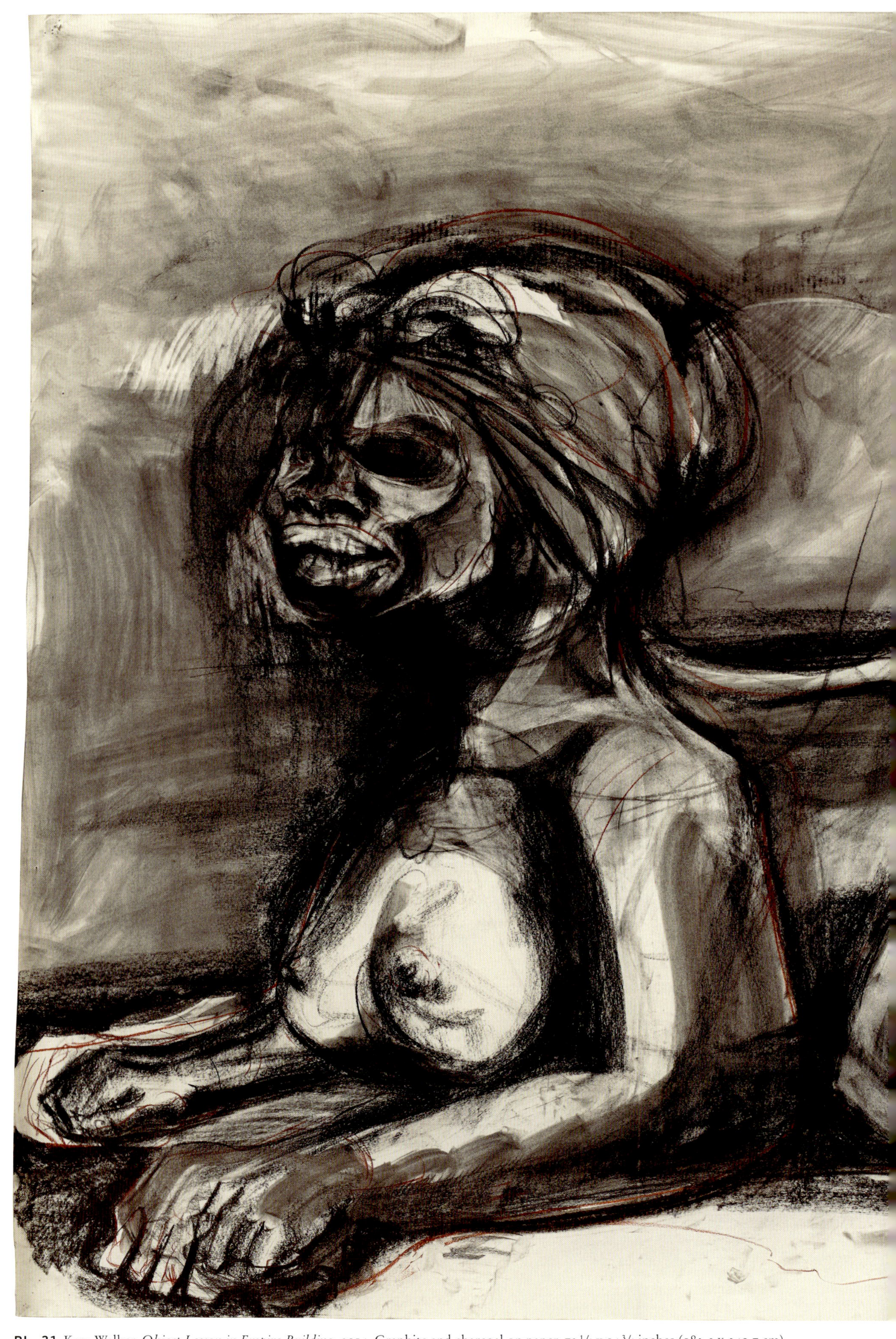

PL. 31 Kara Walker, *Object Lesson in Empire Building*, 2014. Graphite and charcoal on paper, 72 1/4 x 94 3/4 inches (183.5 x 240.7 cm).

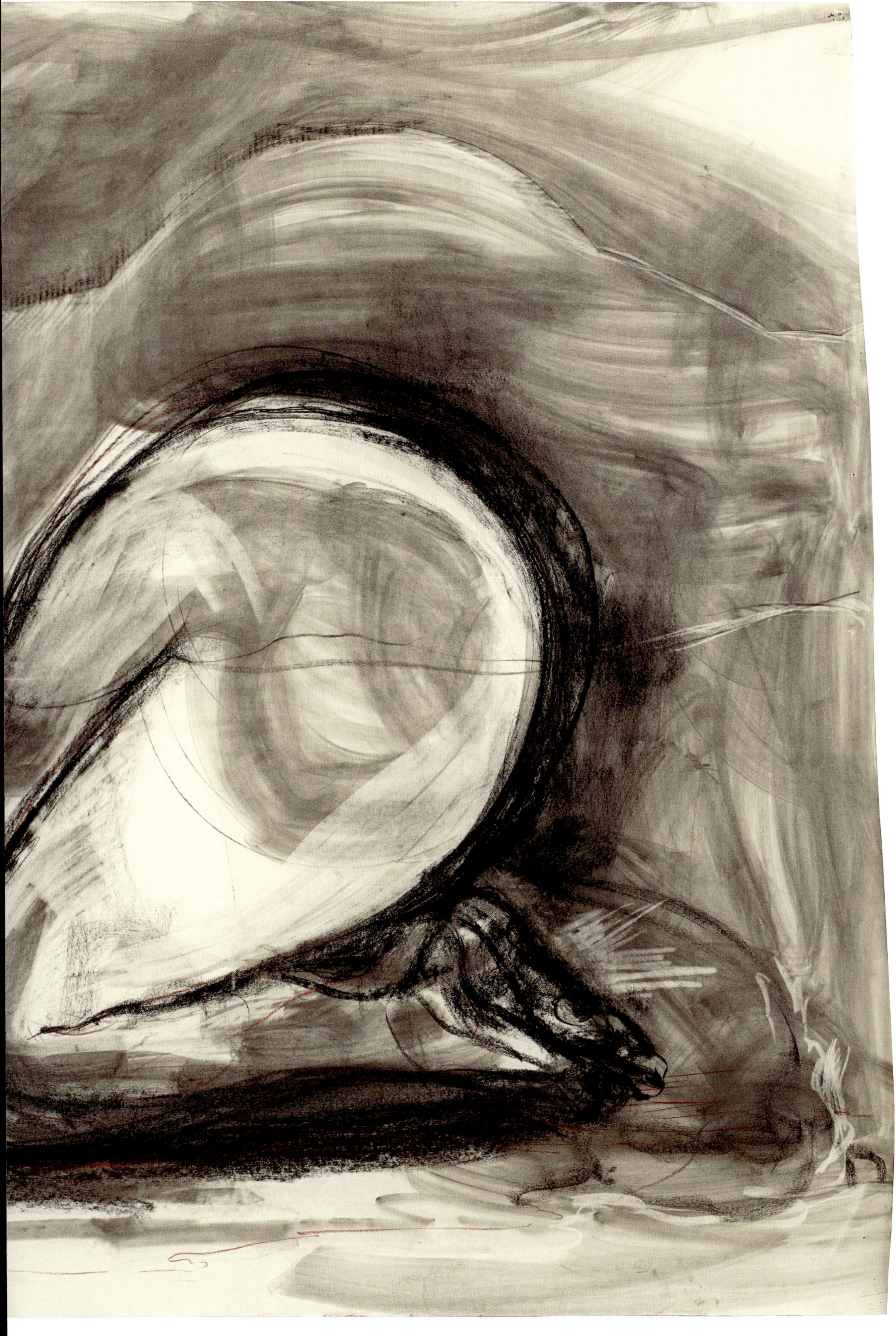

PL. 7 Teresita Fernández, *Nocturnal (Cinematic Sky)*, 2011. Solid graphite on wood panel, 96 x 72 inches (243.8 x 182.9 cm).

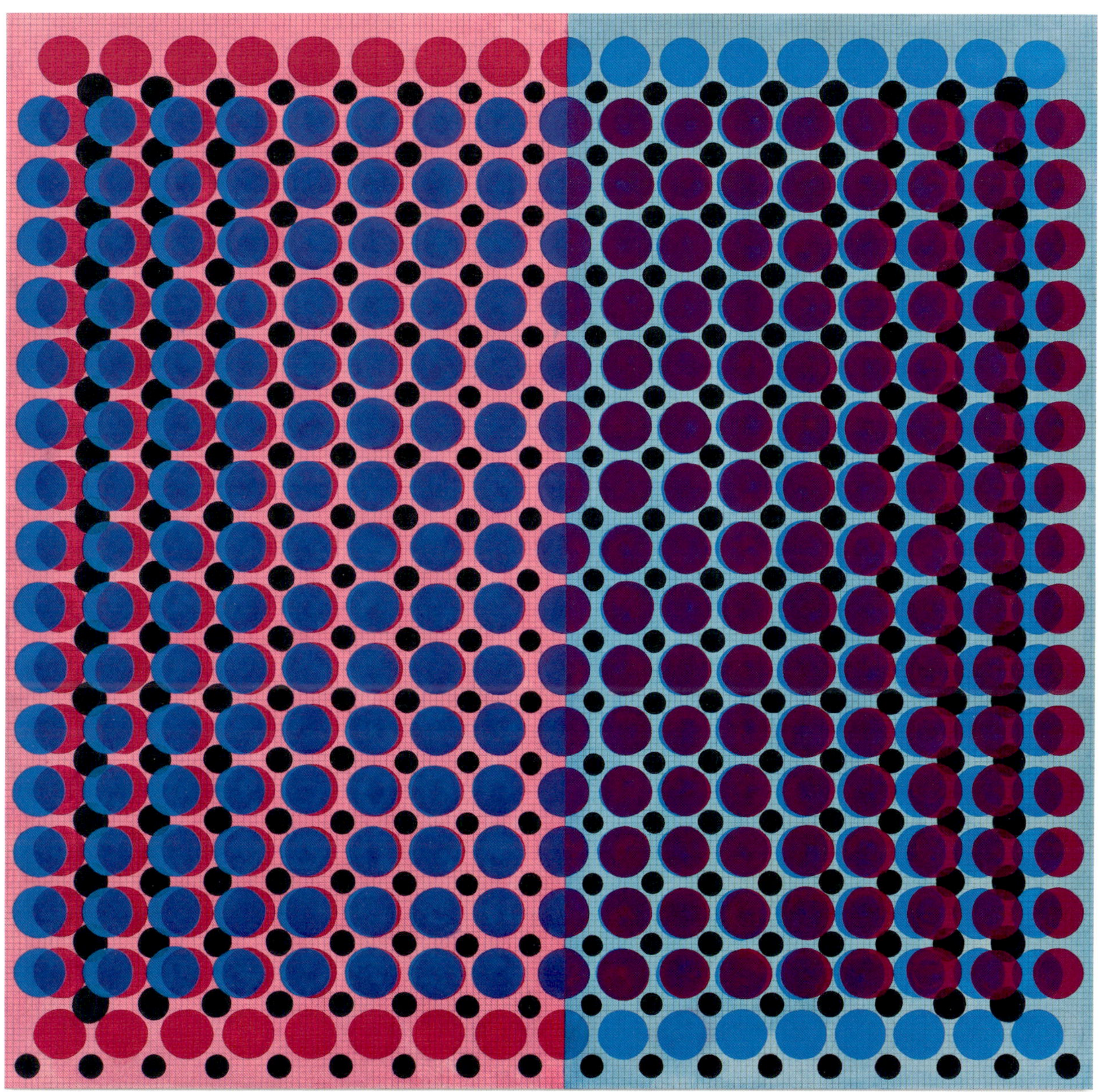

PL. 32 Dan Walsh, *Cycle X*, 2013. Pencil and acrylic on canvas, 70 x 70 inches (177.8 x 177.8 cm).

PL. 29 Rudolf Stingel, *Untitled*, 2014. Oil and enamel on canvas, 83 x 67 inches (210.8 x 170.2 cm).

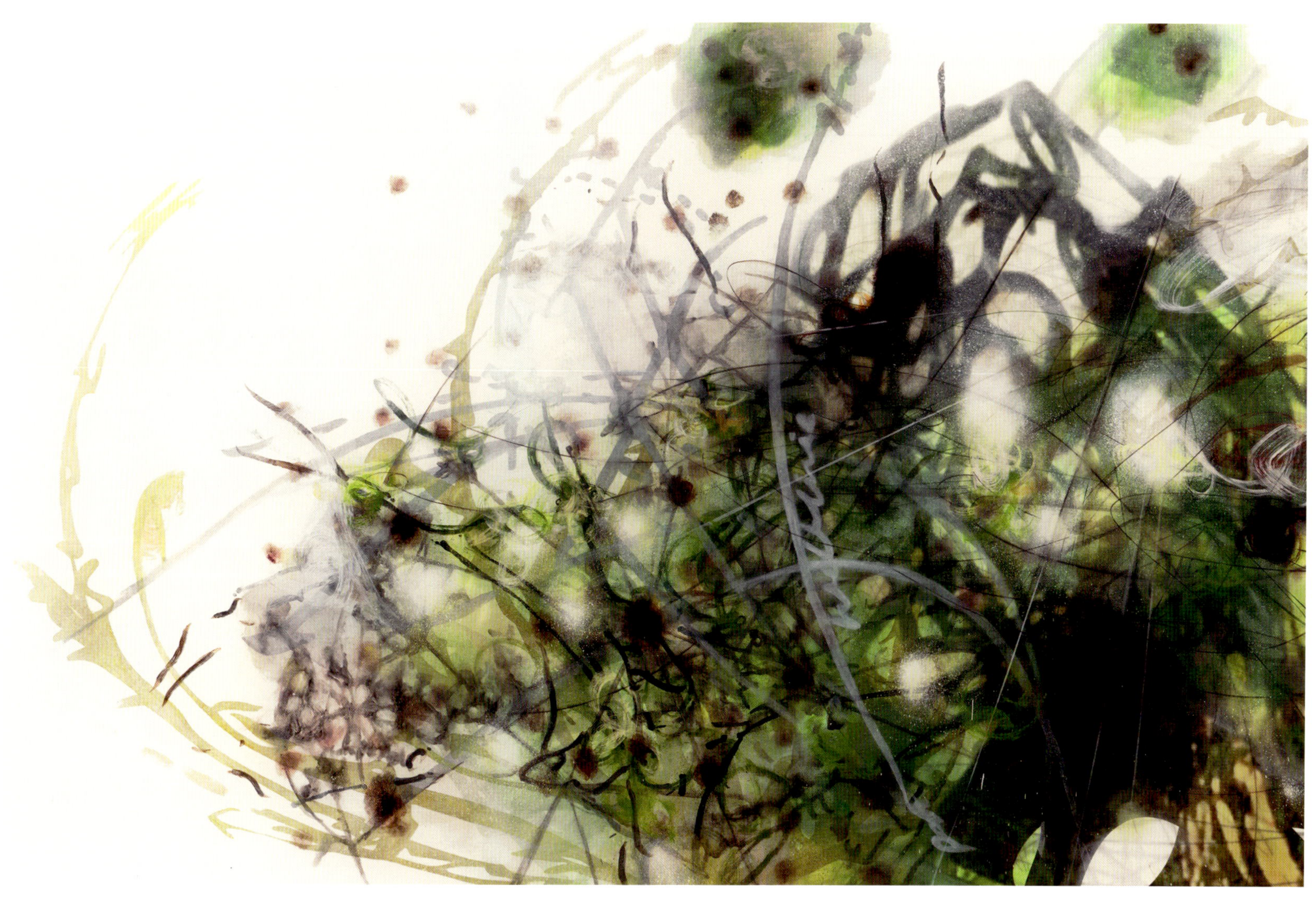

PL. 26 Matthew Ritchie, *Link of Nature*, 2014. Oil and ink on canvas, 78 x 116 x 2 1/2 inches (198.1 x 294.6 x 6.4 cm).

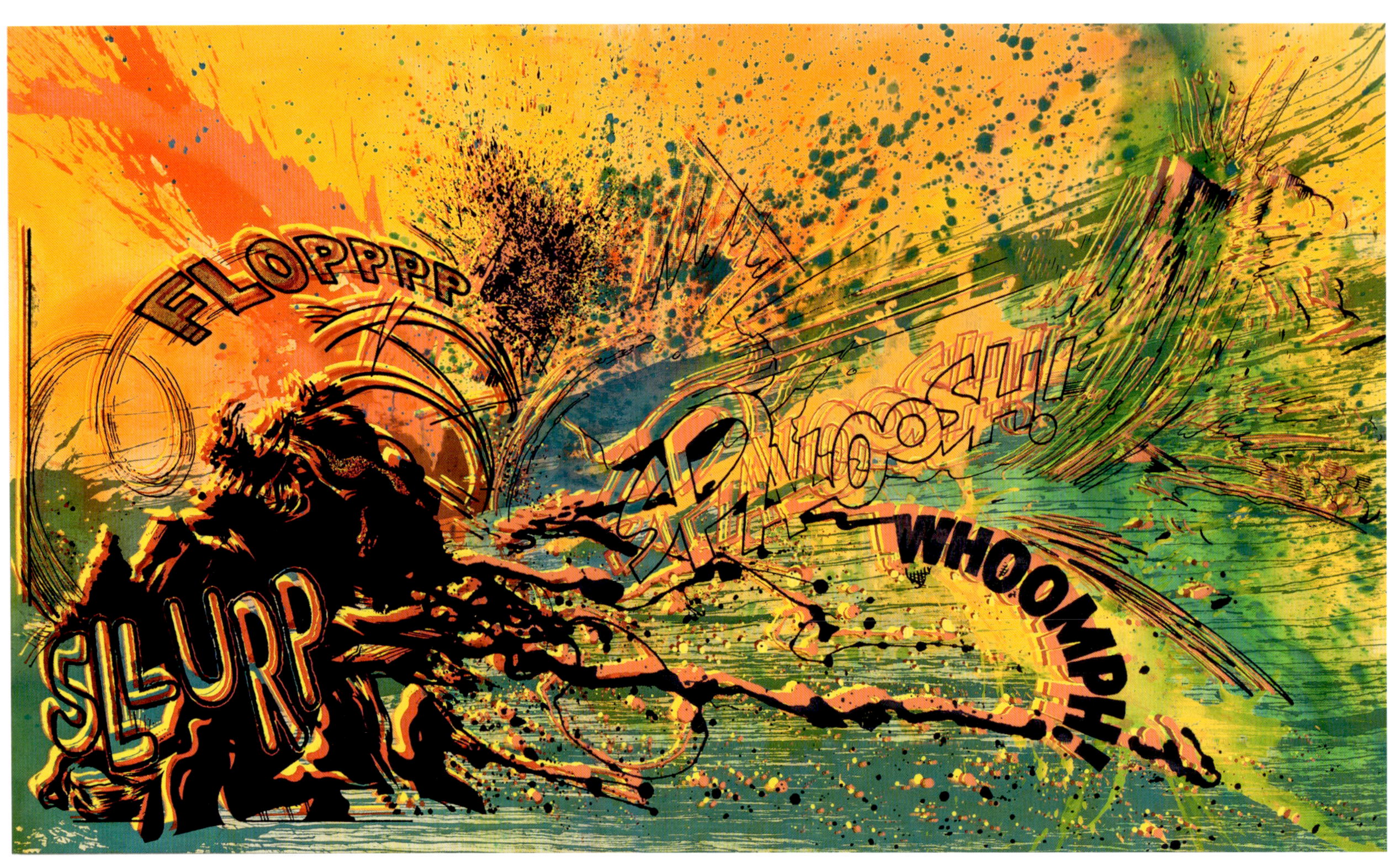

PL. 21 Christian Marclay, *Actions: Flopppp Sllurp Spaloosh Whoomph (No. 3)*, 2013. Screenprint and acrylic on canvas, 61 1/2 x 102 1/2 inches (156.2 x 260.4 cm).

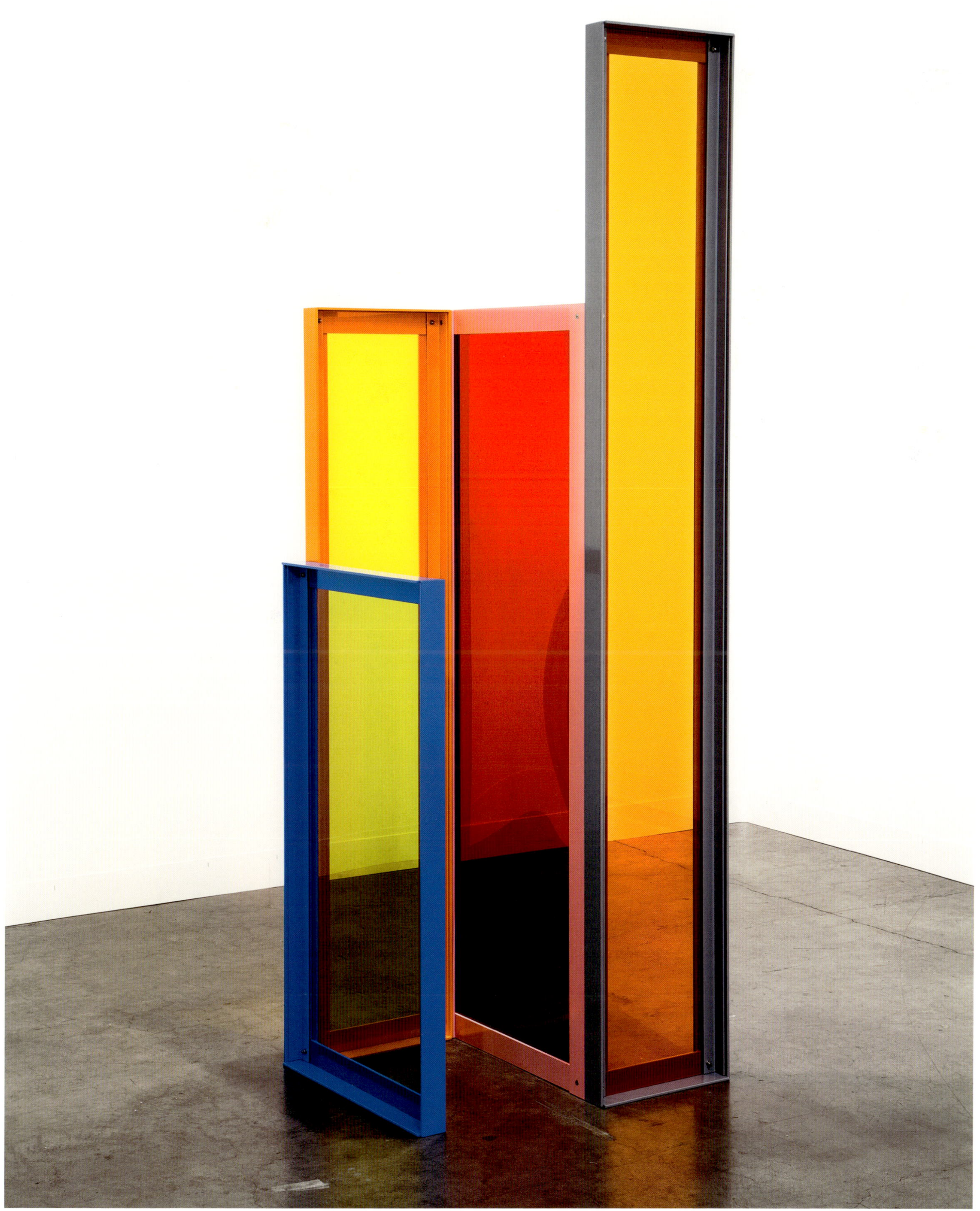

PL. 8 Liam Gillick, *Pascal Elevation*, 2014. Powder-coated aluminum and Plexiglas, 78 3/4 x 24 7/8 x 20 15/16 inches (200 x 63 x 53 cm).

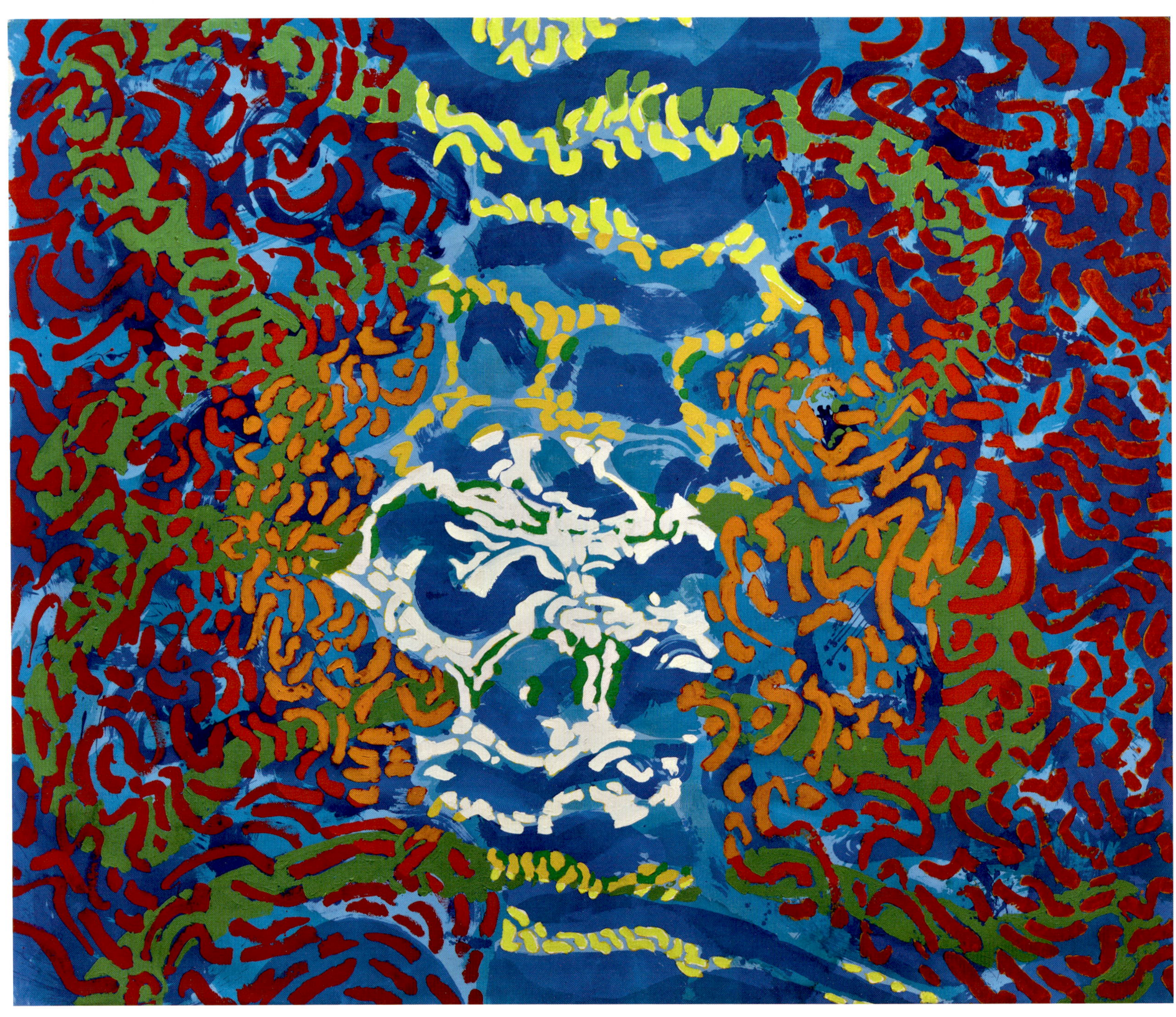

PL. 6 Mark di Suvero, *Untitled*, c. 1995. Acrylic on canvas, 112 x 130 inches (284.5 x 330.2 cm).

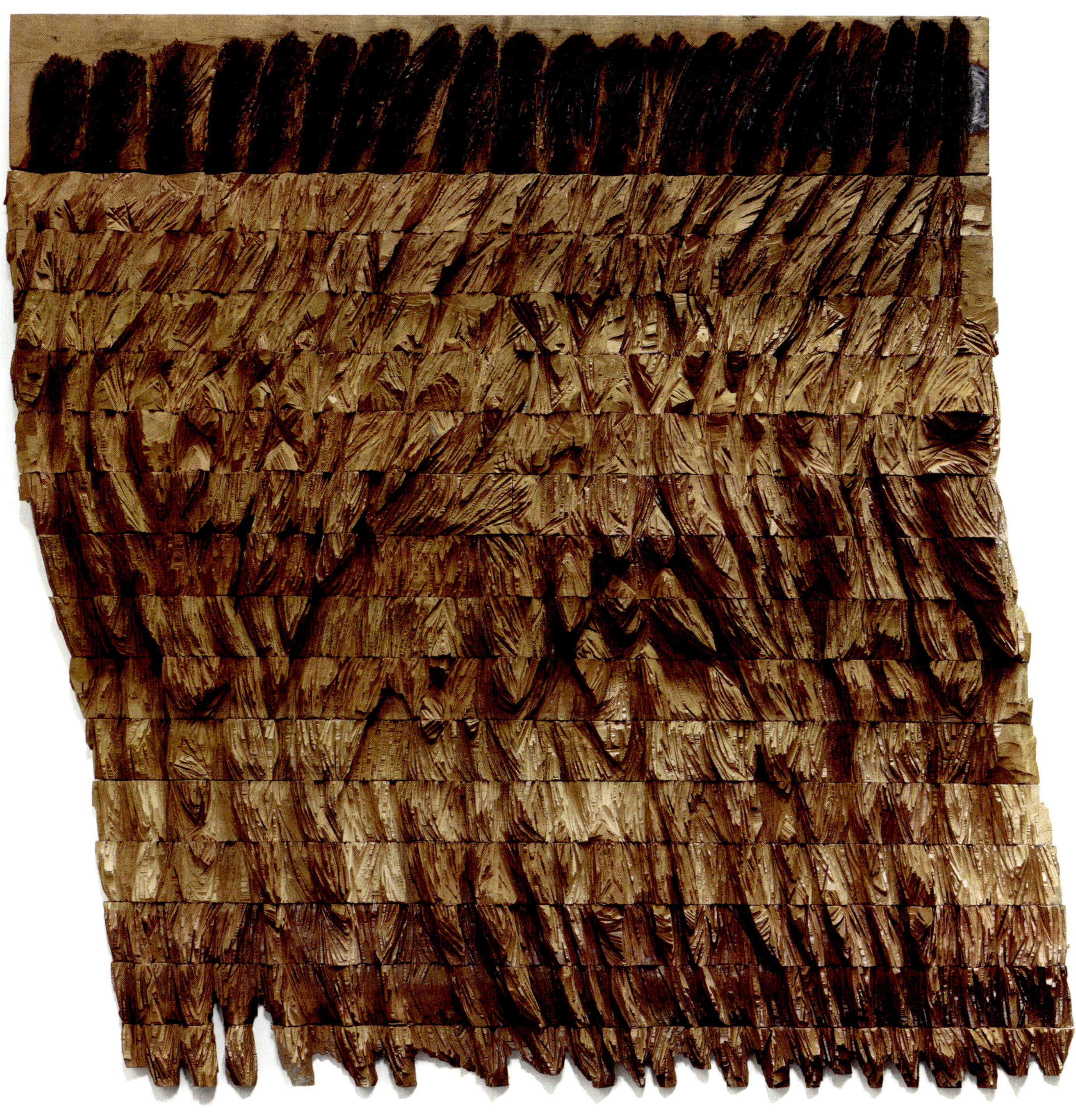

PL. 30 Ursula von Rydingsvard, *Conjugation*, 2012. Cedar and graphite, 62 x 58 x 7 inches (157.5 x 147.3 x 17.8 cm).

Exhibition Checklist

PL. 1
David Altmejd
Born in Montreal, Canada, 1974
Untitled 16 (Guides), 2013
Wood, mirror, Plexiglas, metal wire, glazed ceramic, thread, epoxy clay, acrylic paint, and graphite
79 1/2 x 28 x 21 inches
(201.9 x 71.1 x 53.3 cm)

PL. 2
Huma Bhabha
Born in Karachi, Pakistan, 1962
Chain of Missing Links, 2012
Wood, styrofoam, clay, wire, Plexiglas, acrylic paint, weeds, seedpod, skull, rust, graphite, and oil stick
101 5/8 x 38 1/4 x 29 1/8 inches
(258.1 x 97.2 x 74 cm)

PL. 3
Anthony Caro
Born in Surrey, England, 1924–2013
The Brook, 2012
Steel, rusted
52 3/8 x 105 1/8 x 53 9/16 inches
(133 x 267 x 136 cm)

PL. 4
Tony Cragg
Born in Liverpool, England, 1949
Versus, 2011
Wood
110 1/4 x 116 x 39 1/2 inches
(280 x 295 x 100.3 cm)

PL. 5
Edmund de Waal
Born in Nottingham, England, 1964
breathturn, I, 2013
476 porcelain vessels in aluminum and Plexiglas cabinet
90 3/8 x 118 1/8 x 3 15/16 inches
(229.6 x 300 x 10 cm)

PL. 6
Mark di Suvero
Born in Shanghai, China, 1933
Untitled, c. 1995
Acrylic on canvas
112 x 130 inches (284.5 x 330.2 cm)

PL. 7
Teresita Fernández
Born in Miami, Florida, 1968
Nocturnal (Cinematic Sky), 2011
Solid graphite on wood panel
96 x 72 inches (243.8 x 182.9 cm)

PL. 8
Liam Gillick
Born in Aylesbury, England, 1964
Pascal Elevation, 2014
Powder-coated aluminum and Plexiglas
78 3/4 x 24 7/8 x 20 15/16 inches
(200 x 63 x 53 cm)

PL. 9
Wayne Gonzales
Born in New Orleans, Louisiana, 1957
Waiting Crowd, 2008
Acrylic on canvas
78 x 103 inches
(198.1 x 261.6 cm)

PL. 10
Katharina Grosse
Born in Freiburg, Germany, 1961
Untitled, 2013
Acrylic on fiberglass-reinforced plastic
133 7/8 x 165 3/8 x 283 1/2 inches
(340 x 420.1 x 720.1 cm)

PL. 11
Katharina Grosse
Born in Freiburg, Germany, 1961
Untitled, 2013
Acrylic on canvas
94 1/2 x 152 3/4 inches (240 x 388 cm)

PL. 12
Mark Grotjahn
Born in Pasadena, California, 1968
Untitled (Pretty Lost Blue for My Girls, Italian Mask M30.b), 2013
Painted bronze
52 3/4 x 33 1/2 x 38 inches
(134 x 85.1 x 96.5 cm)

PL. 13
Damien Hirst
Born in Bristol, England, 1965
Beautiful Superheroes Painting (with Butterflies), 2007
Butterflies and household gloss on canvas
48 x 48 inches (122 x 122 cm)

PL. 14
Howard Hodgkin
Born in London, England, 1932
Where Seldom Is Heard a Discouraging Word, 2007–08
Oil on wood
80 1/8 x 105 inches
(203.5 x 266.7 cm)

PL. 15
Thomas Houseago
Born in Leeds, England, 1972
Yet to be titled, 2012
Bronze
Edition 2/3
110 x 46 x 44 inches
(279.4 x 116.8 x 111.8 cm)

PL. 16
Elliott Hundley
Born in Greensboro, North Carolina, 1975
eyes that run like leaping fire, 2011
Wood, soundboard, ink-jet print on Kitakata, string, pins, paper, photographs, plastic, wire, and found embroidery
98 1/2 x 240 5/8 x 11 3/8 inches
(250.2 x 611.2 x 28.9 cm)

PL. 17
Alfredo Jaar
Born in Santiago, Chile, 1956
Life Magazine, April 19, 1968, 1995
Three photographic prints
Edition 3/3
61 x 120 inches (154.9 x 304.8 cm) overall

PL. 18
Anish Kapoor
Born in Mumbai, India, 1954
Full Moon, 2014
Stainless steel
70 7/8 x 70 7/8 x 10 7/8 inches
(180 x 180 x 27.5 cm)

PL. 19
KAWS
Born in Jersey City, New Jersey, 1974
Untitled, 2015
Acrylic on canvas
72 x 120 inches (182.9 x 304.8 cm)

PL. 20
Sol LeWitt
Born in Hartford, Connecticut, 1928–2007
Open Cube Structure, 2007
Painted wood
62 x 87 x 87 inches (157.5 x 221 x 221 cm)

PL. 21
Christian Marclay
Born in San Rafael, California, 1955
Actions: Flopppp Sllurp Spaloosh Whoomph (No. 3), 2013
Screenprint and acrylic on canvas
61 1/2 x 102 1/2 inches (156.2 x 260.4 cm)

PL. 22
Kerry James Marshall
Born in Birmingham, Alabama, 1955
Untitled (Blot), 2014
Acrylic on PVC panel
84 x 119 inches (213.4 x 302.3 cm)

PL. 23
Iván Navarro
Born in Santiago, Chile, 1972
BED (Water Tower), Ladder (Water Tower), ME/WE (Water Tower) from the project *This Land is Your Land*, 2014
Neon, wood, painted steel, galvanized steel, aluminum, mirror, one-way mirror, and electric energy
Edition 1/3
189 x 105 1/8 x 105 1/8 inches
(480.1 x 267 x 267 cm) each

PL. 24
Giuseppe Penone
Born in Garessio, Italy, 1947
Pelle di marmo e spine d'acacia – Marta, 2006
White Carrara marble, canvas, acrylic, glass microspheres, and acacia thorns
39 3/8 x 55 1/8 x 2 3/8 inches (100 x 140 x 6 cm)

PL. 25
Ken Price
Born in Pacific Palisades, California, 1935–2012
Ceejay, 2011
Painted bronze composite
48 x 48 3/8 x 46 inches
(121.9 x 122.9 x 116.8 cm)

PL. 26
Matthew Ritchie
Born in London, England, 1964
Link of Nature, 2014
Oil and ink on canvas
78 x 116 x 2 1/2 inches
(198.1 x 294.6 x 6.4 cm)

PL. 27
Julian Schnabel
Born in New York, New York, 1951
Untitled, 2015
Ink-jet print and spray paint on polyester
108 x 72 inches (274.3 x 182.9 cm)

PL. 28
Richard Serra
Born in San Francisco, California, 1938
Double Rift #10, 2013
Paint stick on handmade paper
84 x 240 3/8 x 3 3/4 inches
(213.4 x 610.6 x 9.5 cm)

PL. 29
Rudolf Stingel
Born in Merano, Italy, 1956
Untitled, 2014
Oil and enamel on canvas
83 x 67 inches (210.8 x 170.2 cm)

PL. 30
Ursula von Rydingsvard
Born in Deensen, Germany, 1942
Conjugation, 2012
Cedar and graphite
62 x 58 x 7 inches (157.5 x 147.3 x 17.8 cm)

PL. 31
Kara Walker
Born in Stockton, CA, 1969
Object Lesson in Empire Building, 2014
Graphite and charcoal on paper
72 1/4 x 94 3/4 inches (183.5 x 240.7 cm)

PL. 32
Dan Walsh
Born in Phildelphia, Pennsylvania, 1960
Cycle X, 2013
Pencil and acrylic on canvas
70 x 70 inches (177.8 x 177.8 cm)

PL. 33
Rachel Whiteread
Born in London, England, 1963
circa 1760 (II), 2012
Resin
73 1/4 x 33 7/16 x 2 9/16 inches
(186.1 x 84.9 x 6.5 cm)

PL. 34
Kehinde Wiley
Born in Los Angeles, California, 1977
Naomi and Her Daughters, 2013
Oil on canvas
180 x 90 inches (457.2 x 228.6 cm)

PL. 35
Christopher Wool
Born in Chicago, Illinois, 1955
Untitled, 2000
Enamel on linen
108 x 72 inches (274.3 x 182.9 cm)

Reproduction Credits

PL. 1 David Altmejd, *Untitled 16 (Guides)*, 2013. Wood, mirror, Plexiglas, metal wire, glazed ceramic, thread, epoxy clay, acrylic paint, and graphite; 79 1/2 x 28 x 21 inches (201.9 x 71.1 x 53.3 cm). Image courtesy of the artist and Andrea Rosen Gallery, New York, New York. © David Altmejd. Photo by Robert Glowacki.

PL. 2 Huma Bhabha, *Chain of Missing Links*, 2012. Wood, styrofoam, clay, wire, Plexiglas, acrylic paint, weeds, seedpod, skull, rust, graphite, and oil stick; 101 5/8 x 38 1/4 x 29 1/8 inches (258.1 x 97.2 x 74 cm). Image courtesy of the artist and Salon 94, New York, New York. © Huma Bhabha.

PL. 3 Anthony Caro, *The Brook*, 2012. Steel, rusted; 52 3/8 x 105 1/8 x 53 9/16 inches (133 x 267 x 136 cm). Image courtesy of the artist and Gagosian Gallery. © Anthony Caro.

PL. 4 Tony Cragg, *Versus*, 2011. Wood, 110 1/4 x 116 x 39 1/2 inches (280 x 295 x 100.3 cm). Image courtesy of the artist and Marian Goodman Gallery, New York, New York, and Paris, France. © Tony Cragg / Artist Rights Society (ARS), New York, New York / VG Bild-Kunst, Bonn, Germany. Photo by Michael Richter

PL. 5 Edmund de Waal, *breathturn, I*, 2013. 476 porcelain vessels in aluminum and Plexiglas cabinet, 90 3/8 x 118 1/8 x 3 15/16 inches (229.6 x 300 x 10 cm). Image courtesy of the artist and Gagosian Gallery. © Edmund de Waal.

PL. 6 Mark di Suvero, *Untitled*, c. 1995. Acrylic on canvas, 112 x 130 inches (284.5 x 330.2 cm). Image courtesy of the artist; Spacetime CC, Long Island City, New York; and Paula Cooper Gallery, New York, New York. © Mark di Suvero. Photo by Steven Probert.

PL. 7 Teresita Fernández, *Nocturnal (Cinematic Sky)*, 2011. Solid graphite on wood panel, 96 x 72 inches (243.8 x 182.9 cm). Image courtesy of the artist and Lehmann Maupin, New York, New York, and Hong Kong, China. © Teresita Fernández.

PL. 8 Liam Gillick, *Pascal Elevation*, 2014. Powder-coated aluminum and Plexiglas, 78 3/4 x 24 7/8 x 20 15/16 inches (200 x 63 x 53 cm). Image courtesy of the artist and Casey Kaplan New York, New York. © Liam Gillick. Photo by Dawn Blackman.

PL. 9 Wayne Gonzales, *Waiting Crowd*, 2008. Acrylic on canvas, 78 x 103 inches (198.1 x 261.6 cm). Image courtesy of the artist and Paula Cooper Gallery, New York, New York. © Wayne Gonzales. Photo by EPW Studio.

PL. 10 Katharina Grosse, *Untitled*, 2013. Acrylic on fiberglass-reinforced plastic, 133 7/8 x 165 3/8 x 283 1/2 inches (340 x 420.1 x 720.1 cm). © Katharina Grosse und VG Bild-Kunst Bonn.

PL. 11 Katharina Grosse, *Untitled*, 2013. Acrylic on canvas, 94 1/2 x 152 3/4 inches (240 x 388 cm). © Katharina Grosse und VG Bild-Kunst Bonn.

PL. 12 Mark Grotjahn, *Untitled (Pretty Lost Blue for My Girls, Italian Mask M30.b)*, 2013. Painted bronze, 52 3/4 x 33 1/2 x 38 inches (134 x 85.1 x 96.5 cm). Image courtesy of the artist and Gagosian Gallery. © Mark Grotjahn. Photo by Doug Parker Studio.

PL. 13 Damien Hirst, *Beautiful Super-heroes Painting (with Butterflies)*, 2007. Butterflies and household gloss on canvas, 48 x 48 inches (122 x 122 cm). © Damien Hirst and Science Ltd. All rights reserved, DACS, London / Artists Rights Society (ARS), New York, New York 2015. Photo by Prudence Cuming Associates Ltd.

PL. 14 Howard Hodgkin, *Where Seldom Is Heard a Discouraging Word*, 2007–08. Oil on wood, 80 1/8 x 105 inches (203.5 x 266.7 cm). Image courtesy of the artist and Gagosian Gallery. © Howard Hodgkin.

PL. 15 Thomas Houseago, *Yet to be titled*, 2012. Bronze, edition 2/3, 110 x 46 x 44 inches (279.4 x 116.8 x 111.8 cm). Image courtesy of the artist and Gagosian Gallery. © Thomas Houseago. Photo by Fredrik Nilsen.

PL. 16 Elliott Hundley, *eyes that run like leaping fire*, 2011. Wood, soundboard, ink-jet print on Kitakata, string, pins, paper, photographs, plastic, wire, and found embroidery; 98 1/2 x 240 5/8 x 11 3/8 inches (250.2 x 611.2 x 28.9 cm). Image courtesy of the artist, Regen Projects, Los Angeles, California, and Andrea Rosen Gallery, New York, New York. © Elliott Hundley. Photo by Joshua White.

PL. 17 Alfredo Jaar, *Life Magazine, April 19, 1968, 1995*. Three photographic prints, edition 3/3; 61 x 120 inches (154.9 x 304.8 cm) overall. Image courtesy of the artist and Galerie Lelong, New York, New York. © Alfredo Jaar.

PL. 18 Anish Kapoor, *Full Moon*, 2014. Stainless steel, 70 7/8 x 70 7/8 x 10 7/8 inches (180 x 180 x 27.5 cm). Image courtesy of the artist; Regen Projects, Los Angeles, California; and Gladstone Gallery, New York, New York, and Brussels, Belgium. © Anish Kapoor. All Rights Reserved DACS London, England / Artist Rights Society (ARS), New York, New York. Photo by Joshua White.

PL. 19 KAWS, *Untitled*, 2015. Acrylic on canvas, 72 x 120 inches (182.9 x 304.8 cm). © KAWS. Photo by Farzad Owrang.

PL. 20 Sol LeWitt, *Open Cube Structure*, 2007. Painted wood, 62 x 87 x 87 inches (157.5 x 221 x 221 cm). Image courtesy of Paula Cooper Gallery, New York, New York. © The LeWitt Estate / Artist Rights Society (ARS), New York, New York.

PL. 21 Christian Marclay, *Actions: Flopppp Sllurp Spaloosh Whoomph (No. 3)*, 2013. Screenprint and acrylic on canvas, 61 1/2 x 102 1/2 inches (156.2 x 260.4 cm). Image courtesy of the artist and Paula Cooper Gallery, New York, New York. © Christian Marclay. Photo by Steven Probert.

PL. 22 Kerry James Marshall, *Untitled (Blot)*, 2014. Acrylic on PVC panel, 84 x 119 inches (213.4 x 302.3 cm). Image courtesy of the artist and David Zwirner, New York, New York, and London, England. © Kerry James Marshall.

PL. 23 Iván Navarro, *BED (Water Tower), Ladder (Water Tower),* and *ME/WE (Water Tower)* from the project *This Land is Your Land*, 2014. Neon, wood, painted steel, galvanized steel, aluminum, mirror, one-way mirror, and electric energy; edition 1/3; 189 x 105 1/8 x 105 1/8 inches (480.1 x 267 x 267 cm) each. Images courtesy of the artist; Paul Kasmin Gallery, New York, New York; and Nasher Museum of Art at Duke University, Durham, North Carolina. © Iván Navarro. Photos by Elisabeth Bernstein, J Caldwell, and Peter Paul Geoffrion.

PL. 24 Giuseppe Penone, *Pelle di marmo e spine d'acacia – Marta*, 2006. White Carrara marble, canvas, acrylic, glass microspheres, and acacia thorns; 39 3/8 x 55 1/8 x 2 3/8 inches (100 x 140 x 6 cm). Image courtesy of Gagosian Gallery. © Archivio Penone.

PL. 25 Ken Price, *Ceejay*, 2011. Painted bronze composite, 48 x 48 3/8 x 46 inches (121.9 x 122.9 x 116.8 cm). Image courtesy of Matthew Marks Gallery, New York, New York. © Estate of Ken Price. Photo by Fredrik Nilsen.

PL. 26 Matthew Ritchie, *Link of Nature*, 2014. Oil and ink on canvas, 78 x 116 x 2 1/2 inches (198.1 x 294.6 x 6.4 cm). Image courtesy of the artist and Andrea Rosen Gallery, New York, New York. © Matthew Ritchie. Photo by Lance Brewer.

PL. 27 Julian Schnabel, *Untitled*, 2015. Ink-jet print and spray paint on polyester, 108 x 72 inches (274.3 x 182.9 cm). © Julian Schnabel Studio. Photo by Lance Brewer.

PL. 28 Richard Serra, *Double Rift #10*, 2013. Paint stick on handmade paper, 84 x 240 3/8 x 3 3/4 inches (213.4 x 610.6 x 9.5 cm). © 2015 Richard Serra / Artists Rights Society (ARS), New York, New York.

PL. 29 Rudolf Stingel, *Untitled*, 2014. Oil and enamel on canvas, 83 x 67 inches (210.8 x 170.2 cm). Photo by Christopher Burke Studio. © Rudolf Stingel.

PL. 30 Ursula von Rydingsvard, *Conjugation*, 2012. Cedar and graphite, 62 x 58 x 7 inches (157.5 x 147.3 x 17.8 cm). Image courtesy of the artist and Galerie Lelong, New York, New York. © Ursula von Rydingsvard.

PL. 31 Kara Walker, *Object Lesson in Empire Building*, 2014. Graphite and charcoal on paper, 72 1/4 x 94 3/4 inches (183.5 x 240.7 cm). Image courtesy of the artist and Sikkema Jenkins & Co., New York, New York. © Kara Walker.

PL. 32 Dan Walsh, *Cycle X*, 2013. Pencil and acrylic on canvas, 70 x 70 inches (177.8 x 177.8 cm). Image courtesy of the artist and Paula Cooper Gallery, New York, New York. © Dan Walsh. Photo by Steven Probert.

PL. 33 Rachel Whiteread, *circa 1760 (II)*, 2012. Resin, 73 1/4 x 33 7/16 x 2 9/16 inches (186.1 x 84.9 x 6.5 cm). Image courtesy of the artist, Luhring Augustine, New York, New York; Gagosian Gallery; and Lorcan O'Neill, Rome, Italy. © Rachel Whiteread. Photo by Mike Bruce.

PL. 34 Kehinde Wiley, *Naomi and Her Daughters*, 2013. Oil on canvas, 180 x 90 inches (457.2 x 228.6 cm). © Kehinde Wiley Studio.

PL. 35 Christopher Wool, *Untitled*, 2000. Enamel on linen, 108 x 72 inches (274.3 x 182.9 cm). Image courtesy of the artist and Luhring Augustine, New York, New York. © Christopher Wool.

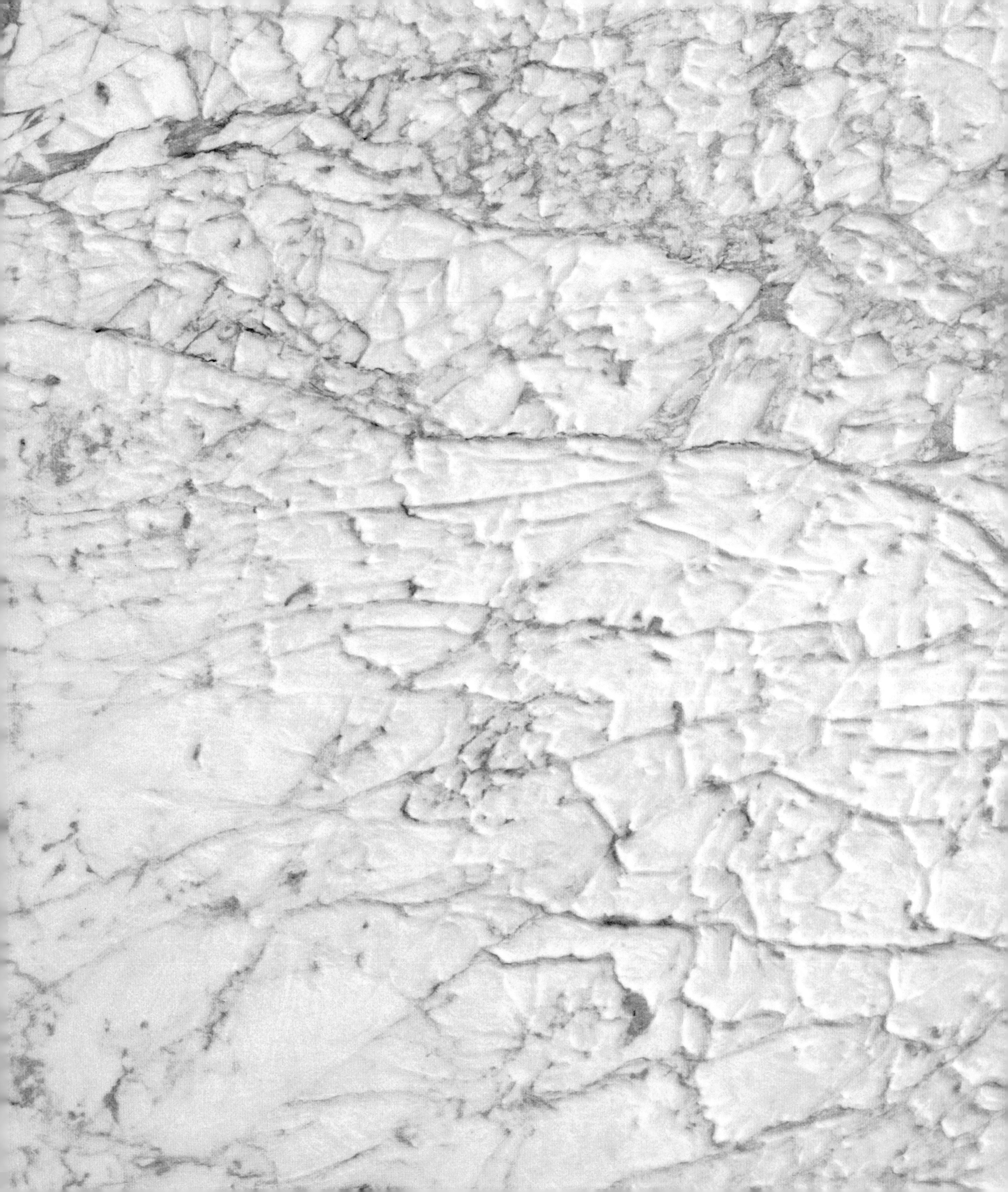

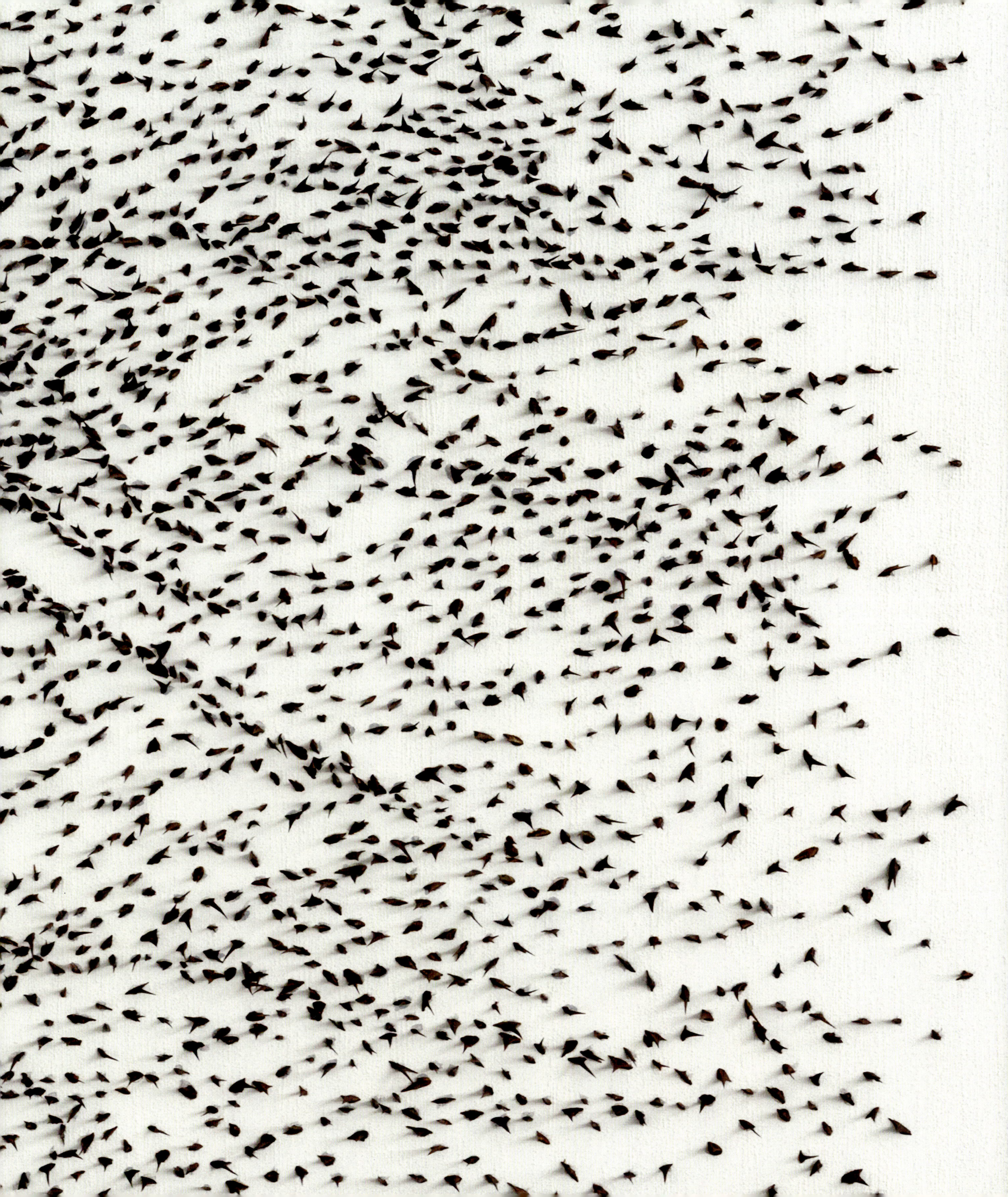